DEVELOPERS ROAD AHEAD

A Complete Guide For Software Architects To Succeed At Work And Life

KARTHIKEYAN VK

INDIA · SINGAPORE · MALAYSIA

Notion Press Media Pvt Ltd

No. 50, Chettiyar Agaram Main Road,
Vanagaram, Chennai, Tamil Nadu – 600 095

First Published by Notion Press 2021
Copyright © Karthikeyan VK 2021
All Rights Reserved.

ISBN 978-1-63606-942-5

Contents

Preface

Why should you read this book?

I am a Computer Science engineer from a very ordinary college, who got into the software profession during the recession period with just Rs.5000 as my first salary. (After TDS it was Rs.4700.)

I found it very difficult to write code even though my engineering major was Computer Science. So I completed my first module with much difficulty and then the next, and then move on to the next, and then the one after that, just like a baby would, planting one arm and one leg. Over time, I began to walk and then run confidently and I continue to run to this date.

Perhaps, I became a better programmer by merely staying in the office, working late and doing things again and again. I was neither gifted nor talented, but my hard work started paying dividends.

I got a little bit of exposure when I had traveled to Japan as a fresher with barely 9 months' experience.

After coming back from the USA on an onsite project (for three years), I had six years' experience and I wanted to take my career to the next level, but I didn't know what to do.

I didn't want to continue as a manager, since I thought it is somehow shady and involves lots of office politics and I was not cut out for it.

I wanted to write code, and I got immense pleasure in producing something and knowing that someone is using it; is the greatest feeling.

So I started searching for things that make an architect, but could get no straightforward answer.

I began looking closely at architects and what their roles were. It looked like some of them were, what one could call, a jack of all technologies and all the architects I knew seemed to have a say in every problem with appropriate technology solutions. I, on the other hand, had no clue for giving multiple solutions. All I knew was .Net.

One of the architects I had worked with said there is something called Design patterns, which is like a packaged solution to well-known problems. Then he explained the patterns that he has used as an architect for our project.

So I thought "Eureka", I have found the elixir of life.

But to my dismay, there were hundreds of patterns and there were also anti-patterns and I was dumbfounded.

After some Googling and soul searching, I came to know there are SOLID principles that lead to these patterns from the "Head First" Design Pattern book.

SOLID principles resonated with me a lot because I am a big fan of "7 Habits of Highly Effective People" by Stephen Covey, where he talks about Principle-based life. So I started learning SOLID principles and applied them in my work, and things started clicking.

But these principles are not enough for one's growth. I realized that in addition to these principles you need to change who you are, to become a successful architect.

You need to change your mindset, communication style, improve your character, change your learning speed, and learn to be compassionate which has nothing to do with any technologies. We will talk more about principle-based life and principle-based decision in Chapter 2 – The **Mindset of an Architect.**

Even though this book is for technology people like you and me, I have made sure this book does not correspond to any single technology.

It is a book to become a successful architect and take your life to the next level.

In the words of Stephen Covey, "**Your economic security does not lie in your job; it lies in your own power to produce—to think, to learn, to create, to adapt. That's true financial independence. It's not having wealth; it's having the power to produce wealth.**"

You can skip the first two chapter of this book and learn all the techniques that I used to improve myself as a great technical person, but believe me, it will give you only short term success.

I recommend that you read in any way you want, to learn the technique first, implement it in the real world as training wheels and then come back to the book and read the core principle that will change you as a person

Book Reviews

"I've known Karthikeyan V K for a couple of years, and I've always admired the contributions he has made to the technical community in India. This is the first time ever I got a chance to read a book written by him and I must admit the fact that he has simply nailed it. The tools and insights he has shared in this book are simply phenomenal and this is a must-read for anyone who's currently working as an architect or in any leadership role for that matter. There are a lot of great topics which Karthik has covered in this book, but I really liked those lines where he speaks about contributing to the technical community, as that's something that we both share in common. To sum it up, this book is definitely a must-read for anybody who's aspiring to become a leader, as Karthikeyan has done a wonderful job in connecting the dots of various leadership principles in this book."

Vignesh Ganesan,
Ex-Microsoft, Deloitte,
Cloud Security Architect.

❋ ❋ ❋

"Developers Road Ahead is a book about the 'must-have' skillsets and qualities of a software architect. The best part is that the author has spoken about everyday challenges and mental roadblocks every software engineer comes across, along with possible workarounds and tested solutions. The first few chapters are meant for every IT employee who started their career with dreams. The book ends with two chapters dedicated to new architects and what they must know. This is truly a book written with one's personal experience based on more than a decade of handling software lifecycle challenges. I strongly recommend this to everyone who is starting their journey to the cloud."

Evangeline Devakiruba,
Google, Partner Manager.

❋ ❋ ❋

"This is not just another self-help book, which you complete and put away. It is a book that is going to grow within you, transform you one page at a time.

First, it makes you ponder your life's purpose and slowly helps you realize your inner callings, and then guides you on that path. It is one of a kind book that you can come back to frequently, to analyze yourself and to keep you right on track to your ultimate goal.

And no wonder Karthik didn't shy away from being real. The book is as honest as it can get. He is going to tell you some realities that you can only realize a hard way otherwise. He also provides super simple and sensible solutions for them as well.

From handling a bad boss to overcoming imposter syndrome, this book possibly covers everything an IT professional would face at a workspace.

And the last 100 pages are pure gold if you really aspire to become an architect. With clear steps and relatable exercises, Karthik not just tells you, he shows you how it is done.

This book is the best mentor any developer could ever have. It is going to transform you into a better professional and content human being."

Bhuvaneshwari,
Principal Engineer,
Imaginea, Part of Accenture.

"A well-rounded book starts with the human aspects, self-discipline, leadership, and most importantly, skills necessary to become an architect. A simple and easy-to-read book from a developer at heart and an architect."

ILyas,
IOT Evangelist, ABB.

This book is consciously written using simple English with the intention to keep the discussion straight and let the readers understand the principles easily.

The Mindset of an Architect

The Burning Why

Those who have a 'why' to live, can bear with almost any 'how'.

– Viktor Frankl, Nazi Camp Survivor
and Founder of Logo Therapy

First, find your "Why" you want to be better than what you are now. It is a very important step and you need to take a clean sheet of paper and write down three reasons why you need to become an architect.

It can be anything, all you need to know is the 'why' because it helps you stay focused on your goal and the prize that you want to win.

It helps you keep away from many distractions and you can always align every action of yours with your own identified 'why'.

Say you are binge-watching a TV series and you came to realize you are wasting your time more than you should be, all that you need to think of is the three 'why' you wrote and whether your current action will get to your WHY or not. Now you can still watch it or switch off the TV and do something that will lead to your WHY.

I am not against any entertainment or any TV series because it has helped me to socialize with my CTO and Sales director, because it shows you have specific interests and you can break the ice when you are having dinner with them. This is better than not knowing what to talk about.

So, if you are doing what you are doing because it will help you get what you want, please continue that action wholeheartedly without any guilt. In the next chapters, you will also learn how you can do all these activities like binge-watching TV series and socializing with friends and still be super productive.

If you don't feel it is good for what you want in life, then don't do it.

Below are samples I think will help you to find your own WHY you want to become an architect. Be honest and dig deep into your motive. Don't be ashamed or guilty to write any of your wishes, because most of the desires in the world are universal. No desire is directly connected with what we say or think. It is always primal. It is either to avoid pain or to get pleasure. These desires could be:

- To get promotion to the next level
- I might lose my current job
- I hate a person in my company and want to prove I am technically better than him
- I feel insecure when people around me talk about the latest technology, but I cannot contribute anything to the conversation
- Give back to the community by learning and doing a lot

Being honest about why you want what you want is the first step. Until you figure out why you need to be a better architect, you cannot go any further.

"What is most personal is most universal."

– Carl R. Rogers, Famous Psychotherapist

Please be extremely honest about your WHY and you don't have to show this to anyone.

Until you find your Why, you will not even complete this book. If you want to learn more and do more, you need motivation.

For Self-motivation to happen, you need to know why you need it. Otherwise, you will feel all excited reading the book and want to try everything, but once you close this book and wake up tomorrow, you will go back to the regular eight hours job with a salary and will fall into your own habit.

Some of the common examples of desires which helps you to make a change in your life and improve yourself to the next level are:

To Get Promotion to the Next Level

Frustration with the current situation is a good place to be, because it helps us to change what we have been doing for a very long time. Until we are frustrated, we will not make changes in our lives. We might be frustrated with our current salary and we want to increase the value of whatever we are earning.

The good news is that it is actually more possible in our software industry than in any other industry. I really wonder why people want to increase their salary but will never really take any steps even to update their resume and attend a couple of interviews.

We get very comfortable with the job we are working on, but with a little frustration piling up every day. We come home, watch television, and distract ourselves from that frustration. If you want to self-motivate yourself, frustration is good.

So if you are frustrated because your salary is less, don't distract yourself from it, let it grow. Then our brain will find a way to remove the frustration, and then you will see all the opportunities around you which you were blind to so far because you got comfortable with what you were doing and distracted yourself away from them by watching television, movies, or unprofitable socializing/gossiping.

Lose My Current Job

In our technology industry, there are too many changes every day, so that keeping up with technology changes is always a nightmare for everyone. How much ever you keep yourself updated, your knowledge will become obsolete within days.

People are contributing to Open-source technologies every day. People find their pain points in the technology or their day-to-day activities and then do something a little better, and it gets into an upward spiral, and so the technology and technique gets better and better every day.

Keeping up with millions of contributions from every developer is very tough. So, people with less experience learn a new technology better because the entry point for the new technology is easier than the old one. So we are stuck with older technologies and we become obsolete. We don't have time to upgrade ourselves, because there are lots of firefighting and pressing issues in our everyday jobs.

So new technology is adopted by less experienced people and we are stuck with our old technologies, which lets us be obsolete sooner and the less experienced people will take our jobs. But we have covered extensively about this problem, later in our book, on how to keep yourself current and still do firefighting every day. This is the common WHY for every developer who wants to improve their life.

Hate a person in my company and want to prove I am technically better than him

Enemy-centric frustration is common, but I would not keep it as part of my life goals because once you have won over that enemy you will only feel empty.

We are humans, right? You identifying the Why is more important, if the enemy is fueling your growth, please use it as a fuel to get better. Friends help us to go through sorrows, building Why around an enemy makes us better.

Keep the enemy centric Why and grow, but make sure you come back to this Why and change to something like contributing back to society and our community, where we have got a lot from the community without paying even a dime, e.g., Stack Overflow, YouTube videos, meetups, etc.

I feel insecure when people around me talk about the latest technology, but I cannot contribute anything to the conversation.

We have all been there, we all feel left out in a conversation when people talk about new technology and we cannot contribute anything to the conversation. This is a good part of the frustration. We can do something about it. Rejection is one of the greatest motivators. In brain science, the part that gets activated when you get physically hurt is the same part that gets activated when you are rejected by society or peer groups. So this can motivate you a lot if you don't distract yourself and use this rejection to grow better.

Give back to the community by learning and doing a lot

Giving back to society is better than anything else in the world because it makes us really good and there's no joy in the world greater than giving something to someone. But just don't write this in your five Whys at the end of the chapter until you absolutely feel so.

Your Turn—Fill in the Blank below

_____

_____

_____

Be absolutely honest, the more honest it is, the better your outcome will be. The sillier and more selfish it sounds, the better it is. Because it is a better place to start from and work the way upwards.

Everybody starts anything with a selfish motive, and we get better and find out that is not enough, so we move away from selfishness and move toward better goals. Can you see the billionaire becoming a philanthropist, e.g., Bill Gates? We can never feel good or feel that something is getting accomplished without giving something back to society.

Write down three Why you want to become an architect, you can repeat any one of the above ones or write your own. But make sure you write them. Writing is a neuromuscular activity that helps you to achieve a lot.

_____

_____

_____

Thinking Long Term

*"We tend to overestimate the effect of a technology in the short
run and underestimate the effect in the long run,"*

**– Roy Amara, past president of
The Institute for the Future**

We live in an instant gratification world where people want everything
now. Long term thinking is having a purpose in life that is larger than
you, where you get up every day and work on the purpose which
you have defined for yourself, the one thing you think is of utmost
importance in your life.

Long term vision can be becoming CEO of a company or becoming
the best dad in the world, or anything that is larger than your whole
life. A purpose that might take more than one lifetime to succeed…
We will be looking into application suggestions later in the chapter to
help you.

If we do not have a long-term perspective, we tend to think on
very narrow lines, and our whole life will be based on current pressing
problems and only working on other people's agenda.

If we have a long-term perspective, problems in our life become
challenges and opportunities. You tend to not waste your energy on
small and mundane things that eat up your time.

People around you will sense your higher burning purpose and you will be attracting lots of people in your life who have the same kind of long term thinking, and you synergize with them to achieve your long term purpose. You will get greater and highly influential people's relationships without doing much to build a network.

Long term purpose lets us start our day with great motivation, instead of waking up every day thinking, again another week to pass by, and waiting for the weekend to relax and rejoice.

Once you have a higher purpose, waking up and planning on getting closer every day to the purpose you have decided is the best feeling you can ever get. You tend to rejoice every day as if it is the greatest opportunity to complete the mission for the day.

"Begin with the end in mind"

– Stephen Covey, author of
7 Habits of highly effective people

Your purpose will help you start every day, every week, every new year with the end in mind. It will help you to always seek and make you curious about what it takes to get closer to your higher purpose.

Thinking long term and having a perspective always helps us to make lots of decisions in a more profitable way which is beneficial to everyone.

If you don't have thoughts on long term purpose, you will be working on fulfilling other people's agenda and their purpose in life. I am not suggesting you to quit your job and start your own company, so you don't have to work for other people's purposes. If you don't have a long-term purpose in life you will be working for someone whose purpose in life does not match with your life.

Everyone in this world has a purpose that we need to fill, we need to find what it is and fulfill the purpose for which we are born. Each of us is unique and we have something to offer to this world. We should be offering something back to this world by all means.

Even being a self-fulfilled happy person, will itself be a great offering back to this world, because happiness is contagious. All emotions are contagious and when we are not in a good mood, we tend to spread it to others and you can always see how one guy in our team brings the whole energy down in a second.

Being happy and fun is the biggest gift you can give back to society. For, being happy without any external factors takes lots of hard work, self-evolution, and mastering your own emotions which you can achieve by working every day on a large purpose, so petty things don't bother you.

> *"You've got to find what you love. And that is as true for your work as it is for your lovers. Your work is going to fill a large part of your life, and the only way to be truly satisfied is to do what you believe is great work. And the only way to do great work is to love what you do. If you haven't found it yet, keep looking. Don't settle. As with all matters of the heart, you'll know when you find it. And, like any great relationship, it just gets better and better as the years roll on. So keep looking until you find it. Don't settle..."*
>
> *– Steve Jobs*

The above quote from Steve Jobs sums it all. You need to find what you love in your life and do it so that it gives something back to society.

We are here to serve all living beings; finding what your major purpose is will help you get to what you want in life.

Once you find your major purpose, you will find ways to get better at what you do, you attract everything in your life and you attracted this book also to your life because you want to get better.

Nobody can define what your purpose is, you have to find what your purpose in life is on your own.

"Ultimately, man should not ask what the meaning of his life is, but rather must recognize that it is he who is asked. In a word, each man is questioned by life; and he can only answer to life by answering for his own life; to life, he can only respond by being responsible."

— Viktor E. Frankl, Man's Search for Meaning

In the book, '*Man's search for meaning*', Victor Frankl, talks about his experience in the Nazi death camp. He asks every man to find his own purpose on his own, and then answer his life with his purpose. He talks about what made him survive the death camp, that it was his having a long term vision, and how he visualized teaching the surviving strategies he followed when he was in the camp to the college students, once he gets out of the camp.

He found that his purpose was to teach people how people cannot take away their freedom even in the worst place like a Nazi camp.

How to Find My Purpose?

As in **Viktor E. Frankl's** quote, you need to find your own purpose, this book only gives you some suggestions about what you can do.

I came back from the USA for my sister's marriage, after completing three years of stay there. When I wanted to return, my visa extension was rejected due to changes in the US travel policy twice. I had all my plans with the USA as the basis.

Once my visa got rejected, I felt some kind of empty feeling because all my plans were around the USA and had become obsolete and I felt empty about it. I started looking out for things to fill my void, and then I come across this idea of finding your own purpose from a Video.

In that video, they spoke about locking yourself in a room until you find your true purpose in life. Luckily, I didn't have to lock myself for days. But I was thinking of this concept for a very long time.

I wanted my purpose to be larger than who I was right then, and it must be something to give back to society. I am always a big fan of people who contribute a lot to the developer community and I adore them. I envy them how they can be updated on the latest technologies and how they have opinions about every new technology.

I am not going to reveal exactly what my purpose is. I figured out it is giving back to society.

You need to figure out your purpose in life, there are no two ways about it. All this chapter can do is to let you know that if you find your purpose and start working on it, you will rejoice more every minute of the day.

I am not suggesting you will NOT find any problems, but you will see those as challenges, and opportunities that take you close to your life purpose.

You change your life to try new things and fail faster, so it will let you grow each and every day.

To achieve your purpose, you need to change your lifestyles, and habits and self-discipline yourself, which we will discuss later in our chapter.

Your life will go in an upward spiral, you will know what you don't know, and you will find people automatically who can teach you or guide you on the path that takes you there.

Your network will grow, and you will find lots of people who have almost the same purpose as yours. At that time, you need to make sure, you are more humble and be more giving from our end.

You need to give more to the mastermind group that forms as a network, than your taking from the group, meaning it can be anything such as organizing the meeting or helping them set up a new meetup group or new conference, or talking in their conference.

Be ready to take their phone call any time, if they have any questions in your area of expertise, and spend time carefully listening to them and giving a well-formed solution.

Write down here about your life's major purpose, in which way you will be contributing back to society.

_____

_____

_____

_____

_____

_____

_____

_____

_____

_____

Taking Responsibility

*"All blame is a waste of time. No matter how much fault
you find with another, and regardless of how much you
blame him, it will not change you."*

**– Wayne Dyer, American philosopher,
author, and motivational speaker**

Taking Responsibility is the first quality that you need to integrate
with yourself in your life. You should take responsibility for everything
that happens in your life. You should see yourself as the person who is
responsible for all the things happening around you which may not in
any way be closely related to you.

Responsible should be read as **response-able**. A person who has the
ability to respond. Once you take responsibility in your life, your whole
attitude toward any circumstance changes. You tend to see problems
from a different perspective.

Instead of finding out who caused the outage or bug, what they
did, and how they did it, you tend to see yourself as a person, who
thinks 'what is my responsibility in fixing the bug or outage and what
can I do about it'.

When you analyze the problem about its root cause, you become
a different person in your team's eye. You can easily see the change in

the way they treat you, people will let their guard down and there is no blaming on who did what. They will work with their full hearts to solve the problem, rather than trying to pinpoint blame.

Once you become a responsible person in your organization, you tend to see every problem as an opportunity, and then your life opens up for more and more new opportunities. You start loving challenges because your brain has become active, trying to solve them rather than finding ways to blame.

You tend to learn a new technology or a new human influence technique that helps to solve any current pressing problem. Since you have taken responsibility for your life and the people around you, you tend to apply your current knowledge and then seek knowledge that might come through.

Let us say you take responsibility for a pain point in the development process, like building your project solution takes more than five minutes. You can complain about it, and still live with it, hoping some senior member of your team will fix it.

But what if you are the most responsible person in your team? You will seek ways to find a solution for that pain point. Your brain becomes active when you see a new video or read a blog article; your brain is very active and will seek the solution in those activities. So you understand the videos and blog articles better because your brain is alert and not generalizing information.

Do you remember when you wanted to buy a new car or a bike and almost finalized the make and model of the car? You tend to see all the cars of the same make and model everywhere on the road, even of the color.

There is a scientific reason for it. Your brain is the busiest, laziest, and most energy-consuming organ in your body and receives almost 50000–60000 signals per day. So if it even attempts to process all the incoming signals, it will burn itself out. So as a survival mechanism, our brain tends to generalize all the signals that come in. That is the reason, when you don't look out for a car, you tend to see all the cars on the road as just vehicles. Because the brain generalizes every car or bike as vehicles on the road.

Once you have thought about buying the car and did a small research about it, your brain gets active and does not generalize the incoming signals about cars. It processes those signals as they are.

So the same thing happens with taking responsibility as a good employee of the organization. You take responsibility for every problem in your organization and you always think about improving your ability to respond to those situations.

So when you learn an article or watch a video, now your brain is active. It does not generalize. Since you have taken responsibility for your organization's success, your brain will actively receive the information and you tend to understand better what you learn.

In the process, you will be learning more because you have understood better. You will remember more, because your understanding of it has improved.

Next time, you will be the person who will be able to suggest a solution even to an upcoming problem. You become the person people seek advice from, because you have a huge bag of knowledge, because you are seeking knowledge by taking responsibility.

Now you are thinking, I don't have the power to change anything, I am just an employee or a developer, how will my responsibility change anything? I am nothing.

You are absolutely right that salary earning employees like us, don't have any power to influence or change anything. The answer is simple: You need to work on your circle of influence and make changes and not work on anything that is not in your circle of influence.

God, give me the grace to accept with serenity
The things that cannot be changed,
Courage to change the things
Which should be changed,
And the Wisdom to distinguish
The one from the other.

– Serenity prayer

As in the serenity prayer, the wisdom to distinguish between things you have control over and the ones you cannot control is the greatest wisdom. Once you find your circle of influence, you can do what is possible to do and which also affects the things you are trying to change.

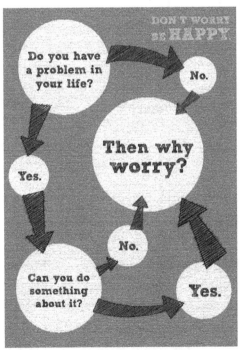

I really like the above flow chart because it clearly explains what to do with the problems in your life. If you can do anything about the problem, then do something about it. If you cannot do anything about the problem, don't worry about it. But you still should have responsibility for the problem. The whole goal of this chapter is for you to understand and get that you are also responsible for the tsunami that happened in India. It means you are response-ABLE.

Finding out the control or change you can make about the problem is the first step, and it is called the "Circle of Influence". It is the circle you can influence that really makes the changes. Once you start working on your own circle of influence, you will see that the circle of your influence widens and you tend to influence your surroundings and the people in it a lot.

When I started as a fresher, I was put into the testing team initially. I managed to ask my manager to move me to the development team and he did. But the way everyone reacted to me was bad and I did not have much knowledge about anything. My lead used to treat me very badly because I was a freshman.

But I started to work on my circle of influence. I concentrated more on my module rather than talking with people or chatting, even though I didn't have any idea what a circle of influence is, at that time.

I put my heart, soul, and all my hard work into the module I was developing, which I have control over, rather than trying to control the behavior of my team lead toward me. I started getting good at the work I was doing.

Once I got a grip of the module and with a little knowledge of SQL, people started asking me to help in their modules because I was completing my assigned modules on time. I used to help people to get their modules and write SQL scripts for them for their modules.

Then my manager one day came and told me, "I see you are helping other people. Did you finish your module?" And I said I did finish mine. He left without saying anything.

After a few days, I became in-charge of other people's completion of modules. Whenever they were stuck on it, my manager asked me whether I could help them. This helped me to get a good name in the team and my organization.

I could have taken two routes, cribbed and complained about my lead's behavior toward me near the water cooler or in the cafeteria, or work on the work assigned to me and then make it a success and start increasing my circle of influence.

I am glad I chose the latter one and it worked out well for me. So that is the reason for this whole chapter, because it works. Taking responsibility and figuring out what is your circle of influence works.

As an exercise, please write down the first five major things that you are complaining about in your life and what is the small step you can take right now, and write it below.

e.g. The road in my street is bumpy – Find the Phone number to complain.

e.g. The technology chosen by the architects might be wrong – Find a blog that is an alternative to the technology that was chosen.

_____

_____

_____

_____

_____

Self-Discipline and Focus

"Whether you call it Buddhism or another religion, self-discipline, that's important. Self-discipline with awareness of consequences."

– Dalai Lama, Monk

As we all know, we lack self-discipline a lot. I am the laziest guy you will ever see. But people ask me, "Where did you find time to write a blog, book, organize the meetup, talk in the meetup, attend meetups, make videos, and write blogs despite your hectic and demanding job?"

To all these questions, I have one answer, that is, forming HABITS. We, humans, are very habit oriented; however much we may deny it, we are habitual and everything we do is unconscious.

Once you form habits and build self-discipline, your success in both your personal and professional life becomes inevitable. You will be seen as a superhuman; if you understand the habits, self-discipline, and power of focus, your time in your hands becomes unlimited.

We fool ourselves thinking whatever we do is out of a conscious choice and nothing is unconscious. Anyone's habit pattern can be read, and we can predict what he will do next.

In late 2011, a teenager's father started receiving all sorts of baby products coupons, so he called Target's (big company in the USA, like

Walmart) shop manager and bashed him, saying that Target is sending these coupons to encourage my teenage daughter to get pregnant. Naturally, the store manager had no idea what the father was talking about, but he apologized for the mistake that had happened.

After working with his IT team, he again called the teenager's father to apologize, and to say he would not receive any more coupons. But the store manager was in for a shock after hearing the father. His daughter was indeed pregnant and she was due in August.

Target had a machine learning system in their system to send coupons, so it recognized the buying pattern of the women who are pregnant, without even the women knowing it, and before they even knew they were pregnant.

So we humans are pattern-oriented people (we are pattern recognizing too). So we all fall into a pattern and live our lives in the same pattern until there are major changes in our environment. And all our patterns are predictable. Just as the Target machine learning algorithm predicted the pregnancy from the teenage girl's buying pattern, success in people can also be predicted by the habits he/she has formed and the things he is doing.

Failure can also be predicted by his/her pattern. We need to use it as an advantage to avoid failure patterns and do all of what is needed to avoid those patterns.

So if you identify which are the habits of successful people and copy them, you will also be successful.

Nature doesn't take sides, there is only cause and effect. As in Newton's third law, 'Every action has an equal and opposite reaction.'

Each and every successful habit has positive consequences, all you need is to find them and copy them and you will be successful.

"Shallow men believe in luck or in circumstance.
Strong men believe in cause and effect."

– Ralph Waldo Emerson

How to make Habits

You may not believe it, but we are all in autopilot mode. We tend to be very habit oriented. Positive or negative. We need to know what all our positive habits are and what all our negative habits are.

Forming a bad habit is easy, but changing a bad habit is hard.

The first step is finding your bad habits and bringing them to your conscious awareness. This will be your first step, as until you are aware of it, you will not be able to overcome them. Awareness is the first step, it will activate your brain to change that habit.

The second step is finding one good habit you are good at and which you are following religiously. For example, I hit the gym four days a week and I have it as a morning habit. You can find your own, maybe you are going to the office early every day, or you wake up early every day.

If you feel you don't have a single good habit, then do one thing, start waking up early every day, just 30 minutes earlier than you usually wake up.

In case you wake up every day by 7:00 AM, from tomorrow, wake up by 6:30 AM, and do this for 21 days. So also in the case of weekends, if you wake up around 9:00 AM, then wake up on weekends at 8:30 AM. So your new habit will be waking up at 6:30 on weekdays and 8:30 on weekends. Do this for 21 days continuously. If you have missed a day, you need to reset it to another 21 days.

Once you do something for 21 days, you will feel the momentum, and you will start following the ritual. You have now built up your willpower a bit.

> *"As people strengthened their willpower muscles in one part of their lives—in the gym, or a money management program—that strength spilled over into what they ate or how hard they worked. Once willpower became stronger, it touched everything."*
>
> *– **Charles Duhigg, The Power Of Habit***

The third step is to piggyback one more good habit to the existing good habit. In our case, it is waking up 30 minutes earlier than our usual time. Start going for a 15-30 minutes' walk. Do that walk for 21 days.

Once you have formed two habits, you can form more habits. Since you are walking for 15-30 minutes, don't listen to the radio or songs, listen to the technical podcast like .Net rocks, Master of Scale, or any technical YouTube video which has been sitting on your 'watch later' video list for a long time.

Can you see the pattern here? You need good habits to append to the good habits you already have. You have to find your good habit and add one more habit. Once you have mastered it, add one more.

We have very limited will power at our disposal, and it is very tiny and it gets sucked by our daily activities. Our brain is lazy to make decisions, and in "*Think Fast and Slow*" Daniel Kahneman divides the brain's decision making into two parts: System 1 and System 2.

System 1 takes decisions on the spur of the moment and they are more instinct-based decisions and can be easily manipulated. The whole media and advertising industry is taking advantage of this knowledge and selling us products which we will never use in our lives. Think about the last time you bought something instinctively, and you are not using that product to date. It may be due to the advertisement or some other way that you were propelled into the idea of buying it.

System 2 is a decision type where you say you need a day to think about it or do research about it. Next time you buy something, make sure you bring System 2 thinking which analyses the current situation, and the decision is made only on analysis.

The next time before clicking the Buy button, think whether it is your System 1 or System 2 thinking at work. If you feel it is System 1, say to yourself, let my System 2 work for a day, and I will buy it tomorrow. I have saved lots of money by just consciously calling System 2 part of my brain to work.

System 2 is hard, and the brain tends to not use it more because it needs energy for the brain to process all the data you have and also research from the memory and external resources. So the brain tends to do easy things.

Decision making is very hard, because the brain has lots of things to do and the decision does trigger lots of emotions like guilt and regret to analyze what, if the decision you made is wrong. So you will have only a certain amount of energy every day to make decisions.

If you are not aware of this simple concept of your brain being lazy, your will power is limited, and you will waste lots of them during the day and you will not have the will power to make important decisions.

That is the reason people like Steve Jobs and Mark Zuckerberg (Facebook founder) wear the same dress every day because they know they have lots of decisions to make in life, and choosing what to wear is the least of them.

Willpower is like a muscle, the more you flex it, the more you get it. Once you start adding will power to your daily life, there is only an upward spiral toward growth.

See if you follow the above routine by waking up early, you have made yourself physically active and you have also made your technology skill grow. All you need to do is start making small changes in your life, and it will automatically have a domino effect.

Growth in your life will quadruple and you will be better than yesterday, and you will be excited every day because you are adding more willpower, which is helping to add value to your life and others' lives.

Value is a topic that will be dealt with highly in the book. You should become a valuable person, you should become a person who provides lots of value to the lives of everyone around you.

In the office, you should be the 'go-to' person for any technology problem that arises and you make yourself valuable by reading and updating your skill. We have a chapter in the book which will help you get the shortcut on how to read and update yourself very fast and remember what you have read for a long time.

At home, you should improve only one habit, and that is the listening habit. Become a great listener, don't probe or don't investigate when your wife or kids or parents talk to you. Just try to understand from their shoes. Give advice only if they ask for, otherwise do not ever give advice. Keep your own autobiography with you. Don't give it for free.

Getting more things done

"People think focus means saying yes to the thing you've got to focus on. But that's not what it means at all. It means saying no to the hundred other good ideas that there are. You have to pick carefully. I'm actually as proud of the things we haven't done as the things I have done. Innovation is saying no to 1,000 things."

— *Steve Jobs*

Focus is one of the things that is getting tougher and tougher these days. We tend to get distracted a lot and it is killing our productivity.

In the book *"Focus"* by Daniel Goleman, he talks about how just uninstalling Facebook will improve the quality of your life. For our creativity to get better, we need our own cocoon, our private space, where we need time to reflect rather than worry about day-to-day problems.

If you need anything to get done, you need to focus on one and only one thing to get it done. Doing multiple things at the same time will get you nowhere.

That is the reason why Steve Jobs, when he returns to Apple after being thrown out, comes back and sacks all the products, and then concentrates only on one product in each segment. Personal computer and Laptop had only one model rather than multiple options.

This gave Apple more time and money to focus on being more innovative, now all they do is make this one product the best in the world.

If you want to get one thing right in your life, it will be getting your focus in line.

In '*7 Habits of Highly effective people*', Stephen Covey talks about what to focus on in our lives and what not to focus on. He has devised a matrix into four quadrants—Urgent, Not Urgent, Important, and Not important.

Quadrant I talks about important and urgent activities such as support calls, server down issues, someone sick in our family.

Quadrant II talks about the technical debts we have in our project, books we have not read which will help in our career, manual activities we are doing in our projects that can be automated, spending time with your wife and kids, spending time with your parents because life is short.

Quadrant III activities are urgent or important, they are emails that need to satisfy someone's agenda, being in a support call, meetings where your presence is needed but no one is prepared and no one knows what should be the outcome of the meeting, interruption from a co-worker who works in another project which you would have some knowledge about.

Quadrant IV talks about not important and not urgent activities where it does not add value or meaning to anyone's life. E.g., Watching News continuously, eating junk food, checking every feed on Facebook, checking every message on WhatsApp.

People ask me where I find the time to do all the activities I do. Initially, you need to figure out your Quadrant IV activities and discipline yourself one by one.

I found myself wasting lots of time on Facebook and WhatsApp. So I deleted the Facebook app from my mobile and got myself out of all the groups of WhatsApp, because there are too many messages you don't need. Friends added me back to my WhatsApp even after I left the WhatsApp. So what I did was delete my WhatsApp account for five days, so no one can add me back.

When I came back to WhatsApp after five days, people were busy with their own lives, so they left me alone. I spend time with my friends like everyone over the phone or meet them personally.

	Urgent	Not Urgent
Important	**Quadrant I** • Crisis • Pressing problems • Deadline driven projects	**Quadrant II** • Relationship building • Finding new opportunities • Long-term planning • Preventive activities • Personal growth • Recreation
Not Important	**Quadrant III** • Interruptions • Emails, calls, meetings • Popular activities • Proximate, pressing matters	**Quadrant IV** • Trivia, busy work • Time wasters • Some calls and emails • Pleasant activities

We want to be on social networks because we don't want to feel left out from the news that happens around us. Do you know what the best way is to make someone feel good about themselves? It is listening to them attentively and respecting their opinion on the things they are talking about. Once you are out of the Facebook and WhatsApp group, you will not know all that happens around you.

Then when your friends tell you about it, you will be genuinely interested to know about it, and they will explain or talk about it, which will make them feel good about themselves and you will learn the things, and also created a quality time with your friends.

Yes, sometimes, some of your friends will ask, "You don't know about this? Everyone knows except you in the world." Then try telling them with confidence, that you don't watch the news or spend time on WhatsApp or Facebook. The key here is telling them with confidence and making it clear that you are not ashamed of it.

You will gain great respect from your peers and friends. The output of this single action will make you feel good about yourself, and friends will have the opportunity to talk about what information they are excited about.

I am not saying that you should walk away from all the news about current trends and the latest scandals that happen on the earth. You need to know them, because it helps you to socialize faster with peers and new groups. The take away here is, don't waste time on Twitter, Facebook, or WhatsApp, learn those current trends from your peers.

Once you have worked on Quadrant IV and avoided those activities, use that time to work on Quadrant II activities, for example, read books you have kept aside for a long time. In the beginning, just read two pages of it, or just check out the chapters. If you already know the chapters, just read two pages of the book. It will surely have a ripple effect.

You can say I am busy and my whole life is a Quadrant 1, where everything is urgent and important. Think again. I have been betraying myself having this talk with myself, but when you reflect on this deeply, all the urgent work was important and was not urgent a few days or weeks ago. If we would have been proactive then, and not kept procrastinating the important ones for a long time, and did things before they became urgent, we would not be under stress or complaining about always being busy.

Driving a bus has been declared as being one of the most stressful jobs on the planet, not because they need to consider the passengers' safety and the people who are running and crossing the road. The main reason for stress is due to the absense of choice. They have to take a certain route, irrespective of traffic, or any congestion. They need to stop at every stop and all are predefined, and the choice they make while driving is almost none.

They have to adhere to those routes and rules very strictly, otherwise, there would be a huge effect on their monthly salary if they get a memo. The airplane is off course most of the time and they keep correcting the course to reach the destination. Even though the airplane has a full autopilot mode, pilots make some choices and decisions. But with the bus driver, it is different.

If you feel out of control, you will feel under stress, that is why you are in full stress when you are in the Quadrant I activity. It is not the job you are doing that stresses you. If you would have done the same job one week earlier, you would have actually felt good about completing something early. But it has become stressful because we have procrastinated for very long and we don't have a choice to do something else. It is the lack of choice that puts you under stress.

Do more Quadrant II activities. It is a sure, pure way to be less stressed and be happier. To do more of the Quadrant II activities, make sure you discipline yourself by piggybacking habits that are discussed in this chapter. Remember it is all about focusing on one thing and doing it over and over to be successful.

List out one thing you will do today that will have a ripple effect (e.g., waking up early)

_____

_____

List out two things you can append to the above activity.

_____

_____

Write down your worst Quadrant IV activities, e.g., Checking WhatsApp every 2 microseconds

_____

_____

Write down three activities you have been procrastinating which are Quadrant II activities.

_____

_____

Self-Talk

"Be mindful of your self-talk. It is a conversation with the universe."

– Wu Wei Wisdom

Brian Tracy is the great-grandfather of self-help. He is amazing! I am what I am because of his audio programs and books. You will move to the next level for sure, just by listening to any of his audios just once. He is that wonderful.

In one of my favorite and Brian Tracy's best sellers, '*The Psychology of Achievement*,' he talks about affirmations, where he says to wake up in the morning and say out loud 10 times to yourself, I AM UNSTOPPABLE, looking at the mirror.

I felt it was weird, but it is a great way to start the day. I have never done this, but I highly recommend you to try it. I have a different type of affirmation that helps me in difficult situations.

When I am in a very stressful situation, I think of the last time I solved a difficult problem and I will tell myself, "I have solved a worse problem than the current one and I am capable of solving this one too."

I highly recommend finding self-talk that gives you positive affirmations and you chant that every day or morning or when you are struggling with any hardship in your life.

The things you talk about when you are under stress or facing challenges or in a struggle, hold a key to your success. Because we are paid to solve problems. Either you can take every problem as an opportunity, or every problem as stress that you need to avoid.

Once you consider every problem as an opportunity, you might want to be around the problem, you will chase the problem rather than it chasing you.

You become the problem attacker and it makes you a better architect, because the architect's/developer's work is to attack a problem and design a solution for it. And then comes a problem from the solution you built and another problem from the new solution. So problem-solving is the skill we are heavily paid for when compared to any other profession in the world.

In the book '*What to say, when you talk to yourself,*' Shad Helmstetter talks about five levels of self-talk.

- I can't
- I need to... I should...
- I never... I no longer...
- I am
- It is

If you are in the first type, 'I can't change, I can't do it,' please change your self-talk to "I Can". Next time you face any situation, try just telling yourself, "I can do it." Never say, "I can't," and you can see the magic happening in your life.

If you are in the second level where you say to yourself, "I need to," or "I should, because I don't have a choice," then tell yourself, you have a choice, and you will choose to respond to that situation and choose to do this one because it makes life better.

The third type of self-talk is better than the first two, at least the self-talk tells you that you are in control of the situation, but the problem with that talk is your brain cannot take negative statements. 'Not' and 'never' have no meaning for the brain. As per NLP (Neuro-linguistic programming), your brain filters the negative words in your statements and only registers the statement as a positive one. For example, if you tell yourself, "I will never smoke," or "I will never be late," your mind cannot register the negative word in your sentence and it will only register the "I will smoke," or "I will be late."

The fourth type is affirming to yourself, that you are already in that place where you want to be, the way you really wanted to be. It is telling yourself that you have already achieved the things you wanted. It is the most effective way.

Instead of being in the third stage, where you tell yourself, "I will never smoke," or "I will never be late," in the fourth, you will be telling yourself, "My lungs are healthy and clean," or, "I am an early riser and early comer."

If you are in the fifth type, you don't even need this book. I am paraphrasing from the book, '*What to say, when you talk to yourself*', "I am one with the universe and it is one with me. I am of it, within it." It is coming from the paradigm that everything in the universe works for you to get better.

Whenever you get into any challenges, you tell yourself the universe is working its way to get the best of me and I'm going to prepare and expose myself, so I get better every day. I am not going to compare myself with anyone, I am going to compare myself with who I was yesterday. Have I improved or deteriorated, is always the question people will ask who are in the fifth stage.

Most of us have experienced the fifth stage at least once. Think of a time, when a person who has been working behind your back, who is not good-intentioned, and an ill-intentioned action by him turned out to be good for you.

Think about the last time you felt lucky, and everything you wanted happened as if the whole universe is working on the thing you wanted, even though you screwed up too many things, but still, everything ended well. These are moments that happen to successful people every time because they think the whole universe is unfolding to do good to them.

I am an Atheist, by the way, and I am into science more. But for certain questions of life, science cannot give us definite answers, Spirituality can. I am not talking about any religion or any religious activities.

One thing I want to touch on here is that most of the suffering in our life is just because of our over-thinking brain, where we project a mental movie of negative things that might happen, that would have never happened in our life. So the suffering is only brain made.

There are two types of pain, mental pain, and physical pain. Physical pain is there for a good purpose, it helps to focus our attention on the body part which is hurt or not healthy, so we move our attention and take care of the situation. But mental pain had its advantages when we were roaming as nomads in the forest.

Until we picture the worst thing that could happen from the sounds we hear from bushes and run, we might be eaten or attacked by any animal that is roaming in the forest. So mentally picturing all the bad things that might happen helped us to flee from such situations.

Right now with our current environment, we don't have to assume bad outcome from every situation. So thinking about the negative outcomes of a particular situation will not be good for anyone. It will bring your energy down because your brain uses more energy than any other organ in your body.

Here is a list of Positive affirmations that you can use:

- I am unstoppable
- I am good at what I do
- I am great at what I do
- I am here to succeed in this world
- Everything that happens in my life, happens for me to succeed
- Everyone around me works for my success
- I get stronger every day

What is your positive affirmation? (Write one from the above list or make your own one)

_____

_____

What did you suffer last time and it turned out to be nothing?

_____

_____

What are the three things you want to change in your life?

1. I need to read every day
2. I will never smoke
3.
4.
5.

Take the above things and change them into positive affirmations that you have already done.

1. I am reading every day morning from 6:30 to 7:00
2. My lungs are healthy and I am taking good care of them
3.
4.
5.

Sense of Deserving

"Agree with yourself, let me tell you, YOU DESERVE"

– Abraham Hicks, Author of
Law of Attraction journal

Lottery winners are more likely to declare bankruptcy within three to five years than any other average citizen. Evidence shows that out of most people who make it to the top, one percent of income earners usually don't stay at the top for very long.

Why people who win millions of dollars go broke after three to five years is because they feel they don't deserve it, and whatever they got from the lottery will be thrown away in gambling and lavish spending because their internal voice says the money they got is not what they deserve. So they have to look rich to the new society they are trying to blend in, and they think they can fake their way by looking rich without feeling rich inside.

Until you feel rich inside, you will not be able to keep your money. All the lavish spending or buying things that we don't need is because we want to prove to someone that we are rich, because we don't feel we are rich.

I am not talking about buying a nice car or home because you want to provide comfort and safety for your parents and children. I am talking about buying something which is not needed, and you buy just to show others that you can afford it. Internally, your mind says you don't deserve it.

This one is big here. Until you feel you deserve it, you will not achieve or get anything or keep it for longer in your life. The first step of getting anything in your life is you should feel you deserve having or possessing the thing you want.

You may have the greatest desire and you may work toward achieving it, but if you have an inner voice telling you it is too much for you, or you are not good enough, or you haven't earned it, then your brain and universe will find all the ways to stop you from getting it, or take away the things you feel you don't deserve.

I personally had lots of experience with this. I will share one experience of mine, when I was working in a top major software solution provider. I used to earn 8 lakhs and I was happy with it. I heard from one of my friends that people are earning 12 lakhs for the same job and experience.

At that time, I was looking for another job and I was asking for the salary increase to be 50% of my current salary, which came to 12 lakhs. The job consultant who used to call for job opportunities yelled at me that I was greedy to expect that much salary hike, because as per the industry standards, you can get a hike of around 20% and the maximum it can go to is around 30%.

But I persisted and told every consultant who called, you don't have a client who can pay me that much, and if you have a client who can pay 12 lakhs, please call me. One guy even shouted at me, that I would never be able to switch to another company because I refused his job offer for a big MNC whose interview I had cleared.

One fine morning a consultant called me, and she said, she has a requirement where the client is ready to pay any amount, if the candidate clears the technical interview.

I attended the interview, cleared the technical rounds, and quoted 12 lakhs, and got the job. Now the new consultant yelled at me for quoting less because the company was ready to pay even 14 lakhs.

I did not quote 14 lakhs because I thought I didn't deserve 14 lakhs. That is the reason I could not ask for 14 lakhs and I thought they would find out that I am not worthy of that much money.

The sense of deserving is a very big mindset you need to work on. Until you work on that, you will not be able to achieve everything you are capable of.

We have less sense of deserving because of society and parents telling us that we cannot get all that we want in our life. We have been programmed by society and schools to be accepting the norms and being average.

When we start permitting ourselves to be whatever we want in our life, we tend to get whatever we want. Lack of a sense of deserving always stops us from getting whatever we want.

Negative programming happens because we have been told by well-intentioned people that we are not good enough, we should try something else.

As a matter of fact, nobody has told us that perseverance is the key, and the more you persist, the more you move toward your goal.

The next time you see yourself talking to yourself, that you are not good enough, stop and take a deep breath, and then tell yourself, "I deserve this."

Meditation helps us a lot in improving our sense of focus which will remove all the cluttering thoughts that run around in your head.

"We always overestimate the change that will occur in the next two years and underestimate the change that will occur in the next ten."

– Bill Gates, *The Road Ahead*

A sense of deserving can be cultivated by first permitting ourselves to say, "It is ok to get what we want," e.g. Becoming the best architect in your company. Tell yourself, "It is ok, I give myself the permission to become the best architect."

Next is to find the greatest fear that stops you from getting better, such as, "People might find out that I am not good enough." You should read Scott Hanselman's blog post. Google for "I am phony". It will be the first in the search result list.

We don't want to become rich and successful because we think our current friends or even our parents might not accept us. This is a very bad programming we have.

Write one thing you want, but you feel you don't deserve.

_____

_____

What do you fear will happen when you get what you want?

_____

_____

What is the worst thing that might happen when you get what you want?

_____

_____

What can you do about handling the worst thing that could happen?

_____

_____

Cause and Effect

"Everything happens for a reason. For every cause, there is an effect,
and for every effect, whether you know it or not, there is a specific
cause or causes. There are no accidents.
You can have anything you want in life if you can first
decide exactly what it is, and then do the things that others
have done to achieve the same result."

– Brian Tracy

Everything in life is caused by something as an effect. You reap what you sow. You receive what you have given. The law of cause and effect is the law which we should understand and make it second nature.

Success leaves tracks, if we do what successful architects and technology giants have done, we can become the same as they are now.

Nature is neutral, it does not take sides. Like the law of gravity, the law of cause and effect works for everyone. You may not be rich, or do not have good communication skills right now. If you do what successful architects have done, you will reach the same place where they are right now.

Pay the price

You need to pay the price upfront because everything has a price. You need to find how much of a successful architect you are going to become, and you need to figure out what you are willing to pay.

In the book '*Think and Grow Rich*,' Napoleon Hill talks about determining exactly what you intend to give in return for the goal you desire. Until you figure out what you are ready to sacrifice in life to become what you want, you will never go anywhere.

Everything starts with paying the price. Like cutting the distractions in your life, removing unwanted socializing in your life, which does not build any long term and meaningful relationships, such as wasting your time gossiping and bad-mouthing about other people...

Remember, when you bad mouth people who are not present, then you are telling the other person indirectly that you bad mouth about him, when he/she is not around.

Channel your energy to do positive activities, rather than holding a grudge which is another energy-consuming activity that leads to stress and hinders your growth to become a successful architect. First thing is to forgive everyone who you think has done bad things to you. You don't have to forget it, but you can still forgive them.

Stop watching TV or the internet that does not give you any information that leads to achieving your goal. I am talking about all the melodrama which sucks your energy and that makes you feel you are a victim. Watch uplifting documentaries or talks or any technical videos that will help you get better at solving challenges as an architect.

Cutting distraction, stopping bad-mouthing, letting go of your grudge, stop watching TV, are the initial prices you need to pay. Once you start doing the above, you will have more time and energy that can be channeled into more productive activities.

Once you master how to avoid wasting your energy and time in unwanted areas, it is very simple to double your productivity and become technology savvy.

Remember, success leaves clues and nature doesn't take sides. Nature is neutral, just as gravity is common for everyone irrespective of your wealth, wisdom, etc.

Think of the people you know who are not smarter than you, who actually earn more money than you. They are not just lucky. They just copy what successful people do, and get to that position.

All you need to do is the below steps that will take you to be a better architect. These are simple to follow:

1. Find your goal on how much of a successful architect you want to become.
2. Find the person who has already achieved that goal.
3. Follow the person and study their success habits.
4. Do what they do every day.

The first step is to find the level of success you want to get in being an architect. It can be even becoming an architect and earning X amount of money.

Find the person who has already achieved what you want to become. It may be someone in your own source community, or an architect in your organization, or even architects of Google and Microsoft. It can be anyone.

Find ways to follow them and find what they do.

You can use social media nowadays to your advantage. Follow the people you want to become and not your friends, so you can avoid getting distracted from your goal.

Always read their blogs, watch their videos and listen to their podcasts, if they have one. So you can follow their footsteps, because they would have removed the obstacles when they walked the path, and now we can walk without much hassle.

Figure out what is the one thing you can start right now that will lead you to the doorstep of who you want to become, which is taken from the successful habits of the person who you want to model on.

List of steps to do right now:

What is the level of success you expect to become from today?

_____

_____

_____

What are you willing to pay to become a successful architect? E.g., Distractions you are going to stop.

_____

_____

_____

Who do you think you can model on, and who is the person who has achieved the goal already?

_____

_____

_____

How can you follow them and what are the resources you can access?

_____

_____

_____

What are their habits?

_____

_____

_____

What is the one thing you are going to model, that your model is doing today?

_____

_____

_____

Characteristics of an Architect

Principle-Based Life

"You Don't Control The Outcomes Of Your Life, Principles Do."

– Stephen Covey

A principle-based life helps to handle critical situations efficiently and effectively. Once you live on certain principles in your life, you tend to strengthen your character. In extremely tough situations, you will know what to do. Silly things will not affect you.

Remember the last time you saw a person who took a solid decision despite the whole world being against him, and in the end, it was THE right decision. Many movies are filled with these types of situations where the man takes a decision and it is opposed. It ends up as the best decision that was ever taken. This is an example of a principle-based life.

A principle-based life helps you to advance your career better. You can learn hundreds of techniques, but those techniques will not work in every situation.

Say, you learn a technique to influence your boss for implementing a new development process that will benefit many developers, and he might get influenced by the new technique you learned. But once you report to some other boss, the same technique may not work with the new boss, because each person is different. Your technique might even backfire, which makes you look like a manipulator.

When you are working on principles, you tend to find long-term solutions, because you don't care about the short-term frustrations that you come across. Once you start thinking about the long term, you won't be getting upset by the small annoyances that you come across in your life. Small things don't shake you. Silly people will not annoy you much.

Once you become more and more of a principle-based person, immature people will start leaving you. You will be attracting successful people. Immature people will automatically not cross your path anymore.

Frustration in your life will go down because frustration is an outcome of excessive expectations without understanding the actual reality, because everything takes time.

Once you are principle-centered, you tend to choose technology and tend to stick with it because you know everything takes time and every technology has a tradeoff. You don't accuse yourself of choosing the wrong technology.

You know that you did all research as much as possible, and you will stick with it and not blame yourself. And you will also ignore the blame of others.

Once you are principle-centered, you tend to choose friends wisely, you don't adjust yourself to fit in any group. You will tend to find people who help with your technical career. You tend to avoid people and conversations that consist of only criticism, gossips, etc.

If you start living a principle-centered life, you will feel more **secure** because your sense of security does not come from the current trends in the market. You will only be improving your knowledge about new technology and will have a firm grip on the basics of computer science.

The current employer's market position does not determine your security. You will be valuable in the market because you have done more and learned more.

If you are a principle-centered person, then you stand apart from the emotions and current situation. You will look at every situation as a whole because you have guiding principles in your life. You will have accurate data when choosing a technology because you don't choose any technology, or a new team member based on current pressing problems. You have a principle that **guides** you because you know where you want to go and also know the current problems are temporary.

If you tend to live with principles, your **wisdom** grows every day because you have principles that guide you. You know exactly where you are right now and where you want to go.

You tend to not get into silly quarrels and not get carried away by the person who challenges your technical decision. Since you seek wisdom, you work on the inclusion of your team's wisdom and see your team members as worthy allies rather than as competitors or persons who just challenge your authority.

You tend to empathetically listen to people because you know, everyone can be right, even if it is conflicting, because you know the situation varies from time to time. There is no right or wrong, it is always "**It depends**".

You will be more **powerful** because you are a self-aware, knowledgeable, proactive individual, largely unrestricted by the attitudes, behaviors, and actions of others. Your ability to influence your team technically goes far beyond the current situation and resources because your inner security, and internal guidance will improve others' wisdom, which encourages a highly developed level of interdependence.

If we are not principle-centered, we tend to take life as it comes with inner resistance. Life tends to worry and annoy us a lot because our inner self says that is not right for us and yet we don't have a choice.

Since we don't have an inner compass, we will not say no to the current pressing and urgent things. So we will be living a dual life, doing things we don't like and longing for things we like.

When you are not living a principle-based life, frustration will be more, because we tend to get distracted by someone's expectations. Our mood tends to be dependent on others' moods. If they are happy, we are happy. If they are angry or frustrated, we tend to be unhappy.

If your life is not principle-centered, you tend to be more constrained with a small perspective about life, because you tend to surround yourself with people you are comfortable with, and not people you are not comfortable with. Because we feel more insecure when people are better than us.

If you don't live on solid principles, you tend to live in a small box of life with less knowledge and skills, and you will be very skeptical in sharing the knowledge because you don't have guiding principles that give a sense of security in sharing things, and you are more worried about your current living than your larger purpose of life.

You will feel powerless because your principles don't navigate you, you tend to get affected by the environment. You feel empowered mainly on two senses.

- Sense of control
- Sense of coherence

First, as an architect, you need your own sense of control. When you read more and follow people who you want to be, you know what to do when there is a solution needed or a problem to be solved.

Once you are fully aware of yourself and well informed, then what you do is make decisions based on your knowledge and wisdom and you feel in control. So you will have better peace of mind. As discussed before in previous sections, an out of control feeling leads to stress.

Once you have better peace of mind, you can influence people because you know what motivates them and how you can build a great team that feels autonomous and also coherent about what they work.

Coherence is the quality of forming a unified whole. You would have heard the expression "Walk the talk". It is coherence.

You are being consistent in who you are and what you do. You don't fake your actions, you don't get anxious when there is a situation with huge pressure, like missing a deadline, or the technology you choose has a tradeoff that we neglected while doing a proof of concept. You tend to actually be cool rather than acting cool.

I still remember my architect whom I worked with while I was in Japan, who is the coolest guy I have ever seen. He would whistle and come to our seat when there was a huge bug that had crept in, or there was a missed functionality and no one knew how to fix it before the day of the client demo.

He would come in as cool as a cucumber, and he would just write a few lines of code, and politely walk away. The whole office would be on fire because of the issue, but I have never seen him slip. He is the guy from whom I learned most of my principles about empathy, mentoring, integrity, etc. He is the most coherent guy I have ever seen. He walks his talk and never lets down his coolness.

When you are coherent in action, thoughts, and words, you tend to become more powerful because people know you don't fake things. Even if you slip sometimes, they will be ok with it because people understand everyone is human. Everyone will understand, that you are not attacking them, you are attacking the problem.

Application Suggestions

You need to find your set of principles, because each and every one is unique. Everyone's life and situation are unique. Principles are like the law of gravity—it works irrespective of the current situation or your current position in life.

Please read the principles I have put together which I strive hard to follow every day of my life and it has done wonders for me. These principles are not invented by me, I have just put them together based on the **7 Habits of highly effective people**. But one thing I know, it works. I have drilled down on suggestions, so every architect can relate and start following them right away. All the seven principles are interrelated with each other, they are closely tied, so that one depends on another to be more complete.

Never compromise with honesty and integrity

Honesty means truthfulness, sincerity, and frankness. Integrity is adhering to ethical principles. You can live with honesty and not have integrity. But you cannot live with integrity and not be honest.

Honesty is being true to yourself; when you are honest, you don't tell lies or do things that are against morals. Integrity is more about taking actions, integrity is about not doing things that are dishonest and doing things to prevent immoral activities. Honesty is about internal character, and integrity is about acting based on your honest principles.

As an architect, you should practice honesty and integrity. You should be known by everyone as a man of words. You gain respect from the team members when you display high integrity in your action and words. No matter what, you don't slip in your integrity, despite pressing deadlines where a small lie will save you, but it will spoil the trust.

Obtain the counsel of others

This one is big. If cultivated properly you can go places. If you know how to get the counsel of others and incorporate them into your work, then you become one of the highest-earning architects ever. People who get counsel make their lives better for themselves and also others.

It is great to be a pioneer or trailblazer, where we find out our own way and let people know about what needs to be done. It does not work every time. Sometimes we must know when we should obtain counsel from others. If you have the mindset of learning everything by yourself then you lose lots of time and energy.

You don't have to reinvent the wheel; in the later chapter Buy vs. Build, we have spoken more about it. If you want to learn everything by yourself, one lifetime won't be enough. Success leaves clues and trails; follow the trails where successful people have already traveled, and then find your own path out of it.

I am not saying here to disturb everyone in the team and get counsel for every small task. You should do research on your own before talking to everyone. You should have all your facts in your hands, and then you should consult them, with the exact problem that is delaying your progress.

If you follow the approach of getting facts in hand before consulting anyone, you will earn better respect and people will be very ready to help you. It lets people come to you when they have doubts. So communication between the team gets better.

One thing I will always do while building a team is to make sure people communicate with each other nicely and jell with each other. As an architect, you should build an environment where ignorance is not a sin. Ignorance is a good thing and it is ok to let people know that you don't know. If you don't know, you should ask around.

If you make it a habit in a team that people are ok with being vulnerable and ask for help when needed, the environment becomes safe and conducive, you get more things done, and the synergy that comes out of the team will be palpable.

Defend those who are absent

This should be the one you should get better at, if you want to be promoted to a senior title. People judge you a lot when you talk about others. If you defend them, then trust about you increases. If you say anything bad about them, they might enjoy the gossip that you share with them, it may even temporarily make you feel a sense of closeness, but they will know deep down and at the back of their minds that you are a person who will gossip about them when they are not around.

Gossip will kill you on all levels. When you gossip with your seniors, then you become the guy who they think is not trustworthy. They will never open up to you and tell you any future policy actions that will happen in the organization because they know you are going to tell this to someone when you gossip to the team. This will also alienate your teammates because they know that any pitfalls or mistakes they make, their personal or professional life is not safe.

When you are gossiping with your team members, you might feel a sense of closeness, but you will become the guy they should never open up to, and they know you are going to bad mouth them when they are absent.

When you gossip or bad mouth someone who is absent, all you lose is trust, you can never create a long-term healthy relationship. You should always defend those who are absent.

Next time, when someone badmouths to you about anyone, tell them, "I think it is not fair to talk bad about people in their absence. If you feel they have done some wrong, we can directly tell them what it is and try to understand why they did what they did." People might not like this when you tell them. It may throw them back. But eventually, you become a very trustable person.

You become the guy to whom people let the secrets out. Sometimes you might be even pushed against a wall to tell them what you know about the other person that is inappropriate. Use these exact words.

"I don't tell anyone what is told to me as a secret. In the same way, if you tell me a secret, I will not tell anyone. So I can't tell you what they told me."

Try this a couple of times, then you will see how much information you will come to know. But NEVER use the above lines as tricks or techniques to manipulate people. People will soon find out if you are not having integrity in what you just said.

Controlling Vs. Being in Control

As humans, we strive for a sense of control. Our whole peace of mind comes from the control we have over the situation. If we feel we don't have a choice in certain situations, then our peace of mind goes down. We don't care about the result, as long as we took the decision and the consequences are from the choices we made.

The problem is when you try to control things that you cannot control or are out of boundaries to control, such as weather, traffic, politics; you can never have peace of mind. The only by-product you get is frustration. **One thing you can control in this world is yourself.** You cannot control what happens to you, you can only control how you react to it.

The way you react makes the situation worse than any incident that actually happened. You should only look out for what you can do from your end that can make your situation better. Trying to be controlling everyone's behavior is not possible.

As an architect, if you want control of your team or your team members, never try to control them. You can never control anyone. The only way you can get things done from the team or navigate the team toward success is by finding a way to influence people. Persuasion and influencing are the greatest skills you need to learn. We will go in-depth about this in the "Leader in an architect" chapter.

Motivation is the greatest skill you should learn for being in control. Everyone is motivated differently, so finding what motivates people is what you first need to understand. To understand what motivates people, you should have your own sense of control. For having your own sense of control of yourself, you should be the person who takes responsibility for everyone, you have a long term goal, your burning why supersedes any current situations or silly/ego problems, you should have an inner sense of security where the external weather or situations do not bother you.

When you understand what influence is, how motivation works, and how to lead a team of A-Players, which you will learn in the "Leader in an architect" chapter, you can be in control of any situation rather than trying to control people in the situation.

Visualize yourself in a room of people and you are in control of the whole without being controlled by every person. When you are in control, everyone wants to follow you. When you want to control, everyone wants to rebel and do things against you even if it is in their best interest.

Examining your motive

This will create lots of suffering initially, but stick with the process. Examining your motive for each and every action leads to one thing. We are extremely selfish in everything we do. You decide only based on selfish motive, and later add some fact that justifies that we are not selfish, to feel good about yourself. So we can have a nice sleep that night. Once you examine the motive for every action, you might lose a couple of days' sleep based on the current maturity level you are in.

As an architect, we need to make lots of decisions based on facts that are currently available. But in the real world, our decision may not be for the well-being of the project and team members; we tend to choose some technology because it was shiny and it adds value to our resume.

Taking decisions for selfish needs, has to be examined. Everyone is selfish, there is no second opinion on that. But selfishness **should have** some **altruism** (concern for the well-being of others).

You should always make decisions based on keeping your needs as a second choice. As an architect choosing the technology, it should be based on the fact that it will make the life of developers better and will fit the current project requirement. Not on making your resume better.

Being an architect, you need to work with different sets of people, you tend to even work with people who are smarter than you. A junior developer can be smarter in certain processes and technology at certain times and he may even challenge your facts. You might not like the way he challenges or behaves with you. You might not want him in the project because he is too arrogant to deal with. Again you need to examine your motive in sending him out of the project, whether he is causing disruption to the project and the team, or you cannot influence him and you feel like you are not respected.

If you feel not respected, then think again. Your needs should not lead to losing a good resource. You should really examine your motives. Have you tried treating him as your ally rather than your enemy? When you try to consider him as an ally, at first he might not trust you because the relationship would have become strained due to past reactions. You should be patient for him to trust you.

I am not talking about him being rude or absurd with you. You should check him then and there and tell him he needs to improve his communication skills if he is overly rude.

If you have tried all ways to get this smart guy to align with the team, and still he keeps on going out of the way to just prove himself right, then you need to take further decisions.

But always examine your motive, why you are doing what you are doing. It is always 'why' that matters, we tend to make mistakes on the way always. When our why is right, then what we do has only fewer consequences because we can correct what we did or what we do. Making mistakes is part of being human. When your why is just right, your successful architect journey is unstoppable.

Building Character Vs. Reputation

"Character is like a tree and reputation like a shadow.
The shadow is what we think of it; the tree is the real thing."

– Abraham Lincoln

In ***The 48 Laws of Power*** by Robert Greene, he talks about reputation and says you need to guard it with your life. I do not fully agree with him completely. But You build your character and your reputation will be taken care of automatically. It is a dark book regarding power and you can read it to see how we are manipulated by the government and corporations using those laws. So you can be aware when those techniques are used against you.

If you have a strong character, your reputation will always follow. People with good character make better leaders and friends. Character building is one thing you need to learn from childhood. Our society gives short term rewards for reputation, but character must be sought by us, to sustain in this changing culture. Character is a very tough path to follow. Having high character is the greatest gift you can get and teach others. You need to build character in each and every action.

Character means the mental and moral qualities distinctive to an individual. Reputation means the beliefs or opinions that are generally held by others. Reputation is doing things when people are looking, and character is doing things when no one is looking. If you do good things even when no one is looking, that shows character, and if you do good things only when someone is looking, then you are working only on reputation.

Start doing things even when no one is looking or policing. It can even start from going to meetings on time. It is completely being true to yourself. It is about revealing mistakes even when you will never be found out.

Avoid being an imposter. If you don't know about something, be the first person to admit it, and as an architect, if you admit it and learn from your peers, it gives them a sense of good feeling that they taught you something. It increases the communication within the team. So when you say something you know, then people will completely believe you, because you have built the character of letting people know what you don't know. Your reputation will automatically increase.

Never hide your screw-up from your boss; we architects tend to screw up a lot in the production and development environment and spend days and nights to rectify the mistakes we have made. Always be the person to admit mistakes and take full responsibility for the situation and then start correcting them. Don't blame others and solve the problem.

When you build the character of admitting the mistake even if no one can find out, people will start trusting you when you really are not at fault. Your words will be respected more and trusted more. Your reputation will be more and your senior management will trust with you more opportunities and promote you to higher levels faster than you ever think of.

Admitting the fault to the client might not be the right thing to do in a certain business situation; you should be a little cautious, how you inform the client about your screw-up. You don't have to lie, you need to investigate a lot and see that you reveal your mistakes professionally.

You also build the character of rewarding the acceptance of mistakes. When you yell at people when they make mistakes, they will start to hide it from you. Because hiding from you is better for them than revealing to you because you are rewarding them when they are hiding from you and punishing them when revealing it to you. People tend to do what they are rewarded for.

"Winning takes talent, to repeat takes character."

**– John Wooden, basketball coach, and author.
Nicknamed the "Wizard of Westwood"**

You can get lucky and win once, but repeated success and moving your technical career on an upward spiral takes character. The characters that are addressed are not new, you know what characters you need to follow. The exercise down below helps you to identify the character you need to follow right now to make you a better man/woman. This character exercise can be done every year because your maturity level changes every year and you will find new characters you need to work on. I got this exercise from Warren Buffet on one of his videos and it has helped me a lot.

Think of the person you dislike, it may be your colleague, peer, college mate. List out five character traits that you hate in the character of this other person.

1.
2.
3.
4.
5.

The character trait you hate the most in the other person is the character you need to work on. That is the character you will slip into when you are under tremendous pressure or you are put into a spot. And you hate yourself for doing that.

That's why you hate the person who has that character as second nature, because part of you knows that it is the character you are trying to avoid. Now list what is the alternative you can choose when the character shows up. E.g. You tend to slip into a white lie when you know you can never get caught. In the list below you write, 'I will never lie in my project.'

_____

_____

_____

_____

_____

Note: Good characters are hard to follow and it is hard to execute, but you need to come back again to improve your character. If it is easy, everyone will cultivate good character. People with low willpower tend to slip, and people with high willpower, despite their circumstances tend to stick with their character, rather than their reputation.

Building Trust Vs. Popularity

"Lack of candor blocks smart ideas,
fast action, and good people contributing all the
stuff they've got. It's a killer."

– Jack Welch

As an architect, you should build trust rather than popularity with your team. Your every action should focus on building trust among your peers and stakeholders, rather than your action concentrating on being the most likable person.

Once you build trust and become trustworthy, you tend to get more opportunities on the way because you express the problems then and there despite the news may be all bad. Higher management trusts people who bring bad news and take responsibility and have a clear cut strategy that is needed to fix them.

Higher management might hate your guts, but the trust factor is so high they cannot miss you. The person who tells them what they want to hear, and is nice and submissive to them does not create a high trust profile.

If your action works on getting people to like you, then it might help you in the short term, but will not help you in the long term, because in professional life lots of things change. If your whole principle lies in getting the liking of people, then it depends also on the mood of the people and you tend to get carried away by their internal and external agenda.

You will not be able to navigate the project to success because you might have to do something that might be liked by some people or sometimes the whole team. So you tend to go for compromise which will catch up later with lots of technical debt and low-quality code, etc.

"The first job of a leader—at work or at home—is to inspire trust. It's to bring out the best in people by entrusting them with meaningful stewardships, and to create an environment in which high-trust interaction inspires creativity and possibility."

– Stephen M.R. Covey, The Speed of Trust: The One Thing that Changes Everything

In the book, *'Speed of trust'*, Stephen Covey Jr. talks about how to build trust and how to sustain trust. He gives various examples of how to build trust even in a very hostile environment. We cannot go deep into this book, it needs a separate book on its own. But let me paraphrase the steps listed in the book.

You need to start with yourself. When you tell yourself I am going to wake up at 6:00 AM to write a blog, then you wake up at 6:00 AM sharp, because you work on yourself first before the external environment. Once you start building trust in yourself and whatever you promised, you should be able to keep your promise for yourself. Once you keep a promise to yourself, where you are only accountable to yourself, then you should move to the next step.

We will talk about self-trust in detail. You can create self-trust when you concentrate on four factors.

Integrity: Deep honesty and truthfulness; who we really are; congruence, humility, and courage.
Intent: Our plan or purpose—our motive, our agenda, our behavior.
Capabilities: Our capacity to produce and accomplish tasks through talents, attitudes, skills, knowledge, style.
Results: Our track record—based on past performance, current performance, and anticipated performance.

Once you start working on improving on the four factors, your self-trust will improve automatically.

In the next step, you can start working on the relationship trust, but you cannot build a trustworthy relationship if you don't have self-trust. One of the main things you need to do while building a trust relationship is keeping your promise in spite of circumstances. If you say you will do or be there at some place, you should be there at that place. You cannot change the plan based on their mood or current situations.

One of my directors will not say 'yes' to anything where she cannot keep her promise. For example, someone invites her to a wedding, and due to circumstances, she cannot attend the wedding. She will say i cannot make it to the wedding, but she wishes them luck. Mostly people will say, "I will attend," even though they know it is not at all possible. She does the same thing with their kids too. She will never give them any false promises. As small as promising them buying toys. She would be able to buy, otherwise, she won't promise them.

Once you build self-trust by keeping your own promise, and also keeping promises made to others, you tend to start being influential in the next levels. Then you can build organization level trust, where people will start sharing information openly, tolerate, and encourage mistakes. The organization will be more innovative and creative, and share credit abundantly.

You can learn more about the market and societal trust in the book '*The speed of trust*', which I highly recommend. It has helped me a lot when I was looking out for answers where I wanted to be trusted by higher management and realized that I have to work from the inside out.

Emotional Intelligence

*"No one cares how much you know
until they know how much you care."*

— Theodore Roosevelt

Technology idiots that we are, we don't even have 1% of emotional intelligence more than a toddler. We lost all our emotional intelligence on the way as we grew up. With the current changing world and Artificial intelligence going to take over most blue-collar jobs, I think emotional intelligence should be a much-learned skill to survive and thrive because it is tough as of now for the robot to be programmed with complete emotional intelligence. How much ever you can model an emotion API, it can never beat a woman in understanding emotions.

We have an inbuilt mechanism called "Mirror Neurons". Mirroring is believed to be how the brain automatically interprets the actions, intentions, and emotions of other people. So the Mirror neuron, which is the cell in the brain, gets activated when you see someone's face, and it copies the same facial reaction and then other neurons are triggered. As per the new facial reaction, your brain will understand the emotions of the other person we saw.

You can see figure (2.2.1), where you can understand some of the emotions. They are from the TV series "Lie to me". A very entertaining series to watch about a guy who interrogates the criminals based on the facial reaction and understands whether they are lying or not.

The whole concept of emotional intelligence is knowing the emotions, understanding what it means, and also building your emotional quotient.

The emotional quotient is nothing but the capability of individuals to recognize their own emotions and those of others. It is improving your emotional intelligence on a scale where you can measure them as in IQ. There are lots of sites out there on the internet which can measure your EQ scale.

Below is my test result taken from the site, https://globalleadershipfoundation.com/geit/eitest.html

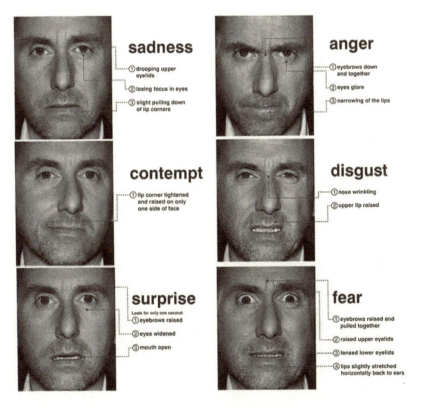

Figure 2.2.1

The Global EI Test Results
(Version 1.0)

Test Date   Thu Sep 24 03:41:28 2020

The following numerical scores are calculated from your answers to the EI test. If you have answered honestly and accurately, your scores, out of 10 for each quadrant, will reflect your capability level within each of the EI quadrants. (You might want to print out this result, if you do not, you will have to retake the last if you want these scores later since they are not saved anywhere.) To gain a picture of what each of the EI quadrants covers, read the short descriptions below.

You have answered all the questions – terrific!

Self Awareness	Self-Management	Social-Awareness	Relationship Management
9	10	10	8

Figure 2.2.2

I highly recommend taking this test and see where you stand. If you have scored more, skip this chapter and move on to the next chapter.

All entire emotion API is built on recognizing facial expression, but the model needs to be trained, so computers can judge our emotions, but we can feel the emotions of the gathering we are in, or the friend, with our eyes closed. It is the power of these emotions that will keep us ahead with computers for a huge amount of time.

As the concept of this whole book is improving and being in control of oneself, once you have mastered yourself, then you can lead others, create synergy, and achieve greater things in life. It all boils down to understanding yourself. As in the Aristotle quote "Know thySelf", once you have mastered yourself, you can master anyone.

The first step as an architect, you need to know the different types of emotions available. List out 15 emotions you know below as comma separated words.

Sad, Happy, Guilt, Regret….

_____

_____

_____

Understanding Emotions

If you have listed more than 15 you can skip the chapter because you are a more emotional person than we are. We not only do not understand the emotion, but we also don't even know most of the emotions available. We know only emotions like happiness, sadness, frustration. But there are more than 25 emotions available. The first step is to know the types of emotions available and then realize it when it arises in your everyday activities.

EQ is more important than IQ for our personal and professional growth

Remember the last time you got so activated by positive or negative emotions and you lost yourself and regretted it later because you did not think logically, and it had a bad consequence in the end? Because your logical brain is taken over by your emotional brain and emotions have more control over you than the logical brain, you were lost in the emotional turmoil. To understand more about emotional intelligence we need to understand the theory of the Triune Brain.

Dr. Paul Maclean, a leading neuroscientist, developed the famous Triune Brain theory for understanding the brain in terms of its evolutionary history. According to this theory, three distinct brains emerged successively in the course of evolution. These three parts of the brain do not operate independently. They have established numerous neuro-pathways through which they influence one another. This interplay of memory and emotion, thought and action is the foundation of a person's individuality.

The Triune Brain theory leads to a better understanding of the survival instinct such as the fight or flight response and its ability to override the more rational neocortex.

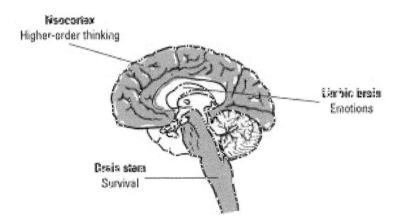

Reptilian Brain or Brain stem

The oldest of the three controls the body's vital functions such as heart rate, breathing, body temperature, and balance. Our reptilian brain includes the main structures found in a reptile's brain: the brainstem and the cerebellum. The reptilian brain is reliable but tends to be somewhat rigid and compulsive. Reptiles like lizards and snakes have evolved only till this system.

Limbic System

Emerged in the first mammals. It can record memories of behaviors that produced agreeable and disagreeable experiences, so it is responsible for what are called emotions in human beings. The main structures of the limbic brain are the hippocampus, the amygdala, and the hypothalamus. The limbic brain is the seat of the value judgments that we make, often unconsciously, that exert such a strong influence on our behavior. Mammals have both reptilian brains and limbic systems. It is responsible for all the emotions such as fear and it is the amygdala that is responsible for fight or flight response. This is the part of the brain which gets activated when your technology decision is challenged.

Neocortex

This hemisphere has been responsible for the development of human language, abstract thought, imagination, and consciousness. The neocortex is flexible and has almost infinite learning capabilities. The hemisphere is divided into two, right, and left hemispheres. These two hemispheres are connected by long neuron branches called the corpus callosum which is relatively larger in women's brains than in men's. That is the reason why women can multitask and men are the worst at multitasking. We will talk more about multitasking and how it hinders our productivity in the chapter on the habits of the architect.

Understanding your own emotions is the first success to be an architect. You cannot skip these steps. You need to understand your own emotions and see how you are feeling every moment and should be able to classify the emotions you are feeling.

Next time you feel happy or sad, dig deeper for the source of the emotions, and see whether they are real. Especially when you are sad, dig deeper into the emotions and see what has triggered the sadness and see what has made you sad, is it the small comment given by your boss or colleague or your relative that is making you feel that way.

When you start classifying your emotions, and then you dig deeper to find the cause of the emotions, you strip the power away from the emotions because you have taken the control away from your amygdala (emotional brain) to your prefrontal cortex which is the logical brain. Once you know about yourself and how you feel the feeling, you get better.

As an architect, this is an important step to understand the science and follow the steps to unwind your emotions. We make lots of decisions every day more than you think of. Our whole work is to make decisions. You decide every second in your work, so if you are not in control of your emotions your decision will tend to violate all your basic principles because the older part of the brain easily takes over.

Writing the code or implementing a technology is just an outcome of all the decisions we have taken. So becoming emotionally stable should be the first step for any architect.

Think of all the cool architects you have met. I am not talking about the way they look. I am talking about how they handle the situation when the whole project is on fire. They may look serious, but you would have never seen them lose their cool.

Application Suggestion

- Think of the last time you were sad.
- Think what made you sad, or what is the situation, or who is the person, or what action by a person, or what words made you sad.
- What were the actual emotions? Was it guilt, regret, revenge, embarrassment?

We will discuss the application suggestions on how you can build your emotional quotient.

Never Criticize, Complain, and Condemn

I learned this from the book '*How to win friends and Influence People*' by Dale Carnegie. This is one habit that, when cultivated, will make you get promotions after promotions and get you connected to upper management easily. This one quality will take you places when you stick to it. People will trust you more and will be friends with you once you cultivate this quality. This quality when made as your second nature will become more powerful than the situation.

You can influence people easily because you have already established trust. But if you don't have the habit, you might look like a person whom people like, but you will never earn their trust. You are the guy who nags about everything; when things get tough, you will be the person on the list to be moved around.

If you don't cultivate this habit, you will be the last person to whom others want to open up about their problem and get a solution from, even if they know, you might have the solution. If you don't follow the habit, you will be avoided in places where decisions need to be made.

Before talking about the habit, let us put one point forward. I am not talking about avoiding or giving people positive criticism in person and in candor even if it will hurt them at the moment. I am talking about complaining and condemning the person at their back when they are not present. If you want to give positive feedback, go for it, there is nothing wrong with it. But you have a method to do it. We will look into it how to do it effectively.

Criticize means indicating the faults of (someone or something) in a disapproving way. You don't have to criticize someone if they have a different view. As an architect, you should be the person who surrounds yourself with people who might have different opinions or different principles and methodology in solving any technical problem.

I am not talking about the person who has a different opinion on the core principles and who brings the energy down from the whole conversation.

Most of my bosses are straightforward and rude, but I like them because they give me straightforward feedback to improve myself every day. They also like my straight forward feedback about them.

So you should never criticize anyone who has a different opinion about the technology you have chosen. First, hear them clearly, then repeat what you understand from them and then state your point of view. Instead of criticizing their different views, you listen, understand, make them feel they are understood, and then express your view. This builds a healthy competitive environment.

Next time you analyze the technology or any development process, you will know at the back of your mind, your colleague or friend will ask you about the aspect that you last discussed and you need to prepare and analyze better, and which indirectly makes you a better architect.

Complaining means expressing dissatisfaction or annoyance about something or someone. You should never complain about anyone to anyone. It might be to your boss, your colleague, or the team you are in charge of.

Complaining does not take you anywhere. It can only give a little satisfaction of being in control; other than that you don't get good from it. When you feel the need to complain, think about what you can do right now to make this situation better and then start working on it.

It all starts with responsibility. Remember, in the first chapter we spoke about how the first step any architect has to take is to take responsibility for yourself, the team, the project, and the company.

So do what you can do about the situation you feel like complaining about. If you still have issues that need to be solved by another person, genuinely tell them your concern (not as a complaint), explain to them what you have done to make the situation better, and ask for help in fixing that concern.

This method takes lots of inner strength to do it. But this is the habit followed by all the successful architects I know. For example, a good architect, will not complain about the low code quality; most of the time they rewrite our code and tell us to follow the same pattern in the next module, rather than just saying your code is not up to the standard. Or set up code analysis that is part of the build system with custom-based rules based on the project and technology and then ask us to make our code pass to the code analysis tool.

Condemn means to express complete disapproval of someone when they express an idea about a new methodology or technology without proper research, and if it does not fit our requirement.

Mediocre architects tend to condemn the technology and reject the idea.

You should never condemn anyone for their new proposal of any technology that they are excited about. You should first listen to them and then ask them questions that will make them think, and from their own mouth, they should tell you it is not fit.

It is a time-consuming process, to rationalize when people are too excited and emotionally charged. Treat them as the ambassador for the technology they proposed, and ask them how they think it can fit the problem we are trying to solve.

Always, as Dale Carnegie says, "Let the other person save face." If they are utterly wrong, don't condemn them; when they leave the conversation, they should not feel humiliated.

Question vs. command

This is one of the top influencing strategies ever. If you understand and cultivate it, you can motivate all your stakeholders from developer to CEO. It should have been taught in school. People who have good parents have been taught this indirectly when they were kids, which helps them to be the most influential ever. You can even try it with your kid if you have one.

If you want to get things, never command or order people what to do, always put your request in question. Ask questions instead of direct orders. If you put your request in question, you tend to get more things done from others than when you command them to do it.

When you ask people, "Do you think that would work?" you empower them, rather than ordering them to do what you want. When they are not part of the decision, they might do what you ordered, but you have spoiled the creativity and relationship.

If you ask any request as a question and then they feel they have a say in what needs to be done, they own the problem. You can avoid malicious obedience, where people do exactly what they are told to do even when they know there are some pitfalls that need to be taken care of. So you become responsible for the action. So never order, always ask them for feedback or help on getting things done.

You become the person who gives them the power to decide on what needs to be done. If you think there is a pitfall or quicksand, you should ask them what you think should be done to attack this problem, rather than telling them what to do. This also helps you delegate better, where you explain about the final outcome and you don't care about the method. If you know a better method of doing it, you can explain to them how it might be useful. But do not force them to use your method.

One of the greatest motivating factors for any human being is being autonomous and having the ability to make decisions on their own in the work they do. If you make them part of the decision by asking the right questions, they automatically feel that they have a say on what needs to be done and they take responsibility for the consequences.

Even if they screw it up, they will take responsibility and spend extra hours fixing it, because they decided what to do and their internal compass knows it is their responsibility to fix what is broken.

Treating Your Boss

"Never Outshine the Master"

– 48 Laws of Power by Robert Greene

Always make those above you feel comfortably superior. In your desire to please or impress them, do not go too far in displaying your talents, or you might accomplish the opposite. You always might need to work with a boss who is not tech-savvy and they are more of management or business stakeholders. So you should know how to work with them.

As an architect, you should know how to work with bosses who are not tech-savvy. You should never make them feel stupid about themselves for not knowing the current technology. It will not make you shine, it will only trigger their insecurity and fear which will cause great friction and strain in the relationship between you and your boss.

Dealing with bosses who are not tech-savvy is also part of our job. You should learn how to influence them and explain to them in the way they understand.

The best way to handle a boss who is not tech-savvy is first understanding the background and trying to fit your current solution into their background experience, and then find an analogy out of it and explain the concept based on that analogy and how it fits into your current technical problem and solution.

Once you understand your boss and know where he is coming from and then you can explain in their own terms, then you got yourself a great ally because you are not making them feel bad for not knowing things. The next time he wants to understand any technical problem, you will be the first person who will come into his mind. Remember everyone is sensitive and insecure about their lack of knowledge.

Suppose your boss has worked in a manufacturing company and he knows more about the manufacturing domain, their work culture, and their work process. You should learn a bit about how the manufacturing process works. You can learn on your own by reading a couple of books or videos.

When you are out with your boss, ask him questions about the manufacturing industry and they usually have very interesting stories to share. You can even ask intruding questions on how things are done and how a particular problem is solved in the manufacturing industry. People love to talk about their past successes and challenges. So you can learn about his life and way of thinking in solving the problem.

Once you have a good understanding of his thought processes, the next time there is a major production issue, like there is an outage on one server going down, because of which the whole process has stopped, you can explain to him, it is almost the same as the manufacturing process, when one of the machines goes down, it will bring down the whole production of the plant.

You can also explain how you are doing something manually to make sure the software still runs as long as the server is up and running, like how they do it in a manufacturing company.

But be careful on using the analogy because it might backfire on you, and if you are not giving an analogy to make them understand the current situation, but to manipulate them, people can smell it.

That too people in upper management can smell your motive as a rat can smell anything. So it all boils down to why you do what you do. This is a powerful technique, but use it with caution. The whole success depends on the integrity with which you treat your boss.

There is also another challenge to it; if your boss understands the problem on his own terms, he might suggest a solution that is analogous to the manufacturing industry. You need to listen to him completely and it might not be viable in software terms, so you should not get annoyed or shrug off the solution.

You should make sure you build enough rapport to tell him currently it is not possible with the current design but you might use the solution later while building the software. This is critical because you make them understand, and if you don't take their solution, you are in deep trouble.

You should be able to take the inputs and work on them, even if it is not directly possible to incorporate them into our software. It is a process you need to stick with for a while to become part of you and it is not easy.

If you fall into criticizing and complaining, don't be hard on yourself, pick yourself up, and stop yourself when you do it again.

Empathetic Listening

> *"Most people do not listen with the intent to understand; they listen with the intent to reply."*
>
> *– Stephen R. Covey*

This is one of my character traits that I really strive hard at improving and find it difficult to follow. I am not even close to where I wanted to be. This trait alone will make you a better person and an aspiring architect. Empathetic listening is one habit that should have been taught in school. We were asked to read and write, but we were never taught to listen. We were just made to listen to boring lectures. But never taught how to listen to other people without probing and waiting to reply.

Once you master empathetic listening, you not only become a trustable architect, but you also will be learning faster. It is a skill that can be learned and should be practiced every day. If you have good parenting then you would be an empathetic listener from your childhood. But if you are like me where we were always told what to do and never listened to, then we can also learn it too.

Empathetic listening is listening not only to understand the person's situation, but also his feeling about the situation.

To become a good listener you should listen to the feelings of the person.

You should never probe a listener by asking questions. When you are listening, you should stop your logical thinking and logical questions should never be asked.

When you are listening to a person, you should always understand the feeling. If you ask any logical question, it will shut people off.

We are all emotional beings and do lots of irrational things that even we know are highly irrational. When we are opening to someone, we don't want them to point out our irrationality in the situation, because we already know when we have done something stupid.

We don't want someone to tell us again how stupid we are. All we want is for someone to listen to us.

You should never probe or give suggestions when anyone is talking to you. You should only listen to understand the feelings and understand where they are coming from.

You should never ask any questions to understand the logicality of the situation. You can reaffirm their emotions though. Women are very good at understanding the emotions of the situation and conversation. They tend to pick up emotions better than men. We men, when coming to understanding emotions, are useless.

When one of your senior developers talks to you about the challenge he is facing for a couple of days and is stuck with it, you can jump and give him a solution or listen to understand and then help him.

If you have faced exactly the same situation and know exactly what to do, then you should let him know what to do and save your time and his time.

But if you know part of the solution, or you know just the gist of the solution, or you have no clue how to solve it, then you should listen to him first.

You should listen to him completely without judging his competence. We developers always tend to blame ourselves for incompetency when there is a technical challenge, and we tend to project the same to other developers when they are stuck in a technical challenge.

When they start explaining and when you sense any emotion such as anger, frustration, regret, or any other negative emotions, affirm them as part of life. You can also tell them how you also were frustrated with a stupid problem and spent days solving it.

If you reaffirm to the person that it is human to get frustrated, and is a challenge or part of our job, you are building an army here. People are going to trust you when you are with them when they are vulnerable. Again you must be genuine and let people know that you understand how they feel. You cannot fake the understanding because people can understand the fakeness even when miles away.

Never Argue

> *"If you argue and rankle and contradict, you may achieve a temporary victory – sometimes; but it will be an empty victory because you will never get your opponent's goodwill."*

> **– Benjamin Franklin**

> *"Why prove to a man he is wrong? Is that going to make him like you? Why not let him save face? He didn't ask for your opinion. He didn't want it. Why argue with him? You can't win an argument, because if you lose, you lose it; and if you win it, you lose it. Why? You will feel fine. But what about him? You have made him feel inferior, you hurt his pride, insult his intelligence, his judgment, and his self-respect, and he'll resent your triumph. That will make him strike back, but it will never make him want to change his mind. A man convinced against his will is of the same opinion still."*

> **– Dale Carnegie, How to Win**
> **Friends and Influence People**

Always stay away from a loud argument. If a person always argues, stay away from him.

Never argue in the office working space loud, you not only disturb others, but you also let other people judge you.

Never argue about politics in the office. If you support the opposite party, it will lead to very bad and ill feelings.

We can see how to handle the technical argument that arises in the organization in detail. But this only deals with someone who works for you. But if you are technically challenged and it is a win or lose project situation, we need to deal with it differently. We will look into that in detail in the later chapter "How to handle when you are technically challenged".

Whenever there is disagreement in technology or methodology with any of the peers, first welcome them and tell them, you are glad, you have someone to discuss it with.

When you feel like you are reacting, stop yourself. The person who argues with you, may even be arrogant and sound rude, don't get defensive. Keep calm and watch his emotions and your emotions that run in your body.

Just realizing emotions in your body is enough, once you bring your emotions into awareness, they will not have power over you. You will have power over them.

Listen first, don't disagree or debate.

Find areas of agreement, once you have heard him well, then talk about the points on which you agree with him. Be honest and sincere in accepting if there is actually a mistake in your doing. It will disarm him.

Once you set the frame right and disarm your opponent, then you can tell him your point of view and thank him for seeing the current situation technology or methodology you have chosen differently.

If he still tries to argue and feels right about his argument, tell him you need time to think through the problem. Please give him a definite time to meet him to discuss the facts you will gather. You can follow the same steps again when you discuss them again.

Once you do the process right, you will be able to get a good sense of yourself. You become the person who takes feedback and corrects himself on the way.

Don't ever beat yourself or apologize in the office environment for the technology mistake, because we did what we did based on the current knowledge, information, and situation.

Never apologize in any office environment; if your behavior is wrong, you can apologize. But never for the decision you have taken in the workplace, don't ever apologize. Take responsibility for the decision's bad outcome, correct it, and move on. Verbal apologies always backfire in case of any mistake in the decision.

If the above steps did not do any good, and the other person is emotionally charged, and you feel like it is pushing your hot buttons, then you always have the choice to walk away from the situation. Even if the argument happens at your desk, it is not a cowardly thing to do. It takes great courage to walk away from anything in your life.

You should always forgive and forget any emotional argument that happened and act as if nothing has happened. You should never have a grudge against anyone who has found the fault and pointed it out to you. A grudge is not a good emotion. You should be thankful because after you reach a certain position, people don't point out your faults to you. They will only discuss it during the tea breaks.

Always think of how pointing out your fault by someone has given you the opportunity to grow. You will grow faster than you realize.

As an architect, we make lots of mistakes, and making mistakes and correcting them on the spot because the environment is changed, is what we are paid for.

So don't beat yourself or apologize for your mistakes, it is part of our life.

Handling Politics

Politics (as per Wiki) is the process of making decisions that apply to members of a group. If you work in any environment, politics exists. Denying it or ignoring it is just being stupid. All we can do is learn them, understand them, and beware of them when someone plays bad politics on us.

You can classify politics into two types, since politics is a process of decision making. There are two types.

- Good Politics
- Bad Politics

Your decision should be based on NOT what you do, it should be based on WHY you do it. If your 'why' is right then 'what' can be corrected at any time. If there is a fault in your 'why' then whatever you do, it does not matter. I am no expert in politics and I have been a victim many times. But one thing, I have learned a lot from them.

Politics is considered bad when the 'why' behind the decision is solely based on your selfish motive. If what you do is selfish, then it is bad politics.

As a leader, your decision should always be centered upon your core principles and also principles that should benefit the company and the team. It will be tough sometimes where you need to balance both the team and your company, so you might have to let go of your team members or reduce their benefits, to sustain the company. Those are the decisions you should take in the long run when you move from architect to technical director and any other higher level.

Next time you feel like you have to do politics, make sure you get your motives right. Motives here is the key to any politics that you will need to handle. You need to reflect a lot before taking any decisions that will affect the team members or company.

Beware of the fact, you might have an internal selfish motive and you are just fooling yourself that you are deciding on a higher motive.

You should be extremely judgmental about yourself and must always put yourself in the court of judgment, whether your decision is driven by selfish motives or for the wellness of the project, team, and company.

Always beware of any type of politics that has a selfish motive, even denying someone new information, or someone a development project, or something that they wished for. It will come back to you anytime soon. Because…

KARMA IS A BOOMERANG

This is the darkest chapter. I wish I didn't have to write this. But we technology geeks have always had some experience being smoked by some non-technical manager or managers who think they are technically savvy.

Learn about politics, to avoid being naive

I am writing this chapter so you don't have to go through some of the pain I went through in my life by being stupid, where I could not see the politics that was played to make me obsolete.

Before getting into the nitty-gritty of politics, you need to understand one thing.

> *"EVERYONE IS A MOON AND HAS A DARK SIDE*
> *WHICH HE NEVER SHOWS TO ANYBODY."*
>
> **– Mark Twain**

We will start by looking into good politics. Politics is considered to be good when the 'why' is based on correct principles and with few conditions.

If your decision is based on the below five conditions, then you can be 100% sure it is good politics. But even if one of the five traits is lacking, then you should reconsider your decision.

1. High Integrity
2. Kindness
3. Intelligence
4. Generosity
5. Self-awareness

High Integrity

The quality of being honest is the single most important characteristic that needs to be cultivated in everyday life. So-called good politics is all about taking decisions, and if your decision is based on honesty and discipline, then every decision we make will yield us good results, even though we might make a bad decision sometimes.

When you are honest and your intention is based on correct principles, then even if you made a bad decision, you will be able to correct it based on the feedback you get, and the next decision you take will generally yield good results.

Kindness

Every decision you take should have a human factor included in it. Even if it is about letting go of an employee when his attitude and turnover is bad.

When you get into people's shoes and see why they are performing badly, and if their current performance is bad only now and he used to be a great/average performer before, then you should always ask him what is the problem that is stopping him from performing at the same level he used to perform.

Most of the time it will be personal problems that are mounting his stress, so he just vents his anger in the office or he has degraded his quality of work. Always be very kind even when you are letting people go.

Jack Welch has fired more people from the organization than anyone else in the world. He has reduced the GE from 4,20K to 3,20K employees, but even he says the process of letting go of people should be more kind than any other process in the organization. Always add a kindness factor into any decision.

Intelligence

As an architect, you should always get facts right. You should never jump to any conclusion without any proper analysis of the problem. You should have listened to both sides before deciding the outcome in case of conflict between the team or between people.

You should always strive to improve your IQ and EQ every day. In the previous chapter we have spoken more about Emotional Intelligence, so understand the emotions and use them wisely.

It is not what you read, or what you say. It is always how you say it. So just being aware of emotional intelligence you can do a better job in the corporate politics arena.

Generosity

Be always generous when you are giving praise or raise in their salary as much as you can. Never underestimate the power of money. Money is never a factor to motivate people. You can buy a man's hand, not his heart. But money helps to get attention for your good deeds.

If you give a good raise to a team member but treat him badly, you cannot buy his heart, and if you don't give him any raise but you are very nice and flexible to him, he might like you, but due to his pressing needs, he might look elsewhere.

Always be generous in everything you do. Always pay from your pocket when you are going out. Never show any kind of miserliness (*Konjoos*) when dealing with money. The team comes first, so do not stop yourself from buying them lunch and dinner and snacks, etc.

Be the first person to pay from your wallet, and if they ask you to split, tell them next time they can pay for you. And don't let them pay next time too.

Self-Awareness

Becoming aware of oneself is the greatest character every developer should work on. You should know what triggers you, and what is your hot button that when pressed lets you show your ugliest side to the world.

The easiest way to realize this is to write down what all you hate in your enemy. This will give you great insight into the dark side of you. You should know your dark side instead of rejecting your dark side. Know your dark side, embrace it, work on it, and take control over it.

What Is Your Dark Side?

We all know what the light in your life is. Even if it takes different names, or is described in different concepts, we all actually know when something is making us shine.

Those are the things we thrive for in our entire life. But what is the dark side in you? It's the opposite of the stuff you like? Not really. In fact, the dark side of your persona is often a rejected and ignored pile of emotions, situations, and phobias that you try to forget with all your power.

Your dark side is what you hate most in yourself. It's your fear of failure, it's your extreme shyness or your selfish motives that pop during pressure.

The dark side is also what you hate most in others. Every time a person is making you go nuts, it's because that person has touched a very delicate part of your dark side. If you hate the person in your team because he gets laurels by just talking his way out, then it is your dark side which you want to hide from others and yourself, which is part of you too and you are not aware of it.

Whenever there is an extreme emotional reaction to other people's behavior, that is the time your dark side is revealed. This is the side of you, you don't want to reveal to anyone. We might be fighting inside ourselves so that no one sees that side of ours.

Why Accept Your Dark Side?

The general approach toward the dark side is to "fight it". From older religion to modern counseling techniques, you are supposed to "kill the anxiety", to "destroy the enemy within," or to "have a victory upon yourself." This is strange. This is a destructive approach. It makes you split your persona in two: the right and the wrong. You can't really be mentally or spiritually split unless you suffer from severe schizophrenia.

The acceptance, on the other hand, has some really interesting advantages.

First of all, when you accept that you do have a dark side and that is part of you, all the energy that you spent in fighting it, will suddenly be available for other purposes. You can start to build on your shiny part if you want because you have an extra energy boost. You don't need to fight and struggle against it anymore; just by accepting that you are who you are, you will have access to a new source of personal power.

Second, when you totally accept yourself, you make a big step toward inner completion or integrity. Integrity here means you know you have a bad side and you are ok with it being part of you. You know you are working on yourself to get better. So energy wasted on fighting the dark side can be used to improve yourself because you have already accepted it.

Find and embrace your dark side, so you can live a simple and joyful life

And third, getting comfortable with your dark side. If you do accept you have a dark side, you establish a starting point. Now I know: "I'm not only this respectable person, but I am also this shy and sad person who fears social contacts. So? This is me, and I know from where I start and where I end. I established my whole territory now. You can accept me or not, but I know that I accepted myself, and that's ok."

Now once you have established the three steps. Accepting, Working toward getting better, and Being comfortable about it when your dark side shows, then you become more powerful. As an architect, people will not bother you anymore. People who want only glory without any hard work will not bother you. You can skip this chapter if you have mastered the three steps. But it is a lifelong process. I have some application suggestions which have helped me a lot.

Again, you should never make enemies with anyone. Always seek to understand them first. Find their strengths and ignore their weaknesses. Make them your ally so you can move your project and company forward and this should be your motive in every interaction— making allies and not enemies.

But in this real world that will not work every time, you might have to face people who are not yet matured to your level, or you will not be mature enough to handle or ignore some people who bring down your energy and the project's energy.

For more understanding about your dark side, checkout 'Meeting the Shadow: The Hidden Power of the Dark Side of Human Nature' by Connie Zweig & Jeremiah Abrams

Application Suggestion

Things you need to be careful about and look out for when handling politics in your office are:

Never Let Anyone Take Credit for Your Work

This is a big piece here. People tend to take credit for your work. It can be any small work. Never let them take credit, don't feel yourself as a God. This rule applies only when the credit is taken by someone of your own level in your organization.

If the credit is taken by the boss and you know he will take care of you, then it is fine. If your work's credit is taken by a developer working under you, cut some slack for them.

But if you find someone is taking credit for your work on your own level or the same hierarchy in your organization, just don't allow it. Initially, it might sound very rude when you confront them, but you will learn how to do it politely and your peers will also learn that they cannot steal your work.

This is a very important rule because I have let many people ride over me and it has bitten me in many bad ways. You never know which small work for which credit is taken by your peer means a lot to the upper management. So always beware and confront them.

Never Run Away from the Limelight

When you are recognized for your work, never undermine the complexity and run away from the limelight. Let the limelight shine on you. You should not get cocky here and let people know "I did it, so I am great," or you should not get to a place where you tell people that the work is nothing and anyone can do it. Both are wrong. If your work is recognized and you are being given compliments, accept with graciousness. Don't comment anything about it. The simplest thing to do is say "Thanks". This way you will look matured and also polite.

If You Don't Like Your Immediate Boss, Leave the Company

This one boils down to a simple emotional intelligence process, never complain. If you don't like your immediate boss or your lead, you should look out for a new job. Complaining and talking about him at his back will do no good and it does waste your energy which will not get you anywhere.

If you get on good terms with him, and you can surpass all his negatives and take positives from him, then you can continue despite his negatives. But if you feel his negative outweighs his positive character, then, instead of complaining about him and wasting your energy, look out for other opportunities. Some people go to the extent of complaining about their manager to HR, but I never saw a positive outcome out of it.

HR will hear your complaints, but they will not do anything in your favor because most probably they will only support your boss. This is how corporates work. Unless the complaint is more of a harassment kind, your complaint will go nowhere.

Never Let All the Cats Out of the Bag

Information is wealth and knowledge is power. I am not against sharing knowledge with your peers and any stakeholders. But you should be careful that you don't share everything you know.

Let us consider that you are pitching for a new project and you are explaining the methodology or technology stack in the meeting and its pros and cons. It is highly probable there will be someone who attends the meeting who wants the same project as you.

Information is wealth, don't tell any more information than you are asked for.

You have done lots of research and got this presentation to this level. So when you have someone who wants the same project as you in the meeting, don't expose all the information you collected. Beware of the information you spill out in the meeting.

What I am saying here is, don't give information that you are not asked for, so you will look like a genius. Always keep the information, and convey it when the place is right. In the corporate jungle, you need to play by the rules. But if you are asked specifically about a new piece of technology, its pros, and cons, then you can explain. Otherwise never let information slip from you for free.

Because people can take your hard work and use it for themselves. You will be stupid and stand to lose what you want.

Again, I am not talking about holding back information when you are giving KT to your team when you move to another project. I am just talking about not giving information when the environment is hostile. Again your core principle is always you should do what is best for the project and the company. But in a hostile environment, you should save yourself first because you are an asset to the company too.

If you don't save yourself, some selfish jerk will take your place and will screw up the whole empire and the project you built up.

Never Attack Anyone Personally

This one is very big, in any kind of politics that is played by you for the goodness of the project or the company, you should always make sure you should never hurt anyone personally either by words or action.

People tend to remember and take revenge when they are hurt personally. You should also become a person who does not take anything personally. Some people will try to hurt you personally by words or actions and want to get some emotions from you. So you will screw up due to your boiling emotions.

Beware of your emotions when you are hit personally. Leave the place, if you feel you are being attacked on your personal issues or problems. We tend to lose our cool when we take things personally.

Never Take Sides

Don't ever take sides for any issues. Don't be part of any gang that is part of or against a company's decision or your boss. This is the most damaging thing that can happen to your career. If you take sides you lose ethics and dignity.

If you feel your management is changing its strategy, automatically, two sets of groups are formed. One supports the strategy and the other opposes the strategy. If you join any one group you are in trouble. If you take sides, you tend not to see the positive aspects on the other side.

As humans, we have instinctual responses that are exacerbated by group influences. What we might not do as individuals we may do as part of a group. People may lose control of their usual inhibitions, as their mentality becomes that of the group.

If the group behavior is violent, the larger the group, the more magnified the violence. There is never a peaceful riot. Humans tend to do all sorts of evil things when they are part of the rioting or supporting some cause.

If you don't take sides, you are not only a better thinker, you will also be powerful. If you don't take sides, both the people from the other sides want your opinion and you will be more influential than when you are on their side.

Never Complain to Your Superior About Anyone

If you want to build trust with your boss, stop bad-mouthing. Bad-mouthing never amounts to anything.

When you talk ill about a person to anyone, some part of them judges you that you are not a trustable person. Stop complaining about anyone to your boss.

It can be the team member who is working for you or someone who is in the same hierarchy as you. When you complain about your team member working for you, your boss will think you are not capable of handling him and the guy you are complaining about is controlling the environment. So you always let the boss know you are in control. I am not talking about discussing the bad behavior of the team member and the steps you have taken to get the situation under control.

If you don't like your boss leave the company

If you explain the situation and let him know the action you have taken, you indirectly let your boss know that you are in control, and also he was made aware of the resources incompetency, either on being a team player or being a rotten apple in the basket who brings the energy of the team down.

If you complain about the peer in the same hierarchy, then you become a nagging person who complains about everyone who works with you. As humans, people think you cannot take constructive feedback and you are too closed.

If you are complaining about their personal or any kind of behavior, then you are in great trouble. Your boss can have the same personal problem or behavior. So it is highly probable he might think you will talk the same way about him to his superior. So never complain about your peers.

But the exception to the rule is if you have a problem with one of your peers and your boss asks you specifically what you think about him. Then you can tell what you want, but it should be extremely professional where you are not blaming him, you are blaming how he handled the particular problem. Your complaint should never be personal, and it should always be professional.

If you have a problem with your boss as in the previous topic, leave the company. I cannot insist enough on this. Complaining about your boss to their superior or HR has never worked and will never work.

Beware of What You Talk About in the Presence of Your Competitor

In the book '*Silent Power*', Stuart Wilde talks about how being silent is the greatest power you can possess. He also talks about "Most people talk too much, and what they do say is often just noise or irrelevant gibberish designed to keep themselves entertained."

If you keep on talking in a meeting or letting your guard down too much and become more vulnerable, you tend to poke the insecurity of the people at the other end.

If you are talking about facts that are not right, then you are hitting the dark side of the people around you. Because you are revealing the dark side of them which they are hiding, so since they hate their dark side, they will hate you too.

Each and every piece of information you expose outside without any need will hurt you a lot. You never know what information about you will be used against you. In places where there are people who are not friendly, beware of all your words.

Talk only when you are spoken to. Convey your knowledge or wisdom, only when you are asked about your opinion. When you are quiet and don't talk, people

Don't let people use your own words against you

will think you have something good to say and people can feel your thinking and you will surely be asked about your opinion.

I am talking about the dinner you go to, the tea break you take with your competitors, where you might spill some information and it will be used against you, or someone steals it and uses it for their own good. During all the breaks you take, never talk about anything concerning the office. You can talk about sports, politics, or anything which is exactly opposite to office work. This will save lots of pain later. You never know what your competitor has in his mind and how he can use the information gained from you against you.

Keep Track of Every Day's Work

As an architect or a senior developer in the team, we tend to do lots of work that might not be directly benefiting the business in the short term. You will be doing lots of work for developers, where developers can be very productive, or any other work that will help our system to scale better, which will not have any direct visible impact currently.

Most of the time we would work on a process where it will never justify it at the earlier stage of the project, like trying to write a common standard logging framework that will be useful for our project, which will be useful in monitoring the app while in the support stage. But you need to write these standards and the framework early in the project, so people can implement them in every module they can code.

In this corporate, when the environment is hostile and the deadlines are not reached, it raises lots of questions about resource utilization and people tend to poke every developer and architect's work to check how much they are contributing toward a single release.

All the managers tend to bring some charts of resource utilization and will ask us what we were doing two months ago. In most of the cases, we would have done some non-functional requirement activities which are not directly related to the release. So we should be in a position to justify any time, what we were doing at any stage of the project. This is where most of the senior developers have struggled, because in the real world "Good deeds never go unpunished."

We would have done work so the project has to be scalable and maintainable in all stages of the development life cycle, but we will be punished for doing things right as leaders if we don't have proper track and justification of what we did. Track your work in an excel sheet.

Correct Yourself When Your Enemy Gives Feedback

In this nice world, people avoid conflicts and once you grow to a certain level in your organization, you generally don't get feedback from your friends or your co-workers. They tend to be very pleasant to your face because it is human to avoid conflicts.

Conflicts in the animal kingdom mean a threat to our survival. So we tend to bear small nuances of peers' behavior even though we grudge and hate those behaviors inside.

It can be as small as telling someone they have body odor and they need to either use deodorant or not wear the shirt twice. We tend to ignore this and work our way out of avoiding close contact with the person.

Look constantly for feedback, correct your mistakes, and move forward

Only the people we don't like will tell us in a hostile situation or in an unpleasant situation that we stink. So always be very attentive to what your enemy talks to you.

Whatever your competitor or enemy talks are the golden nuggets of information that you will not get from your friends.

I am not talking about taking into your heart and emotionally getting activated when there is a sarcastic comment that is passed on you. You should never drool at the sarcasm they pass because they always want to control your emotional stability.

I am only saying to listen attentively when your enemy makes a sarcastic remark and make sure you work on fixing them, so that next time you don't make the same mistake.

Rather than getting upset over his sarcasm or any remarks, correct your mistake and move on. So you get your power back from the situation when you have corrected your mistake.

Never Document Your Disabilities

"Don't be humble... you're not that great."

To sound humble now, we tend to say things that will affect our growth later. Never talk about your shortcomings with anyone. People will take control over us when they know what our shortcomings are and use them against us.

Once I left a project because it had moved to the maintenance phase and the manager of the project was not happy about me leaving the project. But when I joined the project during the requirement phase, I had clearly told him I might not be the guy to work in the maintenance phase, so once the challenges are over, I need to be out. He said yes, but when the project moved to the maintenance phase, he was hesitant to leave me out of the project.

So there was conflict, and finally, I got a release from the project. He asked me to send an email of what I learned and what all can be improved in the project as feedback. Being naive back then, I wrote, my technical lead helped me to communicate properly with clients, he taught me to read the message twice before sending it when you are chatting in the messenger.

I also wrote that I learned new technology coming here and I was very thankful for all the code review that had improved the quality of my code and many other details about all that I learned and how the project has changed me.

To be more polite I wrote I don't find any problems with the project or the way the project was handled, and thanked him for giving me the opportunity.

Be careful of what you write in an email, it might be used against you.

When the appraisal came after four months, I was surprised to see myself in the third bucket (which is next to the last ranking). I always get the first bucket, only once I have got the second bucket. So when I read my appraisal review comments, the comments were exactly what I gave as feedback to him in the email. He had just reworded it as if it is written by him by changing the subject and predicate; the rest was all mine. For example, "We have to teach him everything like how to chat with the client."

This is when I realized that you should never give documented details to anyone about your shortcomings. Always make sure you don't send any emails that portray your disabilities and your shortcomings.

Again, I am not talking about not accepting your faults, correcting them, and getting your power back. I am talking about being extremely cautious about what you write in an email when the recipients are not highly trustable and their intentions toward your success are not their main focus.

A Person's Bad Behavior Doesn't Change Overnight

You are having tough times with your peer and he is getting onto your nerves and you are having a lot of battles with him. This person may be your peer who works with you, works for you, or you work for him, and he suddenly becomes sweet and nice. Exercise caution. People don't change overnight.

I am not saying you should never become friends with your enemy. People tend to misunderstand you first, then they understand who you actually are, so during the initial phase they seem to be distant and a little bit rude to you. But after knowing you, they will become closer friends. But you should be aware of the situation where the other person suddenly becomes nice and sweet to you. It is always dangerous.

You should analyze the situation and be cautious, where you don't suddenly get close with him and then spill all your beans of information and show him your vulnerable points, and he can take advantage of you.

Also, beware when your boss is too nice to you. If he stops annoying you and slowly relieves you from all kinds of responsibilities, it is highly probable that you're in for trouble. Look out for a new opportunity.

Never underestimate the disguise of niceness. It is always the most dreadful weapon that can be used against you. When people become suddenly nice to you, it is highly probable they have some ulterior agenda where they need you in some way.

Become cautious when suddenly people are sweet-talking with you. If they need some help with certain activities, it is well and good. But be sure that their intention is not to take over your projects and your work. Or anything that will affect your career.

Again, I am talking about you not being naive and giving what you build on your own to a cunning person. You should never become prey to cunningness. We, developers and architects, are arrogant idiots who see all in black and white. If people are nice to us, we are nice to them. If they are rude we are rude to them. But we tend to not see through people. This whole chapter is built on not being naive and not getting into the whirlpool of politics and getting affected by it.

If you need to give information about your project as Knowledge transfer, or to someone who genuinely wants to know about the technology so they can be helpful in any way, then you should always share your knowledge.

People Who Work for You, Need Your Attention. It is Acceptable

You will not only be a part of politics, when you are a leader, you will also be a source of politics. People who work for you will do politics to get your attention. Remember, you get more of what you reward. If you reward competition, you will see lots of competition in your team. If you reward cooperation then you will see more cooperation in your team.

When you feel the environment among the people who work for you is too hostile and also very self-centered, then probably it is you who are feeding the hostility by rewarding the hostile behavior of the team.

As a leader, your intentions or motives are very important to build a very cooperative team which will lead to innovations and creativity due to the synergy it creates through cooperation.

Beware of Too Many Compliments

It is good to be recognized for your work and your team members appreciate your hard and smart work. But always beware, too much is too bad. Always be cautious of people who give you too many compliments. They generally might have an agenda. The agenda may be a selfish one.

Always take compliments from others as discussed before and don't run away from the limelight. When too many compliments are given, beware of the person who is paying you the compliments. Watch him closely; he might be playing a double game with your peers too. This is not always true, but being cautious here does not hurt. If you feel a person is paying too many compliments, then you can tell him directly, "I don't trust all your compliments."

Always Have the Company's Growth as the Greatest Priority

You need to take care of the team and your team is your greatest asset, but your team members should work on the company's growth as their greatest priority. If any of your team members does not satisfy the need, you should think again. People tend to undermine the company's growth because they don't like change. We tend to be very complacent with our settings, environment, and current working methodology, and we try to avoid change.

Your current working company is your highest priority, all others are secondary

It is human to avoid change because change creates fear and false insecurity. As a leader, it is your responsibility to address the fears and insecurities that arise because of the changes. You should make people understand about the changes and also how it will be helpful for them in the long run, even though in the short term it will be messy.

But there will be one or more people, who don't like change and will not let you know directly but work in your background to stop the change you are proposing. We might be even wrong in the changes we propose, but someone who is working behind us is not right.

When you feel any team member is working against you, you should investigate properly, and then you should talk to him and find the reason for his behavior. If it is a valid reason, then consider the reason and update your change accordingly, and then warn him, that the next time he should come directly to you to address any issue. If it is not valid, then you tell him fear is acceptable, but you should also warn him. If the back-biting happens again, you should let him go to another project or company.

Everyone is Dispensable

This should be remembered all the time. So never get too arrogant and too naive. Becoming aware of being dispensable keeps you on your edge and out of your comfort zone. As an architect, this is both motivating and stressful at all times.

Thinking long term is the key here. You will be replaced in your project easily, once you have solved the complex problems and the project has moved on to the maintenance phase. It is always our dream to move to a new project and play with new technologies and solve new challenges. But sometimes we will be stuck in an old project because our current employer does not want to invest in a new project until he gets income from the current one.

So we tend to become a highly paid resource, where the amount of challenge is less and also our work has become mundane. But you should never get lethargic and start chilling around.

You should always be working on the pain points of your current project. Our whole job is to solve problems. So never get lethargic and too comfortable in any project. The non-technical managers around us, who we would have made enemies of, will wait for an opportunity to make us obsolete and redundant. So never get too comfortable in a project.

To not be redundant in any project is to find ways to make yourself redundant. You read that right. Think

Only asset and security are your knowledge to produce

of the biggest pain point in your project. You can easily find one in the build process or the development process.

Once you have identified the pain point, start looking for a solution to make it better. It can be as simple as having to copy a couple of files in the build process manually, or that certain part of the code is compiling slowly where you need to wait for minutes to start testing your changes.

Automate the copying process of the build, and in the case of the development compilation, check out whether you can split the process and make it faster. Or upgrading the packages to the latest might speed up the compilation process.

The above is just a simple example, which you can implement even now. You will definitely have any one of the above where you can start working on.

Once you have knocked off one pain point, start with another. Removing your intervention and manual intervention in a build process will free up your time and make yourself redundant because it is now automated. You are not needed anymore. So working on making yourself redundant will not only be non-redundant but also indispensable because you add value to the project, irrespective of your current environment.

You become the person who does things better and makes life better for everyone around you. Make sure you let your boss know how much you have added value to it. This is also important. Just removing the pain points and thinking someone will notice and reward you, is a sure way of being naive and stupid.

Don't brag about your work, but think of yourself as a salesperson who is good at selling good goods to the needy person.

You Pull the Plug Before It is Too Late

As developers, we are either too critical at certain situations or too easy going.

We never tend to analyze the current situation. We are either scared and too closed to human contact in certain situations or too lost in our own minds and work. We never tend to have a real grip on what actually happens around us.

I highly recommend you to read '*Who moved my cheese*' by Dr. Spencer. It talks about three types of mice. That book will be a huge eye-opener for you, if you are someone who gets comfortable on a certain project or a team.

Always beware that your cheese would have been moved and you need to search for your cheese elsewhere. You should always be aware of the current situations, and if your boss treats you with hostility or is too friendly, and people are asking you questions about who can take care of your work, beware and start moving from your current job.

Don't be the person to be let go of, you need to be the person who leaves the company or project before they want to let you go. Don't get attached to any company or any organization or anyone too much. At the end of the day, it is all business and nothing is personal.

Be the first to break up

There will be personal politics and personal favors, but make sure you are always updated with your technology, keep getting strong on your base in computer science, so you can leave the organization anytime if you feel someone moved your cheese. As in the heading, you pull the plug first, rather than them pulling the plug beneath you. Dissociate yourself first from the organization, when you feel something is not right and you might be let go of.

If your skills are updated regularly and you know how to sell yourself properly, you will get a good job outside with a good salary hike. So don't get attached to the organization and pull the plug if you feel they might not need you anymore and they feel you are not adding much value to the organization.

Being Open to Change

*"In the beginner's mind there are many possibilities,
but in the expert's there are few."*

**– Shunryu Suzuki, Zen Mind,
Beginner's Mind**

In the hardware world, change happens every 18 months (Moore's law), but in our software world, it happens every day. With the fast booming open-source technology and GitHub facilitating the contribution from different developers all around the world, change is happening fast.

We have to evolve ourselves and outlearn ourselves every day. We need to constantly look into our perspective about our technology from a third person's point of view, and validate so that we need to break the chain of old thought patterns that are stopping us from growing.

Looking out for better ways to do certain activities makes you better. Changes improve you. Looking for change is part of being human. As humans we always tend to seek what is beyond ourselves, so change always satisfies our hunger for seeking. Change not only makes our lives better but also others' too. Because as you change, you grow, and people around also get better. Change kills boredom and it challenges your current being.

Change makes you move forward in your life if you are open to change, rather than resisting it. Changing and evolving yourself and the organization removes the bureaucracy. The change lets you validate the roots of your core principles and let them rise again.

We need to change as fast as we can. Once we get experienced, we tend to take past experience into the new world. There are an upside and a downside in our experience. The upside is that we don't make mistakes again and move forward quicker in case of any obstacles. The downside is that we tend to get into the old habit of thinking and we don't reinvent our way of thinking.

Since the world is moving too fast, our old fears and concerns regarding a particular challenge would have become obsolete.

But we may get stuck in our old world where we have faced a problem in a particular situation and then we might be still afraid. This bad programming in early childhood or early career can be well understood by the methodology of how Indian elephants are trained and domesticated.

Indian elephants are usually tied to a normal rope made of coir or iron chains which are not of great strength, but the elephants will not try to break the chain and move.

It is because, when the elephants were young and small, trainers would tie them with the heavy chain or rope which was then good enough to keep them safely in the same place.

As they grow up, they have been conditioned to such an extent that they believe that they cannot break away, once they are firmly tied up to a pole or stake. Now the elephant believes the rope still holds it, so it does not try to break free.

It happens to us every day. We tend to have many such beliefs where we are tied to a pole that does not allow us to move forward. Our childhood programming was because of our well-intentioned parents who decided what is doable by us and what is not. So we have to break the program that is hardcoded in our brain in our early childhood.

Being open to change is willingness to change your mindset and methodology based on feedback. Feedback can be from any source; it can be from an individual, a group, or a project.

Approaching any problem with an open mindset is the fastest way to solve the problem. When we handle them with our preconceived notions, we tend to miss the big picture. We tend to miss the bigger picture which is very important for an architect or any leader for that matter.

Be always empathetic to the situation and understand the problem from others' perspectives and then try to find the root cause of the problem rather than trying to fix the symptoms.

Hitting refresh on your whole mindset which you have built all these years is tough to do because it has helped us to survive and thrive in the competitive age, but we cannot move forward with the same mindset which we have had while being a developer and are trying to become the architect with the same mindset.

We should be willing to change our belief system and then also our perception about life and things to move forward.

To move from one level to the next level, you cannot do it with the same set of skills and capabilities. You should be willing to let go of the old skills and learn new skills. Old skills will help you understand the new skills better, but they can also stop you from learning. So you should always be very much skeptical about your perception and your thought process which is resistant to change.

Listening to everyone's feedback and also encouraging them to give feedback are very important characteristics that are open to change. People who are close to you or in the same team don't usually give feedback. And if you are nice to them, people generally will adjust to negative characteristics, so feedback is tough to get. So you should always let people know you are open to feedback.

When they are giving any sort of feedback, never try to justify the action on which the negative feedback is coming through. Listen attentively and ask questions only at the end and it should not be to probe but to get a better understanding of the feedback they are providing.

Being open to change is being vulnerable and you should be very strategic and not let your judgment slide. Because, when you are being vulnerable, you can be easily influenced, so people tend to take advantage too. It is not a bad thing to be taken advantage of.

Approach any problem with a beginner's mind, leave all your assumptions behind

But if the advantage is taken for the wrong reasons, then you should be careful with those relationships and try to avoid them slowly.

Let us look into the characteristics that you need to follow and cultivate so that you not only become a person who is open to change, but also a person who knows exactly how to be open to change without being vulnerable to external and internal competitions.

Identify Your Allies

"Expending energy trying to motivate people is largely a waste of time… if you have the right people on the bus, they will be self-motivated."

– Jim Collins, 'Good to Great.'

Identifying your allies is the greatest thing an architect can do. Until you are sure about who should be in your team and who should do what, the success of the project is always indeterminate. You should always look out for finding allies and encouraging them to try new things. Because if you associate with people who are smarter, hardworking, and motivating more than you are, then synergy comes automatically. You will accomplish more as a whole.

Building Relationships

We spend at least one-third of our time in the office, which is more time than we spend WITH our family. Because, out of the remaining 16 hours we sleep 4-8 hours and hang out with friends, do some chores, travel, etc. Most of us will be spending more time in the office. So it is always good to build good relationships in the place where we spend the most time.

It not only makes you happy and feel good but also helps in getting the creativity and productivity high because you are not thinking about your survival anymore. If there is no good relationship in our office and everyone's a little bit hostile, then we tend to go to our survival mode, where we measure every word we speak and every action we do because internally we know every wrong move will have bad consequences.

Always look out to build relationships with your team members which is beyond the office. Always celebrate all small wins, like a sprint release or any major release.

A relationship is the secret behind any great success

Take your team out and make sure you pay some part of the expenses. If it is too big a team, we can share the expenses, but sponsor completely for the snacks or tickets which are not being shared. People respect you when you take care of them when you are going out.

Seeing the Bigger Picture

Until an architect sees the bigger picture, he cannot plan and execute. It not only applies to the project he works on, but it also applies to personal and interpersonal skills. Change is easier when you see the bigger picture because once you know the bigger picture, you don't worry about the methodology, you know you can correct the method of solving the problem, and you can correct it, if it is the wrong method, on the go.

You don't get stuck up with the single method of solving the problem because you know the final outcome and then you work toward it, rather than your own way of doing things.

Since you are no longer attached to the method which is used to execute, you will be mentally free and you will also be empowering your co-workers to find their methods and correct them if needed.

Because you know the bigger picture and you have explained to them what should be the outcome, you stay away from the way they do it. For example, if your CTO's vision is to build a more digital workforce for your company, meaning he needs more automated BOTs and cognitive services that serve the company, the bigger picture here is getting to know more about the pain points where the AI can be implemented.

Your company has invested more in Microsoft technologies, and then you find that Google's speech recognition API is better than Microsoft's Bing, then you should be open to change your speech recognition application to use Google. If you are stuck with Microsoft products or Google products in any order, then you should reevaluate. Being open to change is easier when you know the vision of the company and you are someone who can see the bigger picture.

Learning from Your Competitors

You should always be open to learning from your competitors. Competitors not only exist outside of your organization. Anyone who wants what you want is also your competitor.

When you start learning and adjusting your activities from your competitors, they become your frenemies. You tend to grow faster when you learn from your frenemies. You become a better leader when you learn from your frenemies.

The shortcut for growth is to look out for frenemies

Your competitors teach you a lot because both of you are interested in almost the same goal, irrespective of whether the method is the same or different. So when you make a single mistake, the competitor waits and knows how to take advantage of it. Only your competitors know your weakness and also your strength. So you get instant feedback from them.

As in the first method in identifying allies, you should know who your competitor is inside and outside your organization. Once you identify your competitor, make sure you are 100% tuned when he/ she is around. Be very careful of the comments he passes about you or the activities he does around you. Mostly those comments are golden nuggets that say where your pitfalls are. You should take those comments with care. But also make sure you don't get carried away by the negative criticism that he gives that is baseless. You should take his comments, validate them, and see whether they are useful.

But you should never make him the center of your life. You should be very clear that his criticism does not affect you emotionally in any way. You just validate those comments or criticism and then change or throw away.

Always asking questions that are centered on your decisions based on what he may think, then you have made him the center of your life. His comments are only to make sure you correct yourself and move on. Remember you work on the bigger picture, not for his comments or to avoid his criticism. People criticize everything, so remembering and getting affected gives us no good.

Let's look into the dark side of this process, sometimes you get more centered toward him and you might even become obsessed with what he does and what he thinks, and what he talks. If that is the case, you are in a dark zone. Always learn from frenemies, never get obsessed because some of your competitors can smell this and take advantage and then lead you to the downward spiral purposefully.

Thinking Outside the Box

When you are thinking outside the box, you tend to be seeing the challenges from a top view, as an eagle sees the forest flying in its top heights. So you get a full perspective on what is going on and your decisions will be better because you are outside the problem. Your mind is not part of the problem.

You tend to be solving lots of problems when you are thinking outside the box. When you are stuck in the rabbit hole of thoughts, you tend to only get frustrated. Remember last time you were stuck in the problem, and you left for home late at night without solving the problem, and then the next morning you came to the office and solved the problem within minutes? This is also an example of 'Thinking outside the box'.

Thinking outside the box does not mean you are still inside the problem and your mind magically fetches the solution from outside. Thinking outside the box means you remove yourself from the problem and are thinking from the position of a person who is alien to the problem.

That is the reason why non-technical people seem to give us great solutions after we explain the problems to them. Most of the time, when we explain the current technical challenge we are facing, we find ourself giving the solution because we saw the challenge from a different angle. Some non-technical people such as Steve Jobs have given great solutions to lots of technical problems in Apple. When the technical team was stuck with the problem for days, he just changed the way of thinking and gave them a technical solution even though he had never written a single line of code in his life.

Remember one thing. Every complex problem has a simple solution. That is the first thing you should tell yourself when you are stuck in a problem. Always walk away from the problem physically, by leaving for home, and then come back and try to challenge the problem. Most probably, you would have solved it, when you were driving back home.

Calculated Risk

Architects are paid for making decisions, and every decision we take, has risk involved and we are responsible for the outcome. When the outcome is good, people tend to share the responsibility of the decision, and when the outcome is bad, they tend to blame you and it is natural.

We would have also behaved the same way to the others unconsciously. So you should always take calculated risks when it comes to the decision we make when choosing any technology because there are lots of costs involved such as resources cost, time, and investments of stakeholders.

Calculated risk is taking risk after thinking through every part of the solution. You should always make sure you choose technology that is already used and successful, it is better to avoid the beta version of any software. Even though you know big giants like Google or Facebook are using the technology, it does not mean that it will work for you too. So you should know when you need to walk away, take a U-turn and move to a different technology.

The simplest example is say you are choosing a technology to create a report in pdf and then you have done a Proof of concept for all the scenarios you know, and then after developing you have found out you cannot report because of a single problem.

Always have a Plan B and Plan C. Be Paranoid about failure

If you have calculated your risk, you would have introduced the interface in such a way that you can replace the current reporting technology with other reporting technology because you have designed the module as plug and play mode.

So you are aware of the risk and you have calculated and you have a fallback and you are also open to take a U-turn because you're not stuck with any decision that is not working. So always have a Plan B because your Plan A may not be successful all the time. Because, being open to change, you should also have solid plans, when change is inevitable.

Address the Fear the Change Brings

Change brings fears because people are comfortable the way they are. All our action is based on either survival or replication, so we unconsciously know when there is a change in the environment, there is a high probability that the survival and replication mechanism that we have learned is challenged.

So we tend to avoid change and get complacent with what we do. Because our animal brain is not designed to see and become our higher self. It is designed to survive and thrive as much as possible with the least energy spent. As an architect and leader, you should take responsibility for handling your personal fear and your team's fear.

The only way to address your personal fear is to face it. When I learned scuba diving in Florida, I could not stay inside the water with a snorkel mask even for 3 seconds with only half feet of water above my head. I saw then what fear for life means. I joined the scuba class, paid around 450 $, and walked away from the practice swimming pool saying that I cannot continue.

I was very ashamed though, so I took the snorkel mask and practiced getting underwater in my gym's swimming pool, and then after some 15 20 days of practice at the gym's pool, I did my first practice dive in the pool.

The first step in scuba diving is, you need to take your breathing pipe off and then again wear it. Then you need to clear the water inside the mask and that was the first exercise in the scuba training. I was scared to death, not figuratively, but literally real death.

Mark of maturity is to face the fear and do it anyway.

But once I faced my fear and did the scuba activities, I felt so good, as if I had conquered the whole world. I made good progress in scuba diving in the swimming pool and stayed more time in the pool.

And the master told me, taking you inside the pool was difficult for me initially, but now taking you out is difficult, because I started loving to stay longer inside the pool with all the gear on and swimming in the depth of 9 feet.

Everything went well until the practice session was over and then we needed to go to real diving sites to get certified, because, without diving in the real sites such as the sea or any area which is 60 feet deep, you cannot be certified.

Again I was scared to death, now I could feel lots of sensations in my stomach. Even when I am writing this, I can feel what I felt then. It was crazy. I was wearing all the scuba diving gear, and yet I was scared. It was a cave that slopes down and it was 60 feet in depth filled with water.

It was extremely dark and you could not see anyone around without the torchlight.

Even with the torchlight, you could see only the people next to you. The visibility was not even 5 m with lights since the water was full of algae. But once I reached the bottom base which was 30 m down, and we settled there, I got cramps inside the water. But I told myself, if I give in to fear, I am going to do worse. We were taught how to handle cramps and how to stretch when you get a cramp. So I took a deep breath and stretched inside the water under 30 m depth, and was relieved of my cramp.

That is the place where I learned that no matter what your environment is, if you accept the environment and then think about what you should do, the fear vanishes and you will be smart enough to know what to do next.

Even now before jumping into the sea, I still have all fears, but I know the other side of the fear is always bliss. When you face the fear and do the things anyway, you will surely feel and experience bliss.

Dealing with our team's fear is also part of our job and we have to deal with their fear and make sure it is addressed when it arises, and also we should be proactive about it because when they are in their state of fear, you will not be able to increase the synergy and creativity in the project. So it is our duty to predict the fear and address it when we are driving for the change.

Fears in a team are mostly the amount of extra work that may arise due to change or their dependability getting reduced which makes them feel vulnerable for replacement.

For example, if we are bringing up automation testing in our team, this might trigger lots of insecurity within the testing team because some testers will not be so good at coding. Or, a developer who plays the key role in getting the build ready, where we are trying to bring CI\CD in the release process, might feel vulnerable that it might remove the key responsibility and control he had in the release process. All the fears when drilled down will be either for their survival or losing control in the project.

You can always make change exciting by the process of inclusion. When you feel a change needs to happen, rather than commanding and making your team execute, call for a meeting and explain the problem that is currently the most painful and hinders the growth and revenue of the project. And then ask them how it can be solved and brainstorm all possible ways the pain can be removed.

Brainstorm means you write down all the ideas on a board and you don't reject any idea that comes from any team member when you start validating the ideas.

Otherwise, the team members will stop talking, and so the purpose of the meeting will fail. Even if you reject or validate or change any idea that is given by the team member in a brainstorming session, people will stop talking. Make sure to keep your mouth shut.

You will be surprised that your team will be more willing and dying for the change to come so they also can be relieved from the pain the problem causes. Make sure you also ask them what they think about your plan for change. By the end of the brainstorming session, you don't have to even address the plan you had. It would have been addressed already.

When they leave the room, people will be very excited because they were part of the solution and their fear of change will automatically be addressed because you followed inclusion rather than exclusion of people in decision making. Now you have a team that is motivated for the change.

Now it is your duty to plan properly, execute, and remove the obstacles that come in the way of the change.

Trust me, there will be many obstacles you need to cross, it will not be easy, but it will be fun. Really fun. After completing the change, you will really feel blissful.

For example, you are planning to bring continuous integration to your project, then call for a brainstorming session for team members and tell them the company is planning to reduce the time of every release. Don't tell people we are planning for Continuous integration and then ask them for suggestions.

Someone in the team will surely bring up Continuous Integration and Continuous Delivery. Write that down on the board. But there will be lots of ideas that people will address that are also valuable; write those down too. Now ask what can be done first that will make a huge difference, and then ask them to plan, and then slowly bring the Continuous integration concept again, and ask them how we can move forward toward it.

Change Requires Hard Work

"We sometimes underestimate what we each can do to make things happen, and overestimate what others need to do for us."

– *'Hit Refresh,' Satya Nadella*

Change is not easy. People are always comfortable the way they are, even though a brainstorming session motivates them, if you have successfully included them in the decision making process and they are all excited about the change as you are.

When it comes to the real world of executing the change, there will always be a little bit of resistance among team members. Real-time problems creep up and the solution that you thought will work for the particular pain point might not be straightforward, sometimes it may be completely wrong. You might have to take a U-turn and then think about the process again.

Sometimes you might even think about stopping the change process because it is more painful than the pain that you are planning to solve. You tend to even be ridiculed and criticized about the process you wanted to change. Please don't take anything personally.

Remember any movie where the hero wants to solve a particular problem, where he plans about it and when he tries to solve it, obstacles come in the way and everyone around him ridicules him. You are in that stage now. So think when the problem is solved, the same people will be praising you. So don't let them get to you.

If the change were easy, it would have been done already, so this is normal. You need to put in lots of hard work mentally and physically to solve the problem. Mentally by thinking and researching the better ways of solving the problem, and physically by sitting in the office for long, maybe work over the weekend. Again don't expect any of your team members to work over the weekend.

If they are working over the weekend, then make sure you facilitate them. Don't ever ask them to work over the weekend until it is absolutely necessary and NEVER expect them to work even if it is very necessary.

You should only try to persuade them and never expect them to be influenced by your persuasion.

Organic change is better than a big bang. Take baby steps

Baby steps are the best way to implement the change. Even a baby step needs lots of hard work from you and your team members. Always expect that for the change to become fully part of the organization, it would take around four to six months.

For example, you are bringing CI/CD into your organization, you make sure there is some code or changes that go on every release. Make use of feature flags to hide those changes. So the final CI/CD implementation will be just a few changes, rather than a big bang.

Make the small win look big by celebrating big, take your team for lunch or a movie or buy them some snacks for the evening and make sure you recognize the hard work that is put in by the team for this small win. You need to ingrain into the DNA of the organization that change is fun and fulfilling.

Get the Right People on the Bus

Technology changes are hard, and you should be sanely insane to change what you are doing and get results from it. Changes hit you hard mentally and physically. So it is really exhausting for people to bring and implement change.

Until you have identified the right people who can implement the change, you cannot go any step forward. Bringing the right people is the first thing for the change. If you have not identified the right people, then change becomes really hard. It is like using a screwdriver to hit the nail on the wall.

Using proper tools not only gets things done faster but also saves lots of energy. You should be very keen and give the right people the right job.

Everything starts with hiring the right people for your team. You should take more time when hiring people and should be very specific, and never try to hire people due to your pressing needs. Hiring the wrong person will always be the biggest mistake of your life. I have experienced myself, and almost most of the CEO interviews I have seen or heard, or read about, also have the same message.

There are two types of people in the software industry. One who is process-oriented does a job with perfection and you can rely on them, that when they are given an existing project they will maintain and support it properly. They don't get easily bored and will be satisfied to do small improvements in bettering the process and technology.

The second one is people who are not perfectionists, who tend to take lots of risks and make lots of mistakes, but they are people who are innovators who will come up with new ideas and also will implement them quickly. But they get easily bored and want new challenges almost every day. You need both of them in your project.

If you are going to do a groundbreaking change, then you need the people who are risk-takers, who will try new technology, and who can help us in figuring out whether the solution is feasible or not, and they will get you a proof of concept very quickly.

When you want to make a change in the existing project which is relatively small and little deviation from the current process, then you need to use the perfectionist to make the small change, because they will be cautious about what might break the current process and will be very careful and will take more time for the change. You need to have both sets of people in the ratio of 70% of perfectionists and 30% of go-getters.

When you are in a project which is in the support/maintenance phase, yet there is lots of development happening as per the needs of the sales, then you need to change the strategy a little bit. You still need to work with both the perfectionist and go-getters. But you have to deal with them in a slightly different way.

Good Communicator

"Think as wise men do, but speak as the common people do."

– Aristotle

As a leader, communication is vital. Until you communicate what is in your head crisply and clearly, your idea will only be an idea. You need to communicate clearly to all the stakeholders you work with. Until you learn to communicate with your boss, your colleague, and your team members who work for you effectively, you cannot succeed as an architect.

Communication helps as a bridge that makes ideas into products or solutions. Communication on all levels will help you climb the corporate ladder faster. When you know how to communicate in writing and speak effectively, you tend to outwit your competition faster, inside and outside the company. Once you understand how to communicate with each and every person, and you know their own personality type, it not only improves your productivity but also theirs because you have communicated clearly in the way they will understand.

If you are not improving your communication skills every day, you tend to be more stressed because you feel you are powerless and everything seems to be not in your control. Your skill of influencing people around you seems to be lesser, and your team will also feel less productive because you are not communicating properly what is expected of them. If you don't understand non-verbal communication, you tend to be very rude and people will avoid you.

When you become an expert communicator, you can understand the team members in a meeting without them saying a word and even with your eyes closed. You will be able to feel the positive or negative energy of the team members easily.

What is Good Communication?

Good communication is not only speaking crisply and clearly, so your audience can understand, but also understanding your audience first before communicating.

Good communication should include all three modes of persuasion, Ethos, which means credibility, Pathos, which means emotion, and Logos, which means logic. You should convey all three modes to be effectively persuasive.

Good communication is not mostly verbal, it is mostly non-verbal. Professor Mehrabian combined the statistical results of the two studies to rule that communication is only 7 percent verbal and 93 percent non-verbal. The non-verbal component was made up of body language (55 percent) and tone of voice (38 percent).

A normal person is not likely to remember a complete conversation from start to finish—only the parts that stick. And worse, whatever the brain forgets tends to get filled in by their imagination, creating false memories. So repetition is not evil in communication.

> *Communication is the one skill that will double your salary.*

Our worldwide statistics show that 78% of the population take in information visually and kinesthetically, and only 22 % through listening. You need to understand people's way of learning and listening to communicate better. A good communicator understands who understands visually or auditorily or kinesthetically and communicates in the way he/she understands.

The way you speak is an important communication tool. Changing the pitch, volume, speed, and rhythm of your voice, like making the tone go up when asking a question, using inflections for sarcasm, or stressing words to add emphasis, can help make your meaning clearer and prevent misunderstandings.

Good communicators always have higher energy and passion than their team members. It helps with a high level of engagement and interest. You can influence more people if you are motivated by the job and those emotions will be passed on to your colleagues. Remember emotions are contagious, good or bad.

Listening with empathy is the only good skill you need to master. The more you can empathize and understand where the other person is coming from, the more you can influence them. Understanding another person's perspective is the best way of flattery and respect to the people.

Improving your vocabulary is a long process to get better at communication. According to a 1999 study by Christopher Winship and Sanders Korenman, knowing a few words more than the average words known in your community raises one's annual income by nearly $10,000. Why should vocabulary size be related to achievement, intelligence, and real-world competence?

Think of the last time you were stuck in communication, where you needed to communicate to someone and you were giving a long explanation and you knew if you told a particular word, the other person would understand quickly.

If you are good with your vocabulary you will communicate crisp and clear. Whole design patterns are introduced in our industry so we can communicate crisp and clear just by saying the name of the pattern we use and the team or the colleagues will understand the logic behind it because it is the vocabulary of the problem that is solved already.

Good communicators have lots of stories to tell. Learn to communicate through stories. Take stories from your life. If your story is authentic and genuine, everyone will like it.

Listen, Talk, and Read More

All three activities are important. If you improve all three activities you will automatically become a better communicator. We are taught in schools how to read and write. We are never taught how to listen.

Our parents are more prone to give us orders, because, in early childhood, we would be talking all rubbish, and their brain is more tuned that we will be talking some gibberish which has no meaning. The same pattern follows with parents when we are old enough to make sense. But they still don't listen to us, and so we learn from them the same habit.

We almost do the same in the office and act as if we are listening, but we are only preparing ourselves to respond, rather than trying to understand what is being spoken to us.

Listening is a great skill we need to learn. There are lots of books available in the market that will help you understand how to get better at listening. You first have to listen to people without disturbing them and you should only talk after the person has completed his talking.

Listening is one skill that will solve 99% of your problem

You should always listen to the speaker completely, i.e., your body and mind should be focused on him. Your body should face him when he speaks to you.

I will explain what works for me and you need to find your own pattern that works for you.

You can follow these steps at the beginning and find your own steps that work for you.

- Always pay attention to the speaker. Give your undivided attention. Take note of their body language. If both their feet are turned toward you, then they are giving full attention to you. You should respect that full attention.
- You reciprocate by leaning toward them, but not too much. It should be close enough, but without violating their personal

space. You will know when you are too close; they will take a step back, so you also take a step back.

- Never judge from what they say. Judging is taking whatever they said and juxta-positioning to their private life and making it who they are. So try to understand where they are coming from, what made them talk that way. You can ask questions like, "Why did you say that?"

- In case of technical discussion, you again paraphrase whatever they said to you and repeat back to them in your own words. Ask them for feedback, to judge how much understanding is right and how much is wrong, and improvise the paraphrasing.

- In the case of personal discussion, never advise anyone until they ask you. Only advise if they specifically ask you, "What do you think I should do?" Then give your wisdom to them. Otherwise, refrain. You only need to listen.

You should never complete anyone's sentences, you should always wait for them to finish. Completing sentences will look as if you are helping them communicate better. But it might also push your perspective into their thinking.

You should start listening to podcasts that talk about technical topics that you are interested in. You can use the podcast app on your Apple phone and any podcast app that is available in the Google play store if you are using an Android phone.

Start listening to podcasts when you are traveling. Give a break for songs that you listen to when you traveling. Reduce the frequency to once or twice a week, and add more podcasts to your commute. You can also download audiobooks and listen on your commute.

So you get better technically without putting in much effort. It is all about being around people who are technically better than you, and podcast is the most efficient way.

If you are a Microsoft based developer then I recommend .Net rocks, the best podcast ever. I highly recommend "Masters of Scale",

"Modern CTO", "The Tony Robbins Podcast", "Darknet Diaries" and "All Angular Podcast".

Talking more helps you to explain things to people clearly and crisply. You tend to find words more often to communicate faster when you talk about the same topic over and over.

When you lose the fear of talking in front of an audience and you become comfortable, you can express better, it not only add value to the audience you are talking to, but also to you personally, because you will become an authority on the topic you are talking about.

People will ask your suggestion on the challenges they are facing and make you think through solutions in different dimensions, which is much needed for any architect.

Talking more means taking every opportunity that comes to you. It can be in an office where they want you to present the feature you have completed. Don't try to give it to your manager or module leader to present. Initially, you will make a fool of yourself but stick with it. If you see the first presentation and the talk I delivered, you would not have bought this book. So make sure you grasp all opportunities that come by.

Nowadays we have lots of meetup groups that are available. Sign up in meetup.com and then make sure you find the group and join in the area you are working in, such as .Net, Java, Angular, RUST, Python, etc. And you join the group. Attend their meetup regularly. When you find a topic that interests you, and you are excited to share, ask the meetup organizer. They will be very happy to give a slot. They might not give one right away, but let them know you are interested.

You will definitely get a slot to speak, I have got a slot six months after I have shown interest to speak. But stay in touch with the organizer by attending the meetup regularly. Don't bother him much. Just a warm smile and a nice 'hi' is enough every time you see him.

Once you start talking in multiple meetups, start going for bigger conferences like a one day Boot Camp that happens around the city on various topics. Find a conference that interests you and try to conduct a hands-on for one day for a crowd of 50-60 members. This will help to realize how to communicate content to people crisply and clearly.

Talking more does not mean you should talk more in the meeting. You should only stick to the agenda in the meeting. It does not hurt to chit chat in a meeting for a while when the number in the audience is less, and everyone can contribute to the chit chat. Small chit chat in the meeting engages the audience and it improves personal relationships. But you should never chit chat when the number in the audience is more than three.

Reading more will help you to talk more because your vocabulary will automatically improve. It will also help you to listen better because you can understand what people are talking about. Reading more will improve your perspective on seeing things the right way, as they are not the way you think they are.

You should read in every genre. I personally cannot read fiction books. If you are a good fiction book reader, then it is well and good. But if you want to become a better architect, you should read all the classics of our industry. All the books that need to be read are available at the end of the book. You should read not only technical books but also science books, autobiographies, your own mother tongue nonfiction books, and successful literature.

For the starters, pick a book from each genre above and read them for a year. Then increase the count every year. The more you read, the more you will know in different genres, and the more conversational you will become. It will not only improve your office life but also your personal life. It will attract more good and interesting people in your life and you will get more opportunities because of the people you have attracted.

Learning About Body Languages

We unconsciously send signals to the world through our bodies about what we are thinking and what emotions we are going through. People can pick up these signals and judge us on what we are thinking and what our intentions are. You cannot stop sending those signals to the outer world. You can only be aware of them and change your body posture so that you don't make others insecure or repelled by your body language.

55 percent of your communication is through body language, so if you need to improve your communication, then you should work on body language.

There are lots of books out there. I highly recommend '*Body Language*' by Julius Fast, which is a good read where you can understand much about it.

You should be aware that you **cannot not** communicate. So whatever you do, communicate something to everyone. Knowing this will make you nervous, but it will build awareness about your body.

Emotions are contagious, and body language conveys your emotions to the outside world, so you should always be aware of what you convey through your body.

Always carry out good posture in your body. Your spine should be straight. Don't bend your back or round your shoulders.

Yoga is a good exercise to make your spine stronger and straight. There are a few exercises also available which you can do at home, such as planks, cat stretches, etc.

Don't move unnecessarily, find all your unnecessary movement and work on it

Walk tall and brisk wherever you go. Whenever you find yourself slumping because of some thought that is bothering you, bring that to your awareness and change your body language and your mood will automatically change.

Don't lean too much toward anyone. And never invade anyone's personal space. The best way to know you are leaning too much is when you find people taking a step back when you go close to them. It means you are too close.

Whenever you sit on a chair, occupy more space, and let your legs be wide apart so you take more space. It shows you are in control of the place and situation.

Remove all nervous ticks and also leg shaking while you are sitting. It telecasts your nervousness. To become a leader and lead a team, you should not be telecasting your nervousness. People don't follow nervous people, people follow only strong people who are in control of situations.

One thing you need to know from any body language book is that your body always transmits your thoughts to the outer world. Every gesture you make communicates something.

So you should bear in mind only one thing. You should reduced your body movement as much as possible and you should move your body only when you need to communicate. That is the reason why adults who are more than 40 seem to have less movement in their bodies.

People will recognize someone is mature or immature unconsciously, and it is usually through the body language that is communicated. Imagine how kids keep moving everywhere and moving their arms and legs all the time. It communicates immaturity. When you find a kid of the same age being silent and sitting in one place, we tend to call the kid a mature one.

Always have less wasteful body motions than your peers. Don't shuffle your feet needlessly. Don't put your hand to your mouth, scratch your head, or tap your fingers.

The difference between maturity and immaturity is often telegraphed by body language. Too much body movement without real meaning is immature. A mature person moves when he has to, and moves purposefully.

Think Before You Communicate

As in body language, you cannot not communicate with every word you speak or write. You will always be communicating subtle things about yourself to everyone. So becoming aware is critical.

In the case of verbal communication, the communication you do gets registered in the memory of everyone around you. Once you say something to someone, you cannot undo it. People tend to build their hopes if you have promised them something. It can be simple promises such as showing up in a meeting at a certain time or bigger things such as giving them a promotion in the next appraisal.

If you don't keep your communication without putting in such promises, then you will start to lose integrity in the eyes of the person to whom you have promised. When you go to a higher level, people tend to value your character more. Character comes first and then comes the skill.

Think before communicating and be extremely aware of what you are talking, writing, and speaking. Your communication should be a response rather than a reaction. Emotions should never get in the way when you communicate. You should not be clouded by emotion when you are communicating.

Don't promise when you are happy, don't reply when you are angry. Think of the last time you said 'yes' to something and later regretted it because you were happy at that time and you said 'yes' instead of saying 'no'.

Also, think of the time when you replied to an email because you were angry and it aggravated the situation and spoiled the relationship. So never promise when you are happy, and don't reply when you are angry.

Always read your very important email more than three times and save it in your inbox. Take a break and then come back again to your draft, then read again and send it. It will save lots of regrets later. Because you will not be clouded by emotions and prejudice if you review it at a later part of the day, where your emotions are different.

While chatting in engines such as Slack, Lync, Skype, etc., make sure you read the text twice before pressing 'Enter'. Also, check your message for proper punctuations.

Always try not to talk initially in a meeting, save all your comments for the end.

Always be prepared for any meeting you attend. If you are conducting a meeting, always make sure you let the audience know what the agenda for the meeting is. And you make sure you don't talk about anything other than what is on the agenda of the meeting. Always value the time of others as much as you value your time.

Always do research before communicating with anyone, it should be about the person you are communicating with, and also what you are going to communicate. You can never be over-prepared for any type of communication.

Be brief, yet be very specific. Avoid "it", "something", "things" in your presentation. Always communicate what you meant. For example, "It can solve the performance problem." Rather than this, say "No-SQL option can solve the performance problem."

Communication is Your Responsibility

Always over-communicate. If you want your messages or technology to get across the team or organization, you have to communicate multiple times.

If your team members don't understand what you are communicating, then being ignorant is not their fault, it is your fault. You are not communicating in a way they understand.

You need to understand what is Visual, Auditory, Kinesthetic type of communication. You should categorize your team members accordingly, and communicate in the category they belong to.

Visual communicators learn by seeing, and memorize by looking at pictures. They tend to be distracted by long verbal instructions.

Auditory communicators learn by listening and by what they hear. They will likely be literal listeners, so choose your words carefully when speaking to an auditory communicator.

Kinesthetic communicators learn by doing, moving, acting out, and hands-on experience. They will often move and talk more slowly.

So take time to understand the person and communicate in the way they understand and make sure you include Visual, Auditory, and Kinesthetic in your presentation.

There are types of people who hate emails and who like emails. So if you send emails to the one who hates, and don't communicate through email to the one who loves it, then you will have a tough time.

Some people will take the phone and call the person who they want to talk to, and get it sorted out. Some people will want a drafted email even before attending the meeting where we are going to talk about what is drafted in the email.

So always make sure you send the agenda of the meeting before the meeting starts and send a quick decision that is taken in the meeting. This will satisfy both types of members who love and hate emails.

Always maintain a positive attitude. If you are communicating anything negative, do it in person or at least on phone. Don't write anything down negative about the person. It will be bad for your career and their career. If they are really a rotten apple, you can document accordingly in their appraisal document before letting them go from your team. Otherwise, it will be a problem for you later, so beware of this too.

Start and end with key points you want to communicate. Because people remember the beginning and the end.

People generally retain more information when presented with novelty, as opposed to routine situations. To help audience members retain information, consider injecting some sort of novel event into a presentation.

This might be something funny, or something that simply catches people by surprise. Engage people in the discussion. You can ask trivial questions and let them answer and this will get them engaged with the discussion.

Technical Talks at Public Events

As an architect, talking in meetups, and Boot Camps will help you get better technically and it will not only improve your technical skills, it will also improve your soft skills. You tend to get better at the topic you are talking about because you want to explain this to someone who does not have any idea what you are talking about.

"If you can't explain it to a six-year-old,
you don't understand it yourself."

– Einstein

You should make your presentation so simple, it can be explained to a kid and he can understand. You can also think of explaining to your grandmother, who doesn't understand technology.

Thinking in terms of explaining to members who are not savvy with technology, will help you prepare a presentation which you can also get better in communicating with higher stakeholders like board members and your boss whose areas of expertise are not computers.

In the book, '***The Presentation Secrets of Steve Jobs***', Carmine Gallo talks about how Steve Jobs would never add more text to the PowerPoint presentation, and he would have only a couple of pictures or a single word in the whole slide.

You should not rely on the PowerPoint, you should rely on storytelling, figuring out analogies to use by understanding the audience.

In the case of webinars with PowerPoint slides, you should rely on words because you will be talking and the audience might need to read your text to better understand it, because webinars will be mostly one-way communication.

Aristotle said it first. Tell them what you will tell them. Tell them. Then tell them what you just told them. Use this formula throughout your presentation

Be authentic in your presentation, do not show yourself as an expert, if you are not. Tell people you have not tried the technology in production and you are also an amateur. You will earn more respect.

While starting your presentation, this one I learned from Brian Tracy. Ask the audience "Why are you here?" Most of the time, initially there won't be any response, and it usually takes 30 seconds or a minute for someone to talk back.

While you are waiting to answer, walk around expecting someone to answer. It is actually the time for people to think about why they are here in the first place, so it will get them alert and look for details about what they want to get out of the meeting.

Then once you are done with the "Why you are here" question, ask them questions like how many of you are aware of the technology, how many of you used the technology you are talking about, how much experience the audience has, and how many of them are developers and how many are IT pros, etc. These questions should be designed to categorize the audience and talk accordingly

If you are not an expert in the area you are talking about, but you are talking because you are excited about the technology, tell them you are talking about this because you don't want the audience to go through the same initial bottleneck you had understanding the technology.

Always focus on earning respect rather than laughter, one or two jokes is fine, but don't get too goofy around the audience. It is a big no, no.

Treat everyone equally and never insult anyone in the audience, irrespective of how stupid their question can be.

Find an analogy to express your idea in a way the audience can understand. If you are talking to developers, tell them how it is related to features they already know. For example, if you are talking about containers, tell them containers are almost like virtual machines. But isolation is at the software level rather than the hardware level.

Always show some demo about your presentation, where the audience can take action right away going home or on the same spot. Don't be all theoretical and abstract.

Sometimes one among the audience will be there only to prove you are wrong and want to show they are the smartest one. You need to handle them by saying you can take the discussion outside, since the whole agenda of the talk is getting spoiled because of the guy who is trying to prove he is smart.

Engage the Audience

You should engage the audience in every part of your talk. If you don't engage them they will get bored and wait for a break to happen. How much ever novelty you add to your presentation, people have a very short time span. Think of the last time your mind wandered during someone's presentation. So audience minds also tend to wander, and you cannot avoid that.

But you can let it wander the way you want. Engaging the audience is all about letting them express their ideas and thoughts.

To make an effective presentation in a meeting, always make the presentation interactive. Don't tell them, don't command them, just engage. That should be your motto for the whole presentation.

Always let people express their idea freely before you try to express your idea

Even if it is one on one with your colleague, ask questions that will make them talk more. When they leave the one on one discussion, they should have felt they have been heard and understood. For that to happen, you need to listen more.

Start your one on one with any personal question that points to the personal message they shared with you and move forward to official topics. Be genuine in the answer they provide you on a personal topic. If you are not genuine enough, you will screw up the relationship.

Always start your presentation with a story, in the case of any technical seminars or talk you present. A good story goes a long way. It can be any short story that is relevant to the topic. If it is a formal presentation, then still you can start with how the presentation got here, and where it is now.

Conduct a poll on any questions and ask them how many of them agree and how many don't. You provide the choices and ask who agrees with the first choice, second choice, and so on. Don't insult anyone if they make a wrong choice. Tell them they are almost right and move on to the person who gives you the right answer.

When you end the meeting or presentation, always end with an action item that they can do as soon as they leave the room.

In case of technical discussion in the workplace, let them know exactly what is the small step they need to do to get the ball rolling is. Communicate this action step for everyone who attended the meeting and it should be specific and tailor-made for each and everyone and should not be generic.

In the case of public technical presentations, tell them the small steps that they can try now, such as create the project from the template and build it and try from the demo.

Ask for Honest Feedback

When your communication is not effective, then there is no point in wasting your energy. You can call your communication effective only when people understand what you communicate. You should always get feedback on whatever you do.

Feedback is not easy to get from people because people tend to be nice to everyone, so if you make mistakes you will never know. The best **way to get** candid **feedback** from your team is to create a culture of open and honest communication.

Encourage people to talk to each other and reward open conversation about any matter.

Once you build an open culture and people are comfortable enough to express their thoughts without being judged, everyone will open up.

People always long to express their thoughts but they fear that it might affect their survival. If you create a culture that will enhance their survival by being open, then you are in for a treat.

Always pay attention to non-verbal cues. It will tell you a lot whether you are doing a good job, and whether they are interested in your talk. An indication of this can be folded hands when you are talking to them.

Never explain or justify when someone gives feedback, Just Shut up and listen

Are they too lethargic and sitting in the chair or are they leaning forward to hear what you are saying?

If they are not leaning forward and sitting very lethargic, you are not doing a good job. Try adding novelty to the conversation or asking an intriguing question to get the attention back.

At the end of any conversation, or presentation, or personal meeting, always ask what they felt about the presentation. Don't talk and let them express what they feel.

Usually, non-verbal cues that come before they utter the words are important, you will understand from these whether your communication was effective or not.

Never be defensive when you get feedback, shut up, and listen. They are valuable points that you don't get often. If you get defensive when you get feedback, then people will not give any more feedback next time.

Build a culture where admitting and correcting one's mistake is rewarded. Once you build that culture of admitting mistakes and you also admit mistakes, people tend to open up a lot and give you valuable nuggets that will help you to improve faster than you have ever imagined.

A Leader in an Architect

"People ask the difference between a leader and a boss. The leader works in the open, and the boss in covert. The leader leads, and the boss drives."

– *Theodore Roosevelt*

Best Motivator

For every 100 employees, 21 are leaving every year in all major software giant companies according to a 2017 survey. What is the reason behind all this attrition? Is it better pay, better company brand name, better social status? Irrespective of any of the above reasons, the main reason is…

Employees Don't Leave Organizations, They Leave Bad Bosses

Employees leave when they don't like their immediate boss. This is the main reason why people leave. There are a few other reasons, where employees leave the organization, but the main reason is they don't like their immediate boss.

Employees stay in a given company longer if they feel they are properly motivated and their motivation is driven from inside.

When people are not motivated, they tend to not work with their full hearts. As Stephen Covey says, **"You can buy a person's hand, but you can't buy his heart. His heart is where his enthusiasm, his loyalty is. You can buy his back, but you can't buy his brain. That's where his creativity is, his ingenuity, his resourcefulness."**

When people are motivated, they tend to take lots of responsibilities and be more creative and synergistic.

You cannot do everything by yourself and you need a team to execute your ideas; if you motivate enough in the right way, you might get your and company's ideas and goals done.

If people are not motivated, there won't be enough trust, and trust is needed to drive your company's goals forward.

Motivation is a word derived from the word 'motive'. **Motivation** is the reason for people's actions, desires, and needs.

Motivation is also one's direction to behavior, or what causes a person to want to repeat a behavior. An individual is not **motivated** by another individual. **Motivation** comes from within the individual.

Autonomy, Mastery, Purpose, Trust are the four main factors of motivation.

These five ways seem to be more effective with personal and professional endeavors.

- Autonomy in Work
- Encouraging Mastery
- Aligned to his/her own Higher Purpose
- Trust and responsibility
- Facilitate to Learn new technology

Autonomy in Work

When you have autonomy in work, people are more motivated than any other factors combined. The deepest need for any human being is having a sense of control. People go to any length to feel a sense of control. That is why we love choices even though all the choices lead to the same outcome.

If we are not given a choice and asked to choose from only one, we get so annoyed. The whole reason boils down to only one factor, feeling a loss of the sense of control.

In a research study with humans, people were given chips to use at a casino. They could use the chips at a table that had one roulette wheel, or at a table where they could choose from two roulette wheels.

People preferred the table with two wheels, even though all the wheels were identical.

The sense of control brings a sense of certainty, people will know what will happen. Autonomy at work gives a great sense of control and this also satisfies the deeper needs of human beings, so it is the highest motivator.

Autonomy at work is letting people make choices and holding them responsible for the choices they make and the result that comes out of it. Nobody dictates what needs to be done and when it should be done.

Autonomy means rather than commanding them what to do, we include them in what needs to be done.

Autonomy is giving more sense of control and making them feel they are part of the problem and part of the solution.

Before digging deeper into how to make your employees autonomous in work, we need to see what is **not autonomous**.

Autonomy does NOT mean working in isolation. Being autonomous doesn't give a person the right to work without supervision or not following any technical guidelines such as code review guidelines, deployment guidelines, development guidelines, etc. Autonomy means the environment encourages to challenge all the guidelines

It's NOT Jumping without a Parachute. Autonomous employees should have their boundaries well set. We should always have proper documentation available for any technical decision taken, stakeholders must be properly consulted and all their fears addressed and feedback taken. When you leave employees to do whatever they want without building any safety net, that's not autonomy; that's a lack of leadership.

Autonomy in work means lots of factors. Some of our employees might not feel they enjoy autonomy, even if you follow all the activities below.

We need to set the goal of what needs to be done and get out of their way and let them decide on how it should be done. Let them make all the decisions on how, where, and who should do it.

The bottom-line benefits to both employees and organizations are that workers who are free to make more choices are happier, more committed to their jobs, productive, and less likely to leave.

Here are **six ways to encourage autonomy** with your employees in their own work.

Always make new mistakes, never repeat. Mistakes are acceptable as long as they are new ones, and you communicate to the employees that this is your mantra. You should make this their mantra too. You are only concerned when they make the same mistake **twice**.

It can be screwing up the database or breaking the build. If you are ok with them making mistakes, but you're not ok with them making the same mistake twice, this brings both autonomy and also articulating the principle for the risks that can be taken.

Hiring Self Sufficient people. Hiring is the key here, you need to hire people who like to work with less supervision. You can encourage people to be autonomous, but it takes lots of effort; some people want to be supervised. So you need to pick people who are autonomous by nature. Identifying is easy, they tend to be rebels. You need to choose wisely and you need to know how to handle them better, otherwise, you will have a bitter life every day.

Define principles for decisions. In the chapter, principle-based life, we have talked more in detail about principles. You need to define principles that should govern everyday decisions. Principles need to be defined at all levels from defining classes in application to deploying your application to production. For example, in the case of defining classes, you should be very strict in following the single responsibility principle. While deployment you should use the "Build once deploy every where principle".

Defining ownership is key in getting people's hearts to work for you. Once they put in their heart, nothing stops them from succeeding in the tasks that are undertaken by them. You need to define exactly what the outcome you are expecting is, and what the definition of done means. Once you define principle, define the outcome, and tell them when you want it to be done, and make sure they understand the results you are expecting, then you should get out of the way.

Checking the results can be done, but it should depend upon the person you are dealing with. If the trust account is high, check sparingly. If the trust account is less, do it often.

Provide tools. We are all knowledge workers and knowledge is our tool that needs to be sharpened. You should facilitate your employees to learn more and make platforms to apply on what they learn too. So it goes back to the first way of encouraging newer mistakes. Buy subscriptions like Pluralsight, and Safari online where you have all the O'Reilly books. Encourage them to attend conferences, sponsor their travel if possible. But you make sure they send you an email on what they learned from the conference as a summary.

Levels of autonomy. You also need to encourage autonomy at the team level and managerial level. An autonomous team is one that is self-managed and receives little to no direction from a supervisor.

Build an autonomous team that encourages the culture of sharing knowledge, the environment of being vulnerable in not knowing it all, ignorance is accepted, and every team member is included in the process of making decisions. Working in such a cooperative and enriching environment can have a positive impact on job satisfaction.

Managerial autonomy is building an organization with almost no hierarchy, where managers can exercise greater authority over employees on incentivizing and giving feedback. Managers are free to reward and motivate employees as they see fit. They also should have the ability to correct/remove the employee if they feel they don't fit with the project or current work.

However, when the manager is not skilled enough, he might do all the wrong things and reward all the bad behaviors which will affect not only the project but also the organization.

Inclusion is the key here, including everyone in all the major meetings, emails, phone conversations that tell where the company is going on their particular project. Once they are clear with what is the outcome expected of them, then get out of their way. Don't worry when they come to the office, or when they leave the office, and be very flexible with the timings of all their personal work. But make sure flexibility is not favoritism, it is a performance recognition.

Encouraging Mastery

"It is easy to live for others, everybody does. I call on you to live for yourself."

– Ralph Waldo Emerson

Humans long for being great at something. It is that drive that motivates us to get up every day to go to work. Think of one thing you get excited to do, you get excited because you feel you are good at doing that activity, but in reality, you seek to get better at doing it.

If you are helping your employees to seek mastery, and you have communicated well enough, then you don't make a team, you make an army who will do anything for you.

Mastery seeking is a very basic human drive that triggers all good emotions. People with good emotions behave and perform better. This will help to trigger creativity and synergy in your team and organization.

Everyone seeks to better on what they do, if you can help them, you will automatically build an army

When your inner motive is bringing out the best in people, then your team members will never leave you and your disadvantages will be overlooked, because they know you care for them.

Guiding them to get better every day means you care more about the employee, you don't have to use words to motivate them, they will know when you care, because your actions will speak louder than words.

Mastery is derived from the French word *"maistrie"* **which** means **comprehensive knowledge** or skill in a **particular subject** or activity or control or superiority over someone or something

> *"Goal of an apprenticeship is not money, a good position, a title, or a diploma, but rather the transformation of your mind and character—the first transformation on the way to mastery."*

> **Robert Greene, Mastery**

There are 10 steps to encourage mastery.

Know them

Until you know the team members' strength, you cannot plan whom to give which work, which work will excite whom. You should always put in lots of effort in knowing the strengths and weaknesses of your employees. This is the first step that will make more masters in your team

Find Apprentice and be Mentor

Identifying an apprentice is always the tough part where you need to understand what is it that you can offer, which is sought by your employee. You should be so tuned to your strengths and you should identify your apprentice who needs help in attaining mastery.

You should never force anyone to become an apprentice, you should become a mentor only when they seek. Your duty is to be available with your doors open. You should know who needs a mentor.

Encourage learning

Encouraging learning in your team will be very beneficial because you can solve challenges with new technology that is available in the market.

If you encourage learning, people will be excited to tell you about what they learned.

You should never dismiss and lessen any new thing they learned and are very excited to share. Show them the same level of excitement that they show when they are sharing the new technology/technique they recently learned.

Always encourage them to attend technical conferences and also provide them a plural sight account that can be shared by the team which is bought on company expenses. Safari online books are also good with all the O'Reilly books.

Guide them through the starting period

When you guide people through the starting period in learning new technology/ understanding new projects, you will earn lots of respect. They will automatically take you as a mentor.

You should be very forgiving when they start on new technology or new projects and you should convey that you understand that the initial phase is hard.

The culture of helping others should be encouraged where people empathize with the struggle everyone goes through in the initial phase of new technology or project. Once there is a culture of empathizing that the initial phase is hard, people will ask for help from others and people will not feel insecure to ask for help.

Positive criticism

When your criticism is positive, you tend to get more work done. People will love you more and want to work under you. Trust level will increase because you care about the growth of the employees.

Getting positive criticism is the greatest gift that can be given to your team members when something is done right. A good master gives good criticism that will help the apprentice grow.

Criticism is positive only when the employee perceives it as positive, so you should understand their personality type and change your words and actions before you criticize.

Some employees will be ok with blunt words and will only see the inner meaning, some will be very sensitive. So criticize accordingly. But you should never avert yourself from positive criticism because you don't want to rock the boat.

Emotional Motivation

"A soldier will fight long and hard
for a bit of colored ribbon."

— *Napoleon Bonaparte*

The above quote might sound really stupid, but it is what it is. Recognition motivates people more than anything that can exist in the world. On the dark side of emotions, we seek validation from peers, society, family, and even strangers.

You need to find what the emotions are that will trigger a person to give his best, and incentivize him on them. If you find the emotional motivation of your employee, you have got the golden key.

Help them to examine their perception

When people examine their perception and recheck whatever they thought might be wrong, then it gives them great strength to learn because they are seeking wisdom.

If this one quality is cultivated and encouraged, then attaining mastery becomes a guarantee. Seeking to examine to understand the world as it is, is very important. You should always help your employees to examine their own perceptions.

Most of the time the problem is not the world out there, the problem is the lens we wear to see the world. If we wear a red lens and complain that the world is all blood, it is stupidity. As a leader, you should always help them examine the lens through which they see the world.

Imagine the last time you got stuck in solving a coding issue and when you stopped your work and went back to the documents, you saw that what you understood was all wrong. Once your perception was changed, you solved the problem within seconds. It is always the way we see the problem, and our preconceived notions about the problem, that is the problem. As a leader, help your employees to see the problem as it is, rather than the way it may be.

Action matters

Until you get things done, nothing matters. An idea will look good and sound good when you talk about it. But until we take action, it really does not matter.

You need to build a culture where you are excited to see when people make their idea a workable piece.

When they learn something and tell you, you should not incentivize them on it. You should only incentivize people who show a demo of the things that they learned.

To take one step further, you should incentivize more if they make the demo and make it part of the project and a workable solution that has helped your project.

Break their ego

Ego in the team environment brings down the whole synergy of the team. In the team, no individual wins, no one employee is shining in the darkness of the others.

Whenever there is "I", there is ego. It is that which is constantly distinguishing "self" from others. It is that intoxicating sense of self-importance and wanting to prove they are better than others.

Appraise the team performance, not the individual

Whenever you find there is conflict because of "I", condemn and become very sensitive to the situation. You should also communicate clearly to the team that you PUNISH when there is "I" being practiced in the team. You work as a team, or you are out of the team.

When highly performing team member is being too much of a jerk, and people don't like to confront them, talk to the team member. If they don't fall in line by helping people, and being open to suggestions, and also learn to communicate the ideas better, then get them out of the team.

Be cautious, that the person who is good at what they do, is not getting along with others because he has better vision than the rest of the team. In this case, you should mentor the person to communicate better and, in a way, to be liked by their peers, and not reject any idea they propose and not ridicule anything they do.

A high performer's ego can be a dangerous thing. They can become monsters if you let them go ahead with it. The minute a high performer seems to be getting arrogant or out of control, you should have a candid conversation about values and behaviors. You should never be afraid of them.

Your whole aim is to build a culture. No one is above the herd, everyone should make others better, so break their ego by having a candid conversation, and if it does not work, then letting them go, is a good way of mentoring the people who stay.

Forced creativity

When pressure is high, people tend to focus and get more things done. Think of the last time you did have to go on a long vacation, and how focused you were, and you did complete all pending tasks that were not humanly possible. It falls down to one thing; when it comes to productivity, it is all about focus.

When you give your team members a challenging deadline and challenging project and squeeze them a bit, you will get more done from them. You need to know they might

Give 20% more work than they are capable of. You will never regret it.

fail and it is ok. Because you have already built a culture of failing is ok if you learn from it.

You should trust their talent, give them challenging deadlines and you should remove their beliefs by telling them you trust their talent and you mean it.

Develop their successful traits

Always be the person who doesn't accept anything less than what they are capable of from your team members. Always set a high standard for yourself and for them.

Identify their success traits such as Drive, Self-reliance, Willpower, Patience, Integrity, Passion, Optimism, and fuel them to improve it more. The more you reward their success traits, the more your mentee will cultivate these traits.

Aligned to His/her Own Higher Purpose

Employees can be driven by purpose in terms of the end result of their work. You can leverage this motivator by getting to know your employees and what they're passionate about and finding a way to connect their work directly to their life purpose.

Finding what type of purpose motivates, is the key to getting your employees motivated every day. Find their strength and align their strength to their day-to-day activity.

Emphasize the positive impact of the work they do. Clarity about how your products or services can improve the world provides guideposts for employees' priorities and decisions. As part of the daily conversation, mission and purpose can make even mundane tasks a means to a larger end.

For instance, if someone in development is particularly driven by ensuring users have a smooth, bug-free experience, you might put them in a role that directly affects end-user experience like UX design or quality assurance.

You might know someone is very keen on getting to know the details of how things work, and they dive, dig, and debug every line of code to understand the nitty-gritty of things. You can give them a long term bug, which is outstanding, and no one knows what the cause of that bug is.

Trust and Responsibility

High trust and a responsible environment is a good motivator and helps people to stay in the organization longer.

When trust is high and people are responsible for the outcome, it will avoid malicious obedience. Stephen Covey talks about malicious obedience where Britain was brought down twice to its knees because the train conductors were maliciously obedient in following all the rules and procedures written on papers.

When the rules are made without proper trust and enforcing proper responsibility on the result, and being authoritative, it will lead to malicious obedience. People will follow the rules commanded by you, but even though some part of the rules might not work in certain situations, they will still follow the rules, which will lead to catastrophic failure.

When employees feel they can't trust leadership, they feel unsafe, like no one is there to back them, and then spend more energy on self-preservation and job hunting than performing at their job. Talent acquisition and employee turnover costs increase.

The more you trust, the more trustworthy they become.

Trust means "reliance on the character, ability, strength, or truth of someone or something."

If you want to be trustable, you have to become trustworthy, and you cannot create trust if you don't trust them. It is a two-way transaction, and thinking of it as a one-way street and expecting people to trust you without trusting them is abysmal.

You cannot do everything by yourself, so you need to trust people and assign them proper responsibility to move far in your career.

Trust and responsibility are about trusting one's potential and fixing them with the responsibility of the result. You don't care how they do it, you only care about the result, and you also provide some guidelines and come to an agreement on the result.

You don't care how they do it, does not mean no standard in the code is being written. You don't care means you are least worried about the method it is done.

There are a million ways to solve the problem, as long as the code is the proper standard, less coupling, readable, and easy to change and add functionality. You don't interfere with what they use to solve the problem. It might be a method that you have not thought about in the first place.

There is a lot of hard work to create trust, but breaking trust is easy. We will look into some trust-building characteristics that need to be improved to better motivate your team members.

Rather than trying to repair the broken trust, try to build a trustable environment where everyone feels safe to share their ignorance. Next time you don't know any particular technology or concept, and any one of the team members has learned about it, be open to what you learned from them. It builds huge amount of trust and encourages people to be vulnerable and trust you.

Take care of your employees. Always support them when they are in a crisis whether in professional or personal spaces. Make sure they know you have got their back and you will never betray them by any means.

Show compassion, improve your listening, and genuinely care about your employees, don't fake it. If you fake even a bit, people are smart enough to find it out. When people are in trouble, think about the last time you were in the same state and empathize with them and maybe share the last screw-up you did, and everything went ok after the screw-up, and make them feel good.

Become generous; Jack Welch calls it having a generous gene. Generosity should be in everything such as praise, recognition, and cash. Always be the first to take your wallet out when you go out. When an employee performs well, give them a generous compliment in front of everyone.

Making everyone part of the conversation builds lots of trust because you show them you care, you want their input, you're not a know-it-all, and are truly interested in what they have to offer.

Facilitate to Learn New Technology

"Train people well enough so they can leave, treat them well enough so they don't want to."

– Richard Branson, Founder of Virgin Group

As automation, Artificial intelligence, and skills retraining dominate conversations about the future of work, there can be catastrophic job loss where current skills can get outdated in a matter of time.

Regardless of which view prevails, navigating this terrain requires a workforce that can adapt to changing environments and acquire the skills necessary to be successful in the future.

In the surveys conducted by the American Psychological Association, training and development consistently emerges as one of the areas employees are least satisfied with, and lack of opportunity for growth and advancement is second only to low pay as a source of work stress.

Employees reported feeling more supported by their supervisor when they were provided with opportunities to develop technical, management, and leadership skills.

Having adequate time available to participate in career development activities and sufficient opportunities for internal career advancement were also related to perceptions of supervisor support.

Making sure you communicate that they are learning new things and trying out new innovative solutions is part of their job. You should never stop them from trying new things, but the proper check and validation is your responsibility.

Encourage curiosity and learning skills

Encourage employees to attend conferences, meetups, user groups, webinars, and seminars of any technical event and treat them as on duty if it is on the weekdays.

Provide both job-specific skills training and development activities that help employees advance within the organization or relative to their broader career goals and align training and development efforts with larger organizational goals.

For the new knowledge and skills gained during training to stick, employees need to actually apply them on the job. In a survey, only 58% of US workers said their employer provided opportunities for them to do so, which means resources invested in training are often squandered.

Also, consider the diversity of your workforce when you design, develop, implement, and evaluate your efforts and ensure that all employees have the resources they need to be successful.

Motivating people has to happen day-to-day. It is not a one-day speech or one-day activity where people get psyched up and it loses its way altogether. If you give people enough autonomy to try their own ideas and let them define the way how it is done, it is the biggest motivator.

If you are interested and investing in getting them to become masters of any technology which they are interested in, you motivate them more.

If you find your employees' purpose and then align their day-to-day work activities to their purpose, then you buy not only their hands but also their hearts to give everything for you.

Trust your employees more and give them more responsibility than they can take, and give them clear guidelines on what the definition of done is.

Building employees so they are well hands-on with the current technology will bring employees to the office with full motivation even if it is Monday. Invest in and incentivize learning that aligns with employees' purpose and organizational goals.

Leader vs. Manager

The word manager has got a very bad connotation due to some of the managers we worked for, who had no idea what the project was, had zero people skills, and finally, they are extremely controlling due to their insecurity.

Also remember those managers who have a great fan following and for whom we are ready to do anything if they ask for it, even though they are not technical.

"If you cannot measure it,
you cannot manage it."

— Peter Drucker

An architect should be both a good leader who defines what the right things are and be a manager to get the right things done.

An architect should be a manager, because if you don't have a process to manage, then you cannot take any decision on a project. When there is a delay, you will not know where we stand, or what is acceptable for the release.

An architect should be a leader, because the manager gets the right things done, and the leader decides what the right things are.

An architect should be a manager because there are tasks that need to be done with formal processes, and should let the team know what they are and how it needs to be done, e.g. for auditing purposes.

Always think of yourself as a leader, always take the blame and delegate the success to the team.

An architect should be a leader because there might be tasks that might need an informal process, and the leader decides how informal you can be, and how much rules can be bent without breaking the organizational goals.

An architect should be a leader because you need to take risks and it may or may not backfire.

An architect should be a manager because you need to be accountable for the risk taken. The risk-taking should not be done without any proper planning and there should always be a backup plan.

An architect should be a leader because he needs to build relationships and they need to focus on people because they need to influence people to realize the company's goals and vision.

An architect should be a manager because he needs to focus on the structures necessary to set and achieve goals. They focus on the analytical and ensure systems are in place to attain the desired outcomes.

An architect should be a manager, because sometimes we need to stick with what works and make sure the project completes by the deadline.

An architect should be both a manager and a leader to take the project on the right path, and also proceed by doing the right things.

The word Manager comes from the Latin 'manus', meaning 'hand.' A good **manager** provides the necessary 'hand' in guiding others. A Manager is a person regarded in terms of their skill in managing resources.

The word Leader comes from the Indo-European root word 'leit,' the name for the person who carried the flag in front of the army going into battle, the person who leads or commands a group, organization, or country.

We will see **five traits** you need to include in your leadership life that have managerial connotations to them, even though it is what great leaders do.

Doing things Right vs. Doing the Right things

"Management is doing things right;
leadership is doing the right things."

Warren Bennis

Doing the right things brings effectiveness, and doing things right brings efficiency. You need to have both efficiency and effectiveness for successful personal and professional life as an architect.

Doing the right things brings harmony and peace to our lives, and it removes the stress because we do things that are not urgent but important.

When more time is spent on doing what is important, we tend to make our life easier because the important things will not be urgent any more. We have planned and thought through and have dealt with what might go wrong and have done an activity based on our plan.

Leaders who are less stressed are people who know what is important and who do not do anything that is not important.

Doing the right things are activities such as code review, and identifying technology that is very easy to adopt and causes less friction for developers to use.

Doing things right are activities such as making sure no code is checked in without any proper code review.

Doing the right things is mentoring your team. Encourage them to make sure they attend meetups, and conferences and share the knowledge by summarizing it in emails and sending them to everyone.

Doing the right things means learning every day about technology and having a cutting edge technology stack that is always in your head that can be incorporated when the time arrives.

Walking on the correct path is doing things right, finding the right path is doing the right things

Doing things right means facilitating learning and making sure subscriptions like Pluralsight, and Safari Online are regularly renewed and also make sure people use them. If any paid learning is not used, you should cross-check with the developer and find the pain points that are stopping them from using it.

Doing the right things is having a handle on your emotional button and not being triggered by verbal or non-verbal abuse and concentrating only on getting things done.

Doing things right means having a contingency plan in case of any problem in the team.

Doing the right things is not to have any personal conflict and handling your in-house competitors only by increasing your quality of work rather than fighting and politicking over petty things.

Doing things right means, in case there is unhealthy competition and politicking, having proper timesheet entries on what you work, and record on how you have spent your time and team members' time are spent, so we can use them when the politicking is truly killing your productivity and you need to justify the time spent to your upper management.

Doing the right things is identifying the cause of all the urgent activities and finding the cause and fixing the cause and not the symptoms.

Doing things right is identifying a module that is causing more outages and more bugs, and trying to rewrite it in your spare time, and release your refactoring in phases in such a way, that people do not have a clue the module was changed.

Doing the right things is writing unit tests for every module you write. You should test all the development cases by using only the unit test and spend less time running the whole project to fix one bug.

Doing things right is having a build mechanism that checks the code coverage on every check-in and makes sure you never reduce the code coverage on any build.

Doing the right things means identifying the easy project to write unit tests, so other developers in your team do not have friction in setting up the unit test framework. Encourage and incentivize your team members for writing unit tests.

Doing things right is making sure when the project is started, the unit test project is part of the project that is created and the build mechanism is set up for running your unit tests.

Collaborating a Project

When you are good at collaborating, your percentage of success of the completion of the project increases. Your team members will feel more motivated and stay focused on the work and they know exactly what to do. Your career path will grow faster because people will trust you more with project handling and people handling.

Project handling does not mean you handle a project like a manager, but like a leader with managerial skills, as discussed in the previous topic "Leader vs. Manager".

When you are good at collaboration, your team will understand the value of working together, and goals and challenges become common among the team. Rather than team members taking the criticism and feedback personally, a good collaborated team will look at the challenges/problems as a third person and try to fix them.

Good Collaboration in a project gives team members equal opportunities and then they will be able to contribute to the project what they are best at, which will not only drive the project to success but also make them feel good about their work. Feeling good about your work is the best motivator ever.

Collaborating on the project is a very important role for an architect or any leader.

Collaboration is the process of two or more people or organizations working together to complete a task or achieving a goal.

Every architect should learn about collaborating requirements to teams, and stakeholders. We will look into how you can become a good collaborator.

Focused Team

An architect who collaborates always thinks and talks in "We" and never in "I". He should always take decisions that are best for the team, which align with the project and organization goals.

Never take any personal credit for any achievement and never blame anyone in an email/meeting when you are communicating with upper management about the mistakes made.

A good architect knows how to collaborate with a team to implement his ideas

Take the blame for the team and in the same email/meeting let them know how you have taken steps to avoid this from happening in the future. And also what is the process you have put in place that will make this mistake go away.

Generous

A great collaborator is generous in taking the first step, starting things, and removing the initial resistance and barriers, even if it does not give him a spotlight. Once the initial resistance is over and the ball gets rolling, a good collaborator will praise and encourage whoever is helping the ball rolling.

Curious

Curiosity, when cultivated in the right way, helps to build relationships, because people like to talk and curious people likes to listen to learn. A good collaborator finds the balance in communication on how much to talk and how much to listen. He understands we have one mouth and two ears. So he uses them accordingly.

Builds Relationships; Breaks Down Walls

When your team collaborates better, the team output is more. The more they talk to each other, the more the work gets done. This might sound counterintuitive, you might think people waste time by talking. But the more they talk, the more they collaborate in their work. The attrition rate will be less, and people are willing to help and take someone else's work in their absence.

When the relationships among your team members are better, the wall gets broken down and people learn to influence each other. The influence circle will become bigger.

For example, one person in your team will have friends with a network team or IT team, so in case of any issue, he will directly contact his friend to sort out the problem faster because the relationship is trustworthy, and it breaks down more walls once the circle of influence gets bigger and bigger.

Diplomatic

The best collaborators are diplomats. A leader knows any mutual relationship is built on trust and it takes time. They also know earning trust is not easy, people are very vulnerable, so they will not easily trust people because they might have been hurt by someone whom they trusted, and this has made them vulnerable.

Trusting makes you vulnerable. Lack of trust has helped us to survive and it is part of the survival process. A good collaborator works on building trust. For them, building character precedes building a reputation.

You need tools to collaborate in your project, and I personally feel Slack and Microsoft teams are very good collaborative tools. I like Teams more because they have hundreds of plugins that we can use in everyday life.

First Who, Then What

"You are a bus driver. The bus, your company, is at a standstill, and it's your job to get it going. You have to decide where you're going, how you're going to get there, and who's going with you.

Most people assume that great bus drivers (read: business leaders) immediately start the journey by announcing to the people on the bus where they're going—by setting a new direction or by articulating a fresh corporate vision.

In fact, leaders of companies that go from good to great start not with "where" but with "who." They start by getting the right people on the bus, the wrong people off the bus, and the right people in the right seats. And they stick with that discipline—first the people, then the direction—no matter how dire the circumstances."

– 'Good to Great', Jim Collins

Get the right people

If you get the right people for your job, external motivation and attrition are minimal. People tend to stick to the project more because they like the people who are already in the project, and they know they can learn a lot even if what they want is not in alignment with the organizational goals, but still, people will stick.

Hire people who take responsibility and they strive till the end and never give up, you can know this quality by asking questions like what were the greatest challenges you faced and how did you overcome them. If their answer is full of energy and their eyes and faces light up, then hire them.

Don't hire people who do not display high energy when they answer this question. High energy is the key here. You can also hire people who have a track record in your company but work on different projects.

People with high integrity tend to succeed more in every part of life. Listen to how they handle things, people with high integrity always avoid even white lies, and people with

Finding the right people will propel success in the right direction

less integrity will tend to praise themselves or be proud of how they manipulated people in getting what they wanted.

Getting the right people means recruiting self-motivated people, whose passion is writing code, and solving challenges. People who like to learn and solve challenges tend to work well for our software industry.

People who have a good passion for contributing to the software society and have some open-source contribution, who talk in technical events or attend technical events are good candidates for self-motivated people.

Get the right people in the right seats

When the right people are in the right seats, there is less supervision and tasks get done faster. Allocating tasks might be the work of a manager, but figuring out who is better at exploiting new technology, who is good to work in already exploited technology, is a leader's task.

Always tune in to see what excites and motivates people and make sure they work in things that excite them and motivate them.

Sometimes you cannot make every work an exciting one, but you can find something in that work that will keep them motivated. E.g. Some people will avoid fixing bugs because they want to do only new things, you can motivate them by saying fix the bug as of now, we need to rewrite to new technology when the time comes, so you will know the functionality and details about the module to rewrite.

Get off the wrong people

Removing the wrong people from your bus will remove the dead weight that has been hindering your speed of progress. Once removed, your project will improve synergy.

Always give people the benefit of the doubt and give them a chance you might have to change their seats. But even after changing the seats, if they don't perform, then get them off the bus.

Do not get emotionally tangled about leaving the people off the bus, you are doing yourself and them a favor. In my experience, people who are left off the bus have moved on, and become great at different company projects, because you cannot give them appropriate work based on their skills.

Drop them off the bus as soon as possible, but always remember to give them the benefit of doubt and switch their seats, if not, then you need to take the tough decision.

Put who, then what

You cannot go far if you put what before who. You should always concentrate on getting the right people and leaving the wrong people out of the project or team.

After reading the autobiographies of CEOs such as Steve Jobs, and Jack Welch, one thing common they all talk about is making the mistake of hiring the wrong person due to the pressing and urgent problem at hand.

They also say Hiring wrong people is one thing they regret and will never do it again. Hiring quicker is the major problem which we will regret later.

Develop a disciplined and systematic way of hiring, and have more than one person in the interview process who is directly not connected to the pressing problem you are trying to solve. You might have a blind spot due to the urgency, and they will help you not to overlook it.

Measure to Manage

You should measure things, because you need to justify why you need to be paid the salary you are paid. Also to justify the spending you have done pertaining to a particular task.

Measuring a key index helps us to take decisions on whether to invest time and resources further or not. It helps us to add more time and resources if needed to a particular task or module.

Take more time in recruiting so you don't have to regret it later

Measuring the right things helps us to grow faster in our career and influence our stakeholders in making decisions for further investment in our current and future projects.

Measuring here does not mean only measuring whether we are on the right track in completing the project. That should not be the deciding factor for the success of the project. Because that is only part of the measurement and does not guarantee any useful output.

"The leader is the one who climbs the tallest tree, surveys the entire situation, and yells, 'Wrong jungle!' ...
Busy, efficient producers and managers often respond ...
'Shut up! We're making progress!'"

– Stephen Covey

Most of the top management decisions are very intuitive and based on their gut feeling, but we need to build data to justify our choices and decisions and it is really bureaucratic. There are certain things that we cannot measure such as how a good relationship with a customer can bring more clients. These are more intuitive and measuring how it impacts our outcome cannot be put on paper.

For example, being nice to customers might be one of the characteristics to get clients. But one customer might take our being nice as a manipulative gesture, and it might backfire; so being nice changes from customer to customer and this is extremely intuitive because it has got a human element to it.

Before getting into what needs to be measured, learn more about Average, Mean, and Standard deviation. There is a beautiful cartoon-based book that is recommended by Bill gates—"*The Cartoon Introduction to Statistics*" **Grady Klein, Alan Dabney**

This chapter wholly concentrates on measuring things that matter. Measuring things that give an overall sense of accomplishment, and those measurements that motivate team members without any psyche up talk…

As an architect, we should measure things that make us more responsible for the business and life of the developer. The topics below are chosen based on how we can be more responsible and proactive on things that matter.

Careful about what you measure, you will start seeing what you measure most

We need to measure things that will help us grow faster in our business, and also improve our support and operational capabilities.

Technology Metrics

You need to measure technology metrics; only then will you be able to manage software and hardware costs. If you don't have any valid data, then you will not be able to justify your point on increasing the hardware or software budget. You will get insight into the design, and also an insight into the product itself.

McCall's Quality Criteria: A quality criteria is an attribute of a quality **factor** that is related to software development.

11 factors are used as attributes of a quality factor, such as Correctness, Reliability, Efficiency, Integrity, Usability, Maintainability, Testability, Flexibility, Portability, Reusability, and Interoperability.

The above 11 factors are guidelines, and measuring all of them is out of the scope of this book, so we will look into the very important ones.

The important ones are Reliability, Usability, Testability, and Maintainability.

Reliability includes the extent to which our software can perform as per its requirement. For example, we might have built the web application for say, 1000 users per second, and it was our initial business requirement then. If the business grows bigger, then it can handle a max of 10000 users per second, more than that you might have problems, so it is a reliability factor.

Load test and Regression testing are two ways to confirm the reliability of the software. For load testing, there are many tools available in the market. A few of them are **WebLOAD, smartmeter.io, and Apache JMeter.**

Regression testing is used to check if any new bugs have been introduced through previous bug fixes. This can be measured by having good coverage and a good amount of unit testing, so each build should have a unit test run and it should show the coverage and also all the unit tests should pass.

Usability includes how easy it is for the user to learn and operate our software. How much easier it is for the user to use without any external training. App Insights and Google Analytics are the best-known tools to measure usability.

Testability includes how much effort is needed to test a program or part of the program. This can be measured by how each piece can be tested easily, how much your developer is feeling it too easy to write the unit test, and how much time he takes to complete it.

If the developer finds any pain point in mocking any services or any other external assemblies, then an architect should be pitched in and remove the pain, so developers can write the unit test with ease.

Testability also means how fast testers can test the system. The time taken for the developer to check in and the tester gets the build should be measured, and should be reduced every sprint.

Maintainability includes the effort required to locate and fix a bug and also how easy it is to incorporate new features, meaning how Open is our software for a change. One can measure maintenance process attributes, such as the time required to make a change, which is influenced by software maintainability.

Based on Frappier's metrics, the maintainability cannot be measured directly by a tool. But you can capture it using attributes. http://www.dmi.usherb.ca/~frappier/Papers/tm2.pdf

Internal Effort per Change (IE): Effort spent in a module for a change. A great indicator is the number of files changed for fixing a single bug or implementing a part of the feature.

External Effort per Change (XE): Effort spent in external modules for a change such as changes needed in external APIs that are being called.

There are two more attributes which are an average number of modules (NB) and Maintenance productivity per project (PP), but both align the same as IE and XE respectively.

When you find module Internal effort change(IE) such as too many files changed, too many lines added, modified, deleted, or your changes need an external module to change, then as a leader, you need to work on refactoring it.

Two things you can do right away:

1. Add a layer of abstraction and find out the class which is violating the Single responsibility principle, meaning a single class is working like a Swiss army knife and doing too many things.
2. Divide the functionality into multiple classes.

These above two actions will make your application measurable in all 11 factors of McCall's Quality Criteria. This is one of the simple step you can perform in every project. And do apply other changes

Business Metrics

Business metrics help us to track trends, not numbers. Properly carefully selected business metrics help us to stop using software metrics that do not lead to change.

A **business** metric is a quantifiable measure **businesses** use to track, monitor, and assess the success or failure of various **business** processes.

Business KPIs can be multiple entities and it is directly related to sales and marketing. Business metrics should be measured to enable sales to monitor their sales trends and also check which feature or module is a bottleneck for their sales.

Some of the examples are below.

Users Currently on Site
Number of User logins
Number of times features/web pages visited
Number of purchases happened because of the new Promocode
Lead Conversion Rate

Customer Metrics

Customer metrics help to measure that we are making money. It helps to understand are we growing, shrinking, or stagnant. It also tells us are we making a profit. In the end, customer metrics help us to tell whether the customers are happy.

Customer metrics are numerical scores or indices that summarize **customer** feedback results. They can be based on either **customer** ratings (e.g., average satisfaction rating with product quality) or open-ended **customer** comments. In short, any information that tells us about the existing customer or metrics that will convert new users to customers.

Some of the examples include,

Cost Per Customer	Measures how much it costs to service a customer.
Burn Rate	A measurement of how much a company is spending as a whole for a particular project.
Customer Acquisition Cost	Useful for marketing and sales team and it is the cost spent on acquiring a single customer.
Customer lifetime value	Total amount spent by the customer starting from the date he joins your organization till he leaves or becomes a dormant customer.

Revenue Per Customer	Self-Explanatory.
Number of paying customer	Metrics that include how many are paying for your product, how many are using trails, and how many left the trail for the period of time.
Customer Churn	Metrics that include how many users have left the product or stopped using it. High churn means some steps have to be taken for stopping the project from going bankrupt.

These metrics cannot be directly measured or calculated, but you can pull metrics from the system that helps to calculate the cost.

Cost Per Customer	Always have metrics that can calculate the number of existing customers, number of users per customer, number of customers who are not using the app. Also, maintain the Cloud or server cost that is affecting your budget every month, so if there is an audit on cost per customer, we can clearly denote metrics from our end with the number of customers and our direct known cost and the auditor can add other Cost to the company for the project and then clearly get the cost per customer
Burn Rate	Always have details about the Cloud cost, salaries of employees easily accessible, so can be used at any cost calculation
Customer Acquisition Cost	This cannot be directly measured but can be assessed when a feature is requested by a sales team based on the particular customer's needs
Customer lifetime value	Start capturing details such as customer start date and end date and the current products he has bought, and have it in a database, so getting metrics will be easier
Revenue Per Customer	Capture from when the customer has bought a product and when he stopped paying for it. Does he pay for annual maintenance? This should be captured
Number of paying customers	This should be straightforward if you have a customer database that captures when the client moved from the trail to paying customer or when he bought a product for the first time
Customer Churn	Capturing the end date of the customer when he leaves will help us to calculate the customer churn

All the above metrics are KPIs and many are available, but the whole point of the topic is not to understand the KPIs, but to know their existence and how you can help your marketing and sales team to measure them.

As an architect, all you have to do is to build a system that captures customer name, customer start date, customer end date, customer bought products, when the product was bought, and it can be a simple UI that can capture with date time picker, text box, and a few radio buttons.

But always build this screen first and then capture it from the beginning. You don't have a complex database to capture this data, no-SQL options that support key-value pairs will do magic here. It is fast and also dead cheap.

Application Metrics

Think of every time a bug is reported and you need to analyze and think, and that we need a proper logging system and reporting system, so we can land to that page and see what happened.

But we need to dig through multiple logs (if we have written any) and write a SQL to find the data and then nothing is working to take a backup of the production database and start debugging.

It is tiresome and too much pressure. We always think we need to do something about it, but we did not get time to do anything about it because of all the urgent problems.

If we have proper application metrics, then we might be able to squash the bugs faster and get back to the customer. Most of the time it is a user error and we cannot tell that customer because we don't have enough data that can be pulled immediately.

Application metrics are metrics that are measured within the application. Any data that can be measured for the application can be called application metrics.

Application metrics are capturing data such as exceptions, log analytics, semantic monitoring data, trace logs, and debug logs.

As an architect, you should have deployed to production or at least to stage and should have analyzed an issue that happened due to server deployment. This will let you know which module lacks in writing logs.

Once you understand the pain of analyzing the problem on the server with your favorite IDE to debug, you will understand how important it is to write log and capture metrics that matter.

You don't even need to read this chapter if you have analyzed an issue in the server because you would already be good at it.

This topic is meant for someone who has no access to the server environments because they work in a very big company where the access is too restricted.

But with the fast adoption of Microservices and Cloud, the high restrictions of the server are going to go away and every team is going to own the server which they are deploying, and this is not far away, it is very soon.

You need to know these measurements to understand how to measure the application metrics.

Average Response Time	Time taken from the request till the first response is made.
Error Rates	Number of errors or exceptions that happen during a period of time.
Request Rate	Number of requests that are served by your server.
CPU Usage	Metrics that measure CPU usage which helps us to decide whether we need to scale up or scale down our server. Higher CPU usage means to scale up, too lower usage means to scale down.
Memory Usage	Metrics that measure Memory usage which helps us to decide whether we need to scale up or scale down our server. Higher Memory usage means to scale up, lower usage means to scale down.
Application crash rate	Application crash rate is calculated by dividing how many times an application fails (F) by how many times it is used (U).

| Exception log | The system should always be in a position to fetch your exception logs as fast as possible. A pie chart representing the exceptions will help us to see where our feature fails and also help us to decide the next sprint on the technical debt. |
| Trace logs | This is very important and should be made default, because if the task is like jobs that run every night, we can enable the trace logs by default, rather than only when needed, because the user is not waiting for it. If the user interaction is part of the request, then it should be switched off and we should be able to switch it on when needed. |

Monitoring is key in case of any applications, we should be able to monitor our applications and be able to respond to any outages as fast as possible.

In the ideal world, we should never be in a position where the server is down because we should have proper monitoring and alerts in place which alert us long before something bad is going to happen.

But there will be outages. Great companies like Microsoft, Amazon, Netflix, Youtube, Whatsapp, etc. have outages too, but there are numerous ways to prevent it and bring back the server when it actually happens.

We need to incorporate what makes our system as reliable as possible. When it breaks, we should know where we should look out. We should know our system is broken, and start working on it, rather than customer complaining about the outage, and then we start going from there.

One of the better ways of monitoring is to implement semantic monitoring which helps to check whether your system is performing well and if there is a problem you are reported quicker even before the client reports to you.

Semantic monitoring

Development teams typically produce tests that specify and validate application behavior but stop running them once the application goes into production.

Semantic monitoring uses your integration tests to continuously evaluate your application, combining test-execution and real-time monitoring.

With the rise of Microservices, we need to understand this level of monitoring and incorporate it into our project to have highly resilient products.

Semantic monitoring approaches Microservice monitoring from the business transaction, or semantic perspective. Instead of monitoring each component that serves a business transaction, synthetic transaction monitoring is employed to ascertain how well the transaction performs for the business and the customers who use it.

For example, your application takes orders for customers, creates invoices, and emails the customer back the created invoice.

The way of implementing the semantic monitoring is to have your integration test create new orders every 10-15 minutes or less based on your requirement, and let the system create the invoice and send the emails to the test customer email id.

If you don't receive enough emails within the stipulated time, you can raise an alert saying the system has a problem. If you write a proper log, you can figure which system failed.

Whether it is while creating new orders, or creating an invoice, or sending an email, now you know your system is up and you will get alerts from your own system rather than the client calling us after the system is already down for two days.

Proper Alerts are always good and lets us know how our system is performing. But the problem with alerts is when we get too many alerts we will stop bothering about them, you should always minimize the alerts.

Think of the time you put a rule in your inbox, so some alerts go to a particular folder and you have never looked at it. Those alerts are a waste of computer resources.

So alerts should be sent to you only if your action is needed. Otherwise configuring alerts is unwise. If the alerts are critical, then an SMS to your mobile is better than an email.

Not to Do as Manager

Architects are leaders but sometimes you have to do some managerial activities for the good of the organization. Managing certain parts of the project is critical for career growth because it showcases your leadership.

In the case of personal management, you should know to manage your own time, learn to say no, be persistent in your work even if the whole world is against you, plan important things and learn to ignore things that look very urgent, etc.

In the case of public management, you should know when to stop researching and start doing your project, when to stop using technology that is reaching its dead-end, and when to take a U-turn on your technology change modules that work in the way you wanted.

All managers are not bad, and all managerial jobs are not bad, but there are certain traits you should never show. You might show these traits unconsciously, which will lead to friction in the team and will affect the synergy in the team.

We will look into the above points one by one in the coming chapters. But in this chapter, we will concentrate on what you should not do as a manager.

By definition, a manager is a person responsible for controlling or administering an organization or group of staff.

As we learned in the previous chapter, a successful architect is always responsible for everything that happens around him. So responsibility is the key.

But administration and controlling is not your job. That should be left to the manager. Administration activities, such as monitoring that everyone is coming to the office on time and being in office for at least eight hours or so, is not your job, even if you feel someone's late arrival is hindering any of your project work, such as a call with a client or meetings need to be rescheduled because of one person. These things should not be handled by you.

You can tell the resources about it, but you don't take charge of keeping people from coming late. If you do, you are a pain in the ass of the developers.

You should never control people; controlling people is a bad habit, being in control is the key.

If you feel a person is not doing his job and is being lethargic, you can yell at them, and threaten them to get it done in a controlling way.

Or you can find out what the real problem is, does he have a personal problem that is stopping him from giving his best, or the work that he is doing is not motivating him enough, or find out whether he needs any help. Become a person to take control of the situation and be in control, rather than controlling.

Never have the goal of finishing the project on time as your goal, you should only be concentrating on getting your project done after the right things are done, such as a proper design that leads to lesser bugs and bugs that arise are easy to fix.

Remember the WHY chapter, your why defines your actions, why you do what you want to do defines your behavior and actions.

A manager and architect both should want to finish the project, but remember the last time you wrote a code of which you feel ashamed even today, because of the time constraint.

As an architect, even you might write code that you might be ashamed of. But those codes are written not because of the time constraint, but because of the technology constraint, so you are aware and you wrote it anyway.

Never be the manager who proves to people that they are wrong in front of others, always let people save their face in front of others and you.

Never win an argument with any of your team members, always let them feel they have won the argument, and even if you prove them wrong, let them save face in front of others.

Never take credit for anyone's work, even if it is a small one. Always give credit to others and it will help you in the long run. This is the big takeaway, if you want to take away one thing from this chapter, not taking credit for someone's work is huge here.

Always take the blame if things go wrong, and accept it saying that it was your responsibility that you should have checked the same.

Don't feel the need to always be right, and apologize in front of everyone if you are wrong. It builds trust because people know when you are wrong you admit, and you are right when you persist.

So when you are right and want your team to carry forward with the work, they will do it without much friction, even when you do not have much evidence and it is just that your gut knows it is right.

Never try to be manipulative, always be straightforward; You might not be popular and likeable but they will understand when you mix your straightforwardness with honesty and integrity. Your straightforwardness will only increase trust and respect.

Never be partial to the guys who are praising you or helping you on any front. Always treat everyone the same. Any personal favor done to you should never affect the way you treat people.

Keep this rule, if you have to give one criticism, then there should be four praises. And keep it 1:4 between criticism and praise. This is tough to follow, but trying never hurts. No matter how mature and straightforward, people love honest positive feedback and a pat on their back.

Getting Things Done

When you become a successful architect, you will be paid more and in turn, the expected amount of work that needs to be delivered also increases.

To cope up with the demand, you need to get more things done in less time. You need to get yourself prepared every day and improve yourself every day.

Your definition of getting things done should change from just developing a module, doing a round of testing and checking in the code, to taking responsibility

Your salary is directly proportional to getting more work done in less time

for any developer's code, designing the system and making sure usage is measured for the new feature, and getting feedback from customers, then iterating your system design and features.

Also, you are expected to code without any bugs and produce 1000 lines of code in one day. Yes, welcome to the world of what is expected from an architect. The trick is to write the 1000 lines of functionality in 10-100 lines.

You are expected to deliver every single time. Suddenly your mistakes are not tolerated and the consequences are severe.

People expect you to know the answer to all the technical problems in the problem domain. And they want that to be implemented yesterday.

Suddenly you are being yelled at and abused for the other mistake in your project. You will be ridiculed at the back for the wrong design that you made a couple of years ago, when the technology was not as versatile as today.

You need to do code review, design the system for new features, propose an architecture for new projects, and also do development.

The development you do is expected to work the first time itself on stage without even having a single bug, because you are an architect.

Become Highly Productive

As an architect, you are expected to deliver many different tasks; you also need to take care of current pressing issues and also think of future versions of the software.

You need to know how to handle both urgent and important matters at once.

If you have not trained yourself to become highly productive, you cannot survive in the architect's job and a senior developer will be a better position for you.

You tend to get caught up in the urgent pressing matters and will neglect the important activities and will pay a heavy fine later for neglecting the important activities.

Ignoring the important activities that are not urgent, will result in their becoming urgent soon enough and you will be firefighting all the time.

Design for high scale is a high leverage important activity. Due to the pressing deadline, you might overlook them and release the product.

Becoming highly productive means balancing both the important and the urgent. In other words, having an eye on important things while solving urgent problems.

You can call yourself a great producer only when you are good at solving current pressing urgent problems and also working on things that will prevent the same problems again.

Productivity requires discipline, focus, and persistence.

Follow the Japanese saying, "**Don't be afraid to make a mistake. But make sure you don't make the same mistake twice**."

This habit will fit nicely into the architect's life where he becomes both a 'Go-to' person for a problem to be solved and also a proactive person who will take responsibility, so the lives of stakeholders are free to create new features and opportunities.

But how can I find time for doing proactive things when attending to the urgent pressing production issue?

Awareness

When you are aware of your own distraction and find ways to get out of it, you will find lots of time to do what you have wanted to do for a long time.

Awareness is being conscious of what you are doing and not feeling guilty about it. Do we not feel guilt when we do things that are not productive such as watching a TV series or a movie to pass time?

When you follow these productive methods, you don't have to feel guilty.

Awareness is being conscious about whatever you do and not doing half-heartedly what you are doing.

If you are watching a movie, or just browsing Facebook/Twitter, don't feel guilty about it. Tell yourself you needed this and you are taking rest, so you are relaxing your mind to be productive and innovative.

Read the previous paragraph properly. I am saying not to feel guilt, and not saying not to think about work. You can still think about work, or think about certain challenges in your work that have been bothering you.

You can be productive in two ways when you are concentrating on a single task and getting it done. And also thinking about the task when you are doing a mundane work like bathing or walking and get it done

The second way applies to all software developers. Remember the last time you were stuck in a problem the whole night and left the office in frustration at not completing it. You went home and then maybe while having dinner, or lying in bed doing nothing, or doing any mundane thing, you figured out the solution. The next day you came in and then you killed it.

So being productive can be both ways—while focusing on a single task, or taking a step back from the task and then building a mental map on how to do it and then getting it done.

So awareness is knowing, you can be productive on both fronts when you are sitting at a desk and also not sitting at a desk.

All you have to do is not to make your mind wander while doing the other job, and becoming aware of your mind wandering.

In Zen culture, it is called "Kill the Buddha". When the disciples are asked to meditate (Eyes Closed) in the group and the Zen master will walk around, if he sees the disciples are not aware of the master's presence by losing themselves in their own thoughts, he will strike him with the stick to bring him back to awareness.

If you are having fun, be 100% indulged in the fun, and do not feel guilty about it. If you are working, then give your 100%. Kill the Buddha

"Zen master will say, 'Kill the Buddha!' Kill the Buddha if the Buddha exists somewhere else. Kill the Buddha, because you should resume your own Buddha nature."

Be aware of your surroundings and your distractions like Facebook, LinkedIn, etc., and minimize the usage. A good tip is to uninstall social media apps on your mobile. So you will never be distracted because of any random notification that pops up on your mobile.

Will Power

The secret to success is using willpower consciously. Will power will help you to overcome poor decision making.

The most well-known experiment, the 'marshmallow experiment', was begun in the 1960s by psychologist Walter Mischel. He offered four-year-olds the choice of one marshmallow (western candy) now, or two if they could wait 15 minutes.

He and other researchers then tracked the performance of these children when they became adults. They found that the children who resisted temptation ("high delayers") achieved greater academic success, better health, and lower rates of marital separation and divorce.

Mischel concluded that the ability to delay gratification constituted "a protective buffer against the development of all kinds of vulnerabilities later in life."

As per Wiki, Will Power means control exerted to do something or restrain impulses. Will power is nothing but to continue whatever you have planned irrespective of your circumstances.

Will Power is taking action even when the odds are against it. Let's say you have planned to go running tomorrow morning, and when you wake up it is raining, you can either decide to quit and roll over back to bed, or get up and go for running despite its raining heavily.

Will Power is understanding the climate is inside rather than outside. Climate change can be anything, it can be a change in the actual environment such as raining, sunny, etc., or it can be emotional climate change.

Someone would have said something that is making you upset, or it can be a financial climate change where you are down financially, but with good will power, you will not be affected by any type of climate change.

Will Power is about keeping your own promises and obeying them, despite any odd circumstances. Winning your own self is more important than others. Once you win yourself, then you might be able to influence others.

Influence starts inside and once you master yourself by influencing yourself to get things, then you can influence the outer world easily. Private victory precedes public victory.

Willpower is like a muscle. If you don't flex and stretch your muscles, then they become stale and resist any action when done sparingly.

You cannot overdo your muscles because they will become tight and it will stop you from normal activities. In the same way, when will power is being overused, you will not have the energy for regular work.

Five things you should do to improve your will power

- Your Will Power is limited; you have only a certain amount of will power during the day. Usually in the morning after you wake up, you have more. So stop using your mobile when you wake up and start doing things like the gym, and meditation which needs more willpower. Activities such as gym and meditation will boost your energy to do everyday activities with high energy and enthusiasm.

- Remove all the activities preventing success from your life, such as Facebook, Instagram, etc. Even LinkedIn has become an entertainment social media. Uninstall the apps such as Facebook, Instagram, and Linkedin from your mobile, so that you will not be checking your mobile often. Make your mobile as boring as possible.

- Schedule your distractions, you cannot live in the world without reading a blog or news or Twitter or WhatsApp. Moving completely from these will make you less sociable. You need topics to talk about in a normal social gathering, so these social media help us. So schedule one hour per day where you will use your social media and indulge in it without any guilt.

- Outsource any work if you're not good at it. If you are not good at cleaning your house, recruit someone who can do it for you. Don't be doing it yourself. If you are not good at, say, SQL, then give it to someone who can do it for you. Do only things you are good at and outsource the rest of it.

- Build habits that make everything you want to do second nature. Think about the last time you forgot to brush your teeth. It would have been a long time ago. It is because it is a habit, so you don't need the willpower to do those activities. It happens without any resistance.

We will be looking into the building of habits in the next section. You need to remember one thing, your WILLPOWER is a scarce resource; you need to use it wisely.

The biggest hogger of your willpower is your mobile, and you need to make sure you uninstall all the apps that distract you. In the section on the 55-10-55-30 Rule (page 114), we will look at how building your willpower and also being productive can happen simultaneously.

Building Rituals

> *"We are what we repeatedly do. Excellence,*
> *then, is not an act, but a habit."*

> *– Aristotle*

Whether we admit it or not, we are creatures of habits. We do the same thing over and over every day. We wake up, brush up, eat breakfast, travel to the office, have lunch, take some breaks in between at the same time every day, come back home, eat dinner, and sleep.

Only a few people are conscious and have a habit of trying out new things every time. Even then they are all monotonous.

It is almost impossible to do anything when we need to remember the steps to do an activity. Remember the last time you needed to set up an environment reading a document. How difficult it was for you to read through the steps.

But once you are comfortable with set-up steps, we just do it without any resistance. Remembering the steps to do any activities is really really hard.

If something is important, you need to make it a habit, so it becomes easy to execute. Remember the last time you thought of steps to brush your teeth. Wet the brush, put the paste on the brush, and put it in your mouth, brush the upper and lower part of your teeth, when your mouth is full, spit out the foam and then repeat brushing and rinse properly. All the steps to brush your teeth are done on autopilot NOW.

If something is important in your life, it makes sense to do it every day and make it a habit, so you don't have to face the resistance to remember the steps.

To build a successful routine you have to remove the initial obstacles that will halt the process. Planning in detail is the key here. Once you have a detailed plan, executing becomes easy.

For example, you are planning to go for a run tomorrow. If you have planned in detail before night on getting the shoe ready, your earphones ready for listening to songs, even downloaded the songs you need to enjoy listening to tomorrow, it will motivate you. You will be more likely to go for a run tomorrow.

If you haven't planned in so much detail, when you wake up, you will think I need to search for my shoe, so I will skip it today, and tomorrow I will do it.

One thing you need to understand is **Transitions** trip us. This is what happens when you look for your clothes, shoes, and earphones, which can cut your time short, and this causes you to fail even before starting the run.

So plan transition ahead of time and reduce the friction around the goal; you want to make it a ritual.

Remember that willpower is scarce and planning the transition will keep you in on-ramp and will not derail you from the goals.

Once you start planning your ritual and also build your day around rituals, you are smart enough to think of all the efficient ways of doing it.

You will become better at building rituals one by one, which will help to be successful in your personal and professional life, where you will have multiple habits that you do on autopilot, such as reading books, going to the gym regularly, writing blogs, contributing in Stack Overflow, which can all be made as rituals if you start with one ritual and keep adding one by one.

Reducing friction

Remember the last time you wanted to read a blog or a book, and you needed to take a pen and left the room and saw the TV or picked up your phone, and you did not realize you wasted 15-20 minutes just like that.

All this boils down to not planning your work in detail, so you don't get distracted in your journey toward your goal.

Friction means inefficiency, things aren't flowing freely and smoothly. We need to reduce the friction, so you can achieve your result with less stress and minimum effort.

Remember the last time you ate a bowl full of ice cream/dessert and you felt guilty and good at the same time. One part of you wants to avoid it, and the other part of you wants to do it.

Remember the last time you wanted to go for a run/gym early in the morning and you were all hyped last night, but the next day some part of you convinced you to stay in the bed.

Remember the last time you wanted to do an activity such as writing a blog, reading a technical book, or developing an open-source project. Some part of you wants to really do it, and another part of you convinces you against it because it is hard to start.

It looks as if there are two people in you. One tells you exactly what to do, get better in your life, and the other finds all the ways and justification to not do it.

In our universe, everything is based on duality. Yin and Yang, Shiva, and Sakthi, Black and White.

Yin is the receptive and Yang the active principle. Shiva is the destroyer, Sakthi is the energy of creation. Black is the absence of light and white means the presence of light.

Seemingly opposite or contrary forces may actually be complementary, interconnected, and interdependent in the natural world, and how they may give rise to each other as they interrelate to one another.

The same applies to the friction that is created by our brain when we want to perform an action that leads to procrastination.

You have two parts inside us, we need to recognize these two parts and introduce each other. I know it sounds weird, but that's the way the universe works; if you resist you are not going to go far.

"By acknowledging, accepting, and embracing our dark side, we create natural steam vents within ourselves. By providing an opening, we eliminate the worry about an explosion because we are allowing the pressure to be released in a safe and appropriate way."

– Debbie Ford

Each part exists for a reason, the most productive way is to acknowledge them and listen to them. And let them listen to each other.

Next time you are tempted to eat ice cream, let both sides talk to each other. One side of you says that eating the ice cream is delicious, and the other side says it has got 250 calories and it takes 1 hour of heavy exercise to burn just one scoop.

Both sides are giving you information about the ice cream, one side is giving you how delicious it is and how good you can feel, and the other side talks about your health and not to have that extra fat in your belly.

Once both have addressed their side's reasoning, you can satisfy both sides by eating your ice cream slowly and letting it stay in your mouth for more time than it usually takes. We tend to gulp ice cream as if we haven't had food for years (at least me), but when you tend to listen to both sides' concerns for avoiding and not avoiding it, you can come up with a synergistic solution where you enjoy the ice cream and also not gain that extra fat.

Next time you are planning to go to the gym, and when you wake up in the morning and one side tells you that you had a tough day yesterday and slept late, and the other side says that you have been planning and failing by giving excuses for not going to the gym, let both sides talk to each other, and listen to their talking.

Both their excuses are valid, you might have slept late yesterday and also you might be physically exhausted. But you have been planning for long, so you need to stick to the plan too.

After listening to others' point of view, what you can do is go to the gym as planned, and not do very strenuous exercises, since you are not very rested physically. What you can do is do some push-ups, pull-ups, some stretching, and some runs on the treadmill.

In real life, you will have more energy once you start exercising. Starting to go to the gym is the problem. If you keep denying the other part, if you listen and find a synergistic solution in your mind, you can go to the gym.

Next time you need to write a blog or read any technical book, one side will tell you that you are not good enough to write a blog, your English sucks, and people will find out how bad you are technically.

The other side will tell you that, you need to write your technical thoughts, so you not only get better at understanding the technology, you can call yourself an authority over certain topics.

So both your sides might be right. The first technique I learned is never to edit while you are writing, just write whatever comes to your mind.

Not to worry about the syntax, grammar, or any spellings. There is some writing software that will blind the screen after you type the word.

Afterward, you need to read it again and take your other side's suggestion, that your English is not good. So you don't publish the blog until you have reviewed it thrice.

The same rule applies to reading a book, where you glance at the chapter, glance once, and then think about what you know already. Find the commonality between the things you already know and the things that are taught here. Find the similarities and differences.

Then you read the book completely. This way you can reduce the friction that is caused by the other side which says you don't know anything about the topic that is described in the book. Now you have taken the feedback and respected the other side, and did what is right.

In the case of open-source projects, always start small because you can never do anything big in the open-source world because most of the friction from the other side is how to use Git effectively, how to fork, and how to send pull requests after you have coded your changes.

Major friction is not writing code, it is doing all the work other than writing code, because you would be a good developer by now, otherwise, you would not have come this far in this book.

https://www.firsttimersonly.com/ will help you to get started easily, do changes such as spelling mistakes in the documentation, or fixing any small validation.

You can also use https://up-for-grabs.net, which will give you a search page where you can search for the areas which you are good at, and then it will lead to the Git hub page, which usually has issues tagged with "up-for-grabs"

Always listen to the negative side when you are doing any kind of activity. It is there to help you. If you avoid and try to build your willpower avoiding your negative side, then you will have huge friction and it is not very easy to overcome.

Remember, everyone wants to be heard. Most of the time if you just listen to a person who conflicts with us, and he believes we understand what he said to us, then the conflict is resolved without even doing any action.

The same goes for your dark side. Always listen to it and make a synergistic solution around it, which will help your architect career faster.

First, we saw the meta of the friction, now we will look into certain friction components and how to avoid them.

You start a job, say reading a book, but you need a pen and start searching for a pen. And then you lose yourself somewhere doing something else other than reading the book.

The same thing happens when you feel thirsty in the middle of reading your book.

This happens even when you want to take a leak, somewhere in between your book reading.

So next time you want to do any productive activity, you make sure you schedule five minutes just to get all the prerequisites met, such as pen, paper, or the book you need to take notes. Take a leak if you have to. And make sure, if you start work you don't have to move from the place for at least 50 minutes, and you can carry on with the work that you have taken up without distraction.

55-10-55-30 Rule

Focused work gets things done faster. Focus is all we want to improve. The more focus you can give to a single work, the more you can get done. Think of the last time you wanted to go on a vacation or go to your native place for the long weekend, and how much you got done.

The secret behind getting more things done is the focus. We will look into how we can get more tasks done by concentrating on one task at a time.

There are two aspects to focus on: **quantity** and **quality**.

As we are building our ability to focus, we want to work on our ability to focus on just one thing at a time, for longer and longer periods of time—that is quantity.

The quality aspect is **WHAT** you are focusing on. For example, the outcome you want to have rather than just passing the day.

We want to work up the ability to work on one task for 55 minutes without any distraction. Most unsuccessful people fail in their lives because they cannot focus on one thing.

Success comes to the entrepreneur who is obsessed and doesn't care about anything around them. This is also true with scientists who are so obsessed with their experiment, who do not shower and don't care how they look. All they care about is their EXPERIMENT'S RESULT.

We don't have to work like a mad scientist, but we can get the same results with the process I am going to tell you.

You need to figure out two things that are important in your life right now, which you have been procrastinating. It can be writing a blog, reading a book, creating technical videos for your YouTube channel, wanting to learn any new technology which you feel will be the future.

Write down the two important tasks that will help your career.

1. _____

2. _____

Write down the benefits you will get when you finish the tasks in order

1. _____

2. _____

Write down what you will lose if don't finish the tasks

1. _____

2. _____

Once you have identified the tasks, all you need is to focus and work on them without distraction. Yes, it is that simple. Simple to hear but very hard to go through.

To be productive, you need to follow one simple rule **55-15-55-30.**

You need to take the first task you wrote down and then concentrate on it for 50 minutes without any distraction. You should not be moving around, checking your mobile, or talking to someone, or doing any other thing while concentrating on your first task for 50 minutes.

You should not even refer to the dictionary when you read the book, you just note it down and refer to it later.

Your concentration should be only on the one task you have taken and you should work on it for 50 minutes, even though you feel like doing something else.

Take a timer and set it to 50 minutes, and get yourself comfortable in the place where you are going to perform the task.

If you are writing a blog, get yourself a nice chair, and also you can switch on the AC, or if the climate is good, open the windows. Keep yourself as comfortable as possible.

If you are reading a book, then make sure you have a pen and paper to take notes, because you might need a pen in the middle and you might wander off.

Always prepare yourself for five minutes and get all you need for the particular task to be done.

Once you are all prepared, switch on the timer and start working on it.

You will lose concentration initially, so tell yourself, "get back to the task" and think of the benefits you are going to get and also the things you might lose or not get.

The first 10 minutes are hard, you might, wander, but afterward, you get into a flow state, and you will not know how the time is passing. Then after 25 – 30 minutes, your mind will wander off. Bring it back to your task.

Then you will again get it into the flow state. You might need to take a rest after 50 minutes because you will be exhausted.

Initially, it will be very tough and exhausting. Like any muscle, your brain will resist this level of focus and concentration. But you will feel good because you would have accomplished one week's work in 50 minutes.

You start doing this every weekend and slowly move it to weekdays, you will find yourself becoming the most productive person that you have ever been.

Second, comes the rest part. Our body has many different rhythms or cycles. One important cycle is called the Ultradian cycle. It lasts 90-120 minutes after which we feel like relaxing or taking a break.

Many people, when they feel this need to take a rest, either drink coffee, smoke, or eat some sugar to power themselves through the energy drop.

All you need to do is drink some water and lie on your bed, or walk away from the place. Flex a bit.

I normally will go to the bed, lie there, close my eyes and relax all parts of the body and try not to think of anything. Relaxing has to be part of an everyday ritual.

It should be conscious relaxing, you can even watch TV to relax, but you might be conscious that you are relaxing and not getting carried away.

If you are relaxing, you should not feel guilty about it, you have to tell yourself you are preparing yourself for better scheduled highly productive hours.

Once you are done relaxing for 15 minutes, you can take the same task or a second task and do it. The key again is before starting your timer, spend 5 minutes thinking about what all you need before starting the task. It might be as small as going to the restroom and getting the pen and paper, but you should not be moving around after the timer starts.

Once both 50 minutes are over, take complete rest for 30 minutes and then do the normal work you do for the weekend, like spending time with your family or binge-watching the TV series, and having a fun weekend.

Renewal is important; you need to renew yourself without any guilt, like doing something that does not need your brain to stress itself.

It can be sleeping and lying on the bed and thinking about things that are mundane.

Renew yourself without any guilt and listen to your body, and also make sure you do that for 50 minutes twice a day, once as the first thing in the morning.

You will feel so good about yourself the whole day because you would have accomplished a week's work that you have been procrastinating.

Do this for 21 days and email me, how you have advanced in your career so far. It will give you the power to control your own destiny.

Once you have mastered this for 21 days, make sure you do two – **55-15-55-30 for 48 days.** Once you have done it, it will be part of your routine like brushing your teeth, where you don't feel stressed or strained to do the activity; it happens automatically.

You will feel so much better about yourself and you know where you are going, and you can see many opportunities will be on your way.

If you lead your life without this one habit you might end up being the same person as Tony Robbins says, **if you are not moving up, then you are moving down.** This one habit will make you more powerful and give you full control over your destiny.

Schedule your distraction

Current society norms and technology can keep you distracted throughout the day. When you schedule your distraction, you tend to get more things done, and also you will look like the most productive person people have ever met.

The more you schedule your distractions, the smarter you become, and the smarter you look to the outside world. People will come and ask you how you get so many things done even though both of us have the same 24 hours.

When you schedule your distractions you tend to spend quality time with your family and also friends. It will look like you are always having fun.

The biggest enemy of productivity is distraction, and the biggest friend of productivity is FOCUS.

Think of the last time you sat to write a blog or read a book, and you saw a notification from your mobile and then started seeing some video and checked some Twitter feed, and suddenly you lost 30 minutes of your writing or reading time.

But checking your phone for those videos is all mandatory because you don't want to be left out of a conversation and look like you escaped to this earth from another planet.

You also need to be current with all the things happening around you so you can have a social conversation and relate with people with views.

So you need all these technology platforms such as Facebook, Twitter, Instagram, and WhatsApp which help you to connect with like-minded people and also get to know what happens around you so that you are not left alone.

It also wastes your time a lot seeing useless videos and reading useless news. To overcome this you need to schedule your distraction.

Scheduling your distraction means finding a specific time each day for all your social media and other non-productive activities.

The first step is finding all your distractions and making note of them; a mental note is enough, but writing down is better.

The second is to find the time where you actually relax after your work or travel in a bus or anything where you don't move or do any physical activity

Third, prioritize your distractions. Always make sure you see posts that will add any social value or add knowledge.

Once you have got all three rehearsed in your mind or on paper, make sure you stick to that for 21 days.

For example, you have identified Facebook and Instagram as being your biggest distractions. Uninstall them from your mobile.

Then find a suitable time such as in the evening after 6:00 when you reach home, or when you travel by bus, when you can be using Facebook and Instagram.

If you have scheduled your distractions during the travel hours, then uninstalling and installing may be an annoying chore, so you won't do it. The best is to disable all the notifications, and you can also use software that is available in the market that helps you to use the app during certain hours, and also for a certain duration of time. The iPhone has a built-in screen time feature that will help you to schedule your distractions.

Become very picky in posts you read and feel free to skip any posts. The technique I always follow is to never read or listen or view any media which you have already watched or listened to or read.

I learned this from Anthony Robbins, never to watch a movie more than once; if you do that you really don't have a life. But I don't follow this religiously because I watch Avengers and Sci-fi movies like The Matrix more than once. For any ordinary movie, I will change the channel and watch something else I have never watched before.

Once you schedule your distractions, your friends will feel how you are currently in trends in social happening and also you have good technical knowledge and you get your work done and do more than you are asked for.

You alone know what the secret is. And make sure you teach your friends, because you will learn more and stick to it if you teach others. Because you have taught someone now, you need to be consistent with what you taught them. This is one of the habits of highly productive people of steps to make your success inevitable which we will discuss as the next topic.

Making Success Inevitable

What if your success is inevitable, what if you know methods such that the outcome can only be success? This is the next level of setting goals.

Inevitable thinking will get you more than goal setting can get you. You will be 1000% more productive than you were ever before if you use just these techniques we are going to talk about.

Making success inevitable means success happens automatically. It is all about creating conditions that make your success inevitable.

How can you set up conditions in your life so that the outcomes you want in your personal and professional life become inevitable?

Promising someone you will do what you hate, if you don't finish a task, will automatically make your success inevitable.

In the book, '*Influence*', Robert Cialdini talks about **Commitment and Consistency.** There's a story Cialdini tells about an experiment where a group of people were given a cancer awareness ribbon and asked to wear it for a week. Most people thought it was a harmless request, and complied.

Some time later, these same people were asked to donate to help fight cancer. Not surprisingly, this group of people donated much more money than did the control group. Why? Because in wearing the ribbon for a week, cancer-fighting had now become a small piece of their identity. They were now more likely to behave as a cancer-fighter would.

This cancer story talks more about commitment. If I don't donate, I tend to look like a fraud for just wearing the badge, and I don't mean it. Even though it really does not matter if you donate or not, but our internal commitment and consistency make us do it.

What if we use this commitment and consistency technique to work for us? Before we can go further, reducing friction is very important. Make sure you set up a physical environment for maximum creativity and productivity.

Get yourself a nice ergonomic chair, a good keyboard, and a big monitor, and make your physical environment as conducive as possible. If you are a guy who likes to work in the dark, get a thick sunscreen for your windows. Make your working place as nice and cozy as possible.

Commit to your friend/wife that you will do a particular task by this date, and if you don't finish the task you will give them x amount. Now you have committed and you will make sure you will be consistent in your actions because you stand to lose x amount.

For example, you say to your wife, if I don't finish reading the book in 30 days, and set the date as 22/12/2021, when if you fail, you will give her 5000 rupees. Keep the amount as high as possible, so that you will not just give them the money for being lazy. The higher the amount, the better you keep up your commitment. Fearing losing something is the biggest motivator, use it to your advantage.

This money technique can be used in any task which you have been procrastinating for a long time. If you're not married, do it with your mom, girlfriend, sister, or cousin who likes and appreciates success in your personal and professional life.

Committing to the public is another great procrastination killer. I usually schedule a meetup or webinar, if I want to learn something very deep, so I know on the webinar day there will be 100 people who will be waiting for me to deliver good content. So I will now learn and prepare because I don't want to be embarrassed.

When you take these steps of committing in private and public and follow through with your task, your success will become inevitable. If you don't have any commitment, you will fail a lot because we are all lazy by nature, and it will take our lives and make us regret it every day.

Becoming a Demon Developer

When you become a demon developer, you tend to stand out in your team automatically and leadership roles and activities come to you automatically.

When you are the developer who delivers more than what four or five developers combined can deliver, you become a demon developer.

You need to get to that stage as soon as possible and it is not a herculean task, all you have to do is follow some simple steps and keep getting better every day.

The important secret for getting highly productive is always FOCUS. That is why I like pressure and deadlines because it automatically gets you focused on a single task.

People either crack under pressure or use that pressure to focus on the single task at hand. If you focus and get things done, you become a demon developer; if you crack under pressure, you become a mediocre developer.

You need to take care of five states to become a demon developer, they are not exhaustive but they are very important. I got this after talking and researching about lots of architects and developers who produce a lot in very little time.

Technical Mindset

People with a good technical mindset seem to solve problems and face challenges with a full heart. When you have a technical mindset, you live stress-free and you accept life as it is rather than what you want it to be.

A technical mindset is all about what you think when you are challenged with a high technical problem. And how you overcome your own insecurities about not knowing enough for doing the job.

It is all about how you talk to yourself in our programming world when you are in the arena of solving the complex challenge you are facing.

We will look into seven strategies every great technical mind I have worked with follows, and how you can take it and implement it right away.

Programming is Hard, not impossible

By now you would have figured out that programming is not easy. If it were easy, everyone would have been earning what you have been earning.

Think of someone who is earning less than you who is not in our developer field. They want to be a software developer like us, but they could not; they may have tried once and left. Only you know, it is hard but not impossible.

Since you have bought this book, you should be a better programmer, this book is for people who want to move from developer to architect, so you should be good at what you do.

Remember your previous success when you are stuck in a problem.

We seek this mindset of NOT impossible. When you get stressed because of some coding issue or any technicality, tell yourself programming is hard. That is why I am paid this much, but it is not impossible because I have been doing this for years, and I have succeeded every single time.

Embrace the pain

Embracing pain is the sure way to grow. When you embrace your pain, you tend to change yourself and it will lead to being better than what you are right now.

Think of the last time you were so frustrated that you wanted to run away from the project and you got too stressed because too many things depended on you completing the module or work you have taken.

Pain is gain, pain has helped us to focus. But the pain only becomes suffering when we resist being in the present moment. When we embrace the present, the pain becomes the flow state.

Next time, when you feel you are in pain, tell yourself once I get through this pain, I will get stronger and smarter. Once you start becoming aware of your pain and you become conscious of it, saying it makes you stronger and smarter, two things happen.

The negative effect of trying to run away from a difficult situation vanishes, so you are more open to challenge. The second thing is you will grow more will power.

The more challenges you start accepting in your life, the better you become. Because it is all about having experience in facing and solving problems.

Not Yet strategy

Learning and incorporating the 'Not Yet' strategy will help us to get one step closer to the solution. I have used it many times and it works like a charm every single time.

Not yet strategy is the step to follow when you are working on a problem, when you are in a flow state where you are going out in all guns to solve the problem, then you get stuck somewhere and you know you need to make a U-turn because the path you have taken is completely wrong, and you are back in square one where you started.

We either tend to give up, or try to work harder in the same direction, or just scrap it all out and start from scratch. Both actions are wrong and right. It is all about finding the middle place.

It is all about getting the one line of code or one function that will solve the whole problem, and all the other lines you wrote are all just a scaffolding that leads to this area of code or configuration for the technology.

When you reach a dead-end, think of it as another turn in the maze, we might even have to come close to the entrance of the maze. Whenever there is a dead-end, think to yourself "Not yet."

This strategy of telling yourself "Not yet," when you are at a dead-end, or your work is not moving forward, will not only help you to reduce stress, it also helps you take every challenge with a smile, because you will remember the last time you told yourself "Not yet", and how you solved it later.

Not forgetting your success story

The problem with programmers like us is that we are absent-minded. Remember the last time you went to the room to get something like a key or mobile and you forgot why you went there, or you left something in your car or bike and walked back from your home to get it. The incidents of being absent-minded are countless, but we remember complex configurations, complex programming languages, and each and every scene in the sci-fi movies we love. But can't remember to lock the door or take things from our vehicle and walk back to get them.

Sometimes, I will get one item from the car and forget the other one, and will again walk back cursing myself for being so stupid. Are we that stupid? Probably not. We are a little bit smarter than most crowds we know.

The same forgetfulness applies when we are stuck in a problem and we are frustrated and think that we are not good enough. We forget how many problems we have solved in our career which were challenged and ridiculed as not solvable.

The best way is to keep a journal every day about the technical problems you had and how you solved them. Some days might consist of only how you are stuck in a problem, while another day you might be boosting yourself on how you solved a complex problem with a few lines of code, or sometimes not even writing a single line of code.

This way of maintaining a journal will help you to remember the success we had. Don't use this as something to boost your ego and walk around the world pumping your chest and looking down on others. Karma is a great teacher, it will slap you in your face if your ego gets to a high level, and the universe will put you in your proper place.

You need to remember your success story. It will help you to talk to yourself and self-motivate yourself that you are capable of facing complex challenges, and this is just the phase you had like last time where you solved a complex problem and had felt the same way in the middle.

If you don't remember your success story, you will always be feeling low about yourself and it will spill into every part of your life. It is all about confidence, and if you project confidence, it will attract positive and successful people to your life.

Feeling good about yourself, about your success story without boosting your ego will help to attract more success in your life.

Beginner's mind

When you have a beginner's mind, you tend to solve problems faster. Architects who think they don't know and are curious seem to be the best learners. They ask the right questions and they are very curious to learn anything that is brought to the table.

Shoshin (初心) is a word from Zen Buddhism meaning "**beginner's mind.**" It refers to having an attitude of openness, eagerness, and lack of preconceptions when studying a subject, even when studying at an advanced level, just as a beginner would.

Preconceived notions are always our enemy. That is the reason why when we explain the problem to someone and they ask you mundane questions, or ask you to try a step that is too trivial, the light bulb lights in our head. Because we think we are smart, we don't think of trivial steps that might solve the problem.

Next time you approach fixing a bug, remember to forget all your previous knowledge about the module.

Architects like us should always approach any problem with curiosity and also listen to people who have already done some research on the problem and get input from them.

Not listening to them because we think we are smart is rude, and inefficient, because listening builds trust and people feel their work is valued rather than you throwing off their work and giving a solution.

Everything is learnable and the beginning is always hard

"Change is hard at the beginning, messy in the middle, and gorgeous at the end."

– Robin Sharma

When you have a mindset of learning, and you know everything is hard at the beginning, you tend to take up new challenges because it gives you a sense of high, to work in new technologies. The newer technology you know, the more opportunities pop up. Your life will become some kind of magic, where people will consider you as a guru.

Think of the amount of time you will give your child to practice walking during infancy. It should be infinite times, right? We don't stop them from trying, they start trying to hold something and stand, and see they can balance, and they take the first step and fall, and again take another step and then fall.

Then they walk a couple of steps, walking by holding onto things, and they try to walk without holding any things and then fall.

But we never de-motivate our child from trying, and you know the more the kid tries to walk, the sooner he is going to walk better. But in our own professional work, we tend to forget this simple evolutionary process which has helped us to walk and forget the principle of learning.

My successful friends and most successful directors I have worked with know this and they anticipate friction when trying anything new. Our own minds will not allow us to change because change from an evolutionary point of view is a risk.

Unknown territory comes with unknown risks in which we are not trained yet, because there might be a predator that might be waiting to kill us in the jungle. We are not living in the jungle, but our brains are still the old brain which has millions of years of wiring of living in the jungle.

We are now in a different type of jungle. There are different types of predators out there, that will disturb our survival, are not learning, and not trying out new things. Evolution has not changed our brains yet.

Since you are reading this book, you want to learn something and be better, because the book has promised that you will become a better architect. Since you have come this far, you realize the book will make you better. Kudos for trusting me.

Learned to walk away and come back

Walking away is the most productive activity when you are stuck in the turmoil of stress, or in a rabbit hole of thoughts, or deep layers of problems. When you learn to walk away, you are more likely to solve the problem than if you are sitting in the same place and banging your hand or head on the desktop.

Whenever you are in deep technical problems, learn to shut down your computer and leave for home and not think about it any time sooner.

There is some kind of magic that happens when you do that. Most of the time you would have the solution in your head when you wake up, or sometimes worse, you will have a solution when you walk down your steps or are in the lift, and you will be running back to your desk to try that solution.

Learn to go back to the step zero at any point in time.

The mindset to go and start back from zero, when cultivated, will not only help to handle our technical problems but also our personal issues. When you are willing to go back to ground zero and start again, you will have more opportunities than only one solution in your hand and you are adamant about letting it go.

Whenever you get stuck in a technical problem, think to yourself that I am in a rabbit hole and the further I move toward this path, it will lead to a dead-end.

Sometimes we are attached to the way to the solution that we don't want to turn back when even we know it is the stupidest path we have chosen.

Next time if you are attached to the path of solving, catch yourself, and be detached from the path to the solution. You are not here to solve it the way you wanted to solve it.

You are hired to solve it in the best way that satisfies the principles of design and programming, not the way you have chosen first and with your ego attached to the process and path chosen.

Developer's developer

Remove noise for developers

As an architect, it is your utmost duty to remove the unwanted noise that hinders your developer's productivity. Removing noise is one of the high leverage activities that differentiate a sole architect who spends the rest of his life as a senior developer with a fancy architect title, from the one who goes to CTO level.

When you start thinking of things that will make a developer's life easy, then your career skyrockets and you will start getting more and more responsibility which will help to climb the corporate ladder faster.

Removing noise for developers means clearing any roadblocks that stop a developer from delivering his module. It changes from project to project, but the principle is the same. Find the noise source, block the noise communication path, and protect your developer from the noise.

For example, there might be a support team that is directly communicating with the developer and getting things done which might be some of the support team activity, *Learn to say no for your developers* so the source of noise is the support team or support member. He might come to his desk or message him to get things and the communication channel is either direct or through message or email. You need to tell the support team member (source) to stop communicating directly with email or message and it should only come through you (source channel). Then the developer will have time to do his actual work rather than the work of the other member.

I am not saying the support team or sales team should not communicate with your developer; he cannot contact him for the same issue or same type of issue more than once. The support team should be proactive enough to understand the issue themselves and handle it if it comes up again.

Removing the most painful

Competition is intense nowadays; in order to just keep your head above water, you need to solve your business problem as soon as possible. Your developer should be working on things that matter. Just like the previous topic, removing the most painful is as important as removing noise. When you strategically remove the pain points of your developer, your developer not only will become productive, you will also become a highly productive person because you can produce more with few people in your team.

Painful things are the ones that come in the way of a developer when he is trying to debug an issue, work on a new feature, or set up an environment as a new developer in the project.

You can create an environment where debugging an issue is easier because you worked on getting the log set up properly and easily accessible by the developer. For setting a new environment you can create a docker based environment setting where the environment can be set in two minutes by pulling the docker image.

Trying out new tools

Using the right tool for the right activity makes you more efficient; it also helps you to avoid procrastination because we always procrastinate if it is hard to start. If you have the right tool, the tool does the plumbing and so you can concentrate on solving the actual business problems that are pressing you.

As an architect, you should be the one who takes care of the productivity of the team. When you come across any tool which is ranking high in the order, you must try it, and if you feel it will make the developer productive, then you should be advising the team to use it.

Also, be open to developers trying out new tools, and let them select tools which they are comfortable with, and encourage developers to try new tools and be thankful and praise them in public, if they suggest a tool that they have used and found useful.

But you make sure when the developer suggests a tool. Do research from your end, and also don't directly impose tools on developers. Then there might be resistance. Ask people what they think of the tool, and if you show them how painful it was before, and after using the tool how easy it has become, the resistance from their side will be less for using the tool.

Learning how to write a framework

If you know how to write a framework, you not only become an aspiring architect, you also leave a legacy. A legacy that will be there as long as the project exists. You will be making the life of the developer easy if you write a good framework.

If you write a framework that is not right, you make the developer's life hell. Think of the last time when you were stuck and felt like a prison, and your hands are tied because of the underlying framework of your project.

Writing a framework is **a standardized set of concepts, practices, and criteria for dealing with a common type of problem**, which can be used as a reference to help us approach and resolve new problems of a similar nature.

The best way to write a framework is to follow principles rather than techniques. The framework should be simple, designed to evolve, and the final main point is it should be consistent.

A good Architect always thinks about standardizing practices to help developers.

Consistency should be the key, the framework you wrote should be consistent across. If it is not consistent, it is only going to make a huge entry barrier, and developers will be confused and start breaking the framework apart. Learning about writing a framework is out of the scope of this book, but you can read more about the principles and implementation in '*Framework design guidelines*', a book by Cwalina.

DevOps Expert

As an architect, you should be a DevOps expert. Being DevOps makes you a more productive worker and also it is one of the greatest high leverage activities. The benefits of being a DevOps person is not only making you a developer's developer, but also a sales team developer. You build a strong foundation for faster delivery of your features. Developers' time is more spent on fixing bugs rather than fixing build errors at the time of the release.

I highly recommend reading the book 'Phoenix Project: A Novel about It, DevOps, and Helping Your Business Win' by Gene Kim and Kevin Behr to improve your own DevOps and engineering practices.

Every architect should be a DevOps Expert, he should be able to implement DevOps on his own in any project.

Being a DevOps expert means you should know one tool such as Bamboo, Jenkins, Azure DevOps, CircleCI, or Github Actions. I personally prefer Github Actions, because it has lots of inbuilt tasks that can be written in Yaml, so it is bug-free and more innovations poured in. You should know how to make your Greenfield projects and also Brownfield projects DevOps compliant.

Principles

Principles help us to decide what to do, when to stop, and make decisions even when our ego is high, or our ego is hurt, or we are insecure. Principles are a secret sauce that helps strong people to make decisions and secrets that make people strong when they are vulnerable.

Three principles should drive your decision making in DevOps. **Reduce the time to market, reduce the friction around deployment, and work constantly on removing a manual dependency.**

Reducing time to market means when the developer checks in and how much time it takes to be in a stage environment. You should work constantly to reduce the time from check-in to stage. The best way is to find the build task that is taking more time and fix it. Once you have optimized the picked up task, then find the next task and then optimize.

DevOps need to be constantly taken care of like a pet. Remember maintenance cost for DevOps is always high as are its returns. So your principle is to find the friction that is stopping the developer from using your DevOps.

Also when the developer seems to be violating your DevOps pipeline or CI, talk to them and understand what is stopping them from using it. It is the architect who has to find the friction that stops the developer from using the DevOps pipeline.

All your principles will help you make decisions when you are planning for a tradeoff; you can choose any two principles and leave one alone. And next time weigh in the other principle which you have ignored. It is a process of balancing between three principles.

Knowing how to initialize DevOps in any project

As you become a successful architect who got DevOps for your own project and people start seeing the results, and your developers start bragging about your DevOps pipeline which makes their life easy, you will be asked to work on other projects or asked about suggestions on how to start.

As an architect, you should be able to know how to work on any projects which have zero or little DevOps in them.

The best principle to use as a silver bullet while starting any type of project is to find the most annoying manual process in the release process and then automate it.

DevOps is a recurring process

Build breaks almost every day might be due to developers checking in some code, or there is an update in the release process of a mobile app store, or the build agent's machine just got a windows update or any 100 different reasons. So as an architect you should own the process of keeping the DevOps up and running every day.

You don't have to be responsible for maintaining it and you can delegate it to any responsible person, who is doing this in a better way. But in his absence, you should be able to fix it when there is a problem, or you need to develop one more functionality.

In order to be in a place where you can fix the DevOps by yourself, you should have been the person who was responsible for creating it. If you are in a project where you weren't responsible and you just moved in, then your DevOps process must become your first pet you take care of in the project.

Always make sure you review the DevOps changes if possible, keep the DevOps developer sitting close to you or almost in the same bay so you know what changes are being made. It is very important because once DevOps becomes implemented, business stakeholders will be mentally tuned that the development is over, and the release can be sooner. If the DevOps breaks and you are not aware of how to fix it, then your business stakeholder might not be happy.

You are responsible for DevOps

When you feel completely responsible, then you will design for release from the beginning of the project. This will help to estimate the project considering DevOps activities and current DevOps changes.

The more you take responsibility, the more you will think of a cleaner approach to solve the problem, the more you will tend to keep the future in mind.

Responsibility means you should know the DevOps process in and out and tasks that are used in the DevOps cycle, and even if all the members leave, you should be able to take it from there. It should also run in a proper state, even if you leave the company or the project.

Get good at one technology and keep updating your knowledge about the DevOps process and technology changes. Always keep an eye on the CI/CD pipeline and the time it takes to market. Make sure you reduce the time and also remove any manual intervention.

No exception in spite of releases schedule

When you accept the breaking of the build due to the pressing schedule, you will fall into the pit where your build is always broken and you will switch to the cumbersome manual process. Initially, you will feel like you are moving things faster, but your developer will be spending more time in the operations rather than thinking and solving the actual problem which makes our business better.

Always make sure once your DevOps process is on, there is no going back to manual. Any process that is automated should stay automated; if it is broken you or another developer should fix it and you should always keep it as the rule not to break the build process. Whoever breaks it should fix it even if it is postponing the release.

Learn Methodology

YAGNI

There is a thin line between designing for the future and over architecting. Most of the time, when you are a midlevel architect, you will complicate the solution where a simpler approach should have been better. Simple solutions are sustainable and also easy to implement.

Think of the time you implemented an interface and you added "throw not implemented exception", that is definitely YAGNI.

YAGNI means "You Ain't Gonna Need It". Don't design or implement anything extra where you are not going to use it now.

Strive to become a minimalist Always implement and design what is needed for the immediate future. Anything more than that is a waste of time and makes the system complex. You never know, after six months you might re-architect the whole solution when the business changes.

Don't implement any interface if it has no implementation, don't choose any technology if there isn't usage of 70-80% of the features. Always make sure you need to reduce the number of technologies you have chosen.

YAGNI

It may look like overkill, but I'm sure we'll need it eventually.

Always remember that you might never use the code or design and it just increases your operational cost.

Follow Pareto's principle of 80-20 and find the 20% that will make the 80% difference, and make sure you follow this religiously in business requirements. While doing UI design or exposing the APIs, choosing technology, or any other work you do in our industry, always find the 20% and put your 80% of work in that area, no more no less.

Rapid Application Development

This type of development process is done in a project where the company is a startup and you need to reach a market for the survival of the company. This methodology should not be tried for the enterprise project because those systems should be designed for scaling which will not be possible in Rapid Application development.

They are done in three phases:

Requirement collection: It involves the use of various techniques used in requirements like brainstorming, task analysis, form analysis, user case analysis, etc.

Build Prototype: Start building a prototype with the requirement gathered and budget figured out. The prototype should be an iterative process and it is complete when all the use cases gathered are completed.

User Feedback: Start releasing into the market and work on only the modules where the users are using and ignore the modules where the user is not interested. Make sure you have built in user feedback mechanism build into the system.

Repeat this process again, so the product starts making revenue for your startup. I am going to skip Agile methodology for all the obvious reasons.

Lean Development methodology

Lean development methodology helps in getting our team to work effectively and efficiently. It also helps to design our project according to what is needed and not to do anything extra which might not be used. It not only creates a better environment but also creates a better culture of design and development. It aligns closely with the YAGNI principle.

Lean production is a systematic method originating in the Japanese manufacturing industry for the minimization of waste (無駄 Muda) within a manufacturing system without sacrificing productivity, which can cause problems.

Let us look into the seven Mudas in our software context and see how we can use them to our advantage. The seven principles were adapted from lean manufacturing by Mary and Tom Poppendieck to our software industry.

Overproduction a.k.a. Avoid 'Good to have' features. Any feature that is added to the project or sprint will always delay the project. So don't do any features that are good to have. Take only features that you feel are completely necessary for the release. Don't produce anything ahead of demand.

Overprocessing a.k.a. Embrace YAGNI. This is about thinking in design and development in terms of you ain't going to need it. Choosing tools that are overkill for the job is one of the examples. For example, choosing Service bus instead of an ordinary queue for technical problems, will not only overkill but also slow your response rate because the service bus is a heavy option. If you are not using all the features, which might not be needed for the project, validate your choice again.

Unnecessary Transportation a.k.a. starting more than is to be completed. Choosing more work than what needs to be completed creates context switching, unnecessary delay, and adds stress to every day's work and the resource working on it.

Don't add new functionalities initially or at the time of release unless we have promised it to the customer or client. Always delay the release if new functionality is added.

This might look counterintuitive for the speed we need to increase in our project, but when people know release will be delayed because of last-minute changes, they will make sure they add the requirement early in the process and not add anything in late. Because when we say it is a small change, the business does not understand the amount of work and risk involved. It might be two lines of code, but testers have to test the whole scenario because it should not break.

Inventory a.k.a unnecessary resources. It increases the overall production cost of your product or project, so always keep it minimal. Remove any unnecessary tools that are used. As an architect, you are the guy who keeps a tab on the cost of the Cloud resources, and other tools costs being paid every month. Always make sure you only pay for what you use, this also can be implemented in our design by moving to serverless wherever possible.

Motion a.k.a Avoid Context switching. Context kills productivity; when people work on more than one task they are less productive. This not only diminishes productivity, but also reduces the overall morale of the developer because he feels every day that he has not contributed for the day. Context switching is asking developers to start looking into other work because something urgent came up. As an architect, you should be a gateway for developers. It takes leadership to say no to things even if it looks very urgent and not disturb the developers and take up the urgent work after he has finished the current job.

Waiting a.k.a unclear requirement or Job details. When there is an unclear requirement, developers tend to be least productive and nothing actually moves forward. You tend to do something just to move forward which will only kill the creativity. When the requirements are 100% clear, you can see how fast we write code, and as an architect, it is your responsibility to keep the requirement clear. You will not get a 100% requirement from the client, but the task whatever you have allocated should be clear and precise so there is no ambiguity in work and the developer should never feel ambiguous.

Defects. More defects not only reduce the credibility of the product but also reduce the credibility of the developers, QA, and the whole team. Speed does not mean defects can be pushed to production. As an architect, you should build a culture where it is not the QA's jobs to identify defects, it is everyone's job to identify the edge cases and bugs in the module or feature, the developer should make sure he has thought through all the use cases and edge cases, and business analyst should make sure he has added edge cases in the requirement document, and QA must make sure there is no regression whatsoever and the new functionality works solidly in stage environment on all possible cases. When you build a culture as an architect that everyone is responsible for zero bug release, it becomes a different project altogether. I know zero bugs are ideal, but it can be really tried and the closer you get to zero bugs, the better your work-life balance will be.

Become a Sales/Marketing Guy

When you learn about sales and marketing, you tend to influence people better. You can pitch a technology to a boss and start implementing it in your project. You become a star performer and you will be noticed across projects. You will become the front runner for any promotion because you will be known in all upper layers.

You need to sell yourself constantly, let us do it better.

It is familiarity that breeds trust. When you go to the supermarket and you want to buy a product which you have not bought before, when you look at the rack, you tend to pick the one which you have seen an advertisement for, or a hoarding somewhere, or you heard someone talk about it. You might not know the quality of the product, but you will still buy the one you are familiar with.

Similarly when you are competing for the promotion and all odds are the same between you and your competitor, the promotion goes more likely to the guy whom the upper management is familiar with. You might have given a presentation to the client or cc'd your stakeholder in some of the emails. N-number of things they know about you determines your promotion.

When you know sales and marketing, you tend to earn more because you know how to sell your own value to others. Selling and marketing have a very bad connotation, so we techies hate those sales and marketing guys because they oversell and put a burden on us.

But you should get over it and start to learn the methods and process, so we can sell ourselves and also our ideas which make our company, team and also our family better. We should know how to influence people, otherwise when in conflict we know only two techniques which are Flight or Fight. Flight and fight behavior is too primeval and we should evolve from animals to proper human beings.

When you don't learn sales and marketing techniques and processes, you tend to hit and miss a lot of opportunities when it comes to influencing people and selling your technical ideas. You will only be frustrated that your ideas are tossed to the dust-bin. In the worst case, it will not even be heard. You can improve your life 10x by learning a few sales and marketing techniques which will make you stand out in the crowd.

You Are a Salesperson

Regardless of Your Role, Everyone is a Salesperson – Unknown

Welcome to the real world, one way or another we are salespeople. You are selling either your programming skills or design skills. We are paid for these values and you should be a better person to sell and project your skills.

First, you need to get out of the notion of sales and marketing being a bad thing. It took me a while to get over it and once I got over it, my life got better and I started learning more about presenting my ideas and also marketing myself. This is not about selling someone what they want and I still hate that too, being conned by the marketing technique. The more I learned about marketing and sales, I could see lots of patterns around us which makes me save lots of money, because I know it is designed in a way to make me greedy or fearful of losing a deal. So I take a deep breath, laugh about it, and do not buy it.

No matter what industry a company does business in, sales are at the core of success. Sales are the one that makes the company thrive and survive. The same goes for us, if you are not good at selling yourself, you are destined to be doomed.

We programmers do not want the limelight, we expect people to recognize how good we are from the code we write, which most people never see, especially the one who is going to give you a promotion or raise. Even if your boss does a code review, he might not review all the code, or when you are in a senior developer position, your code might not be reviewed at all. Your immediate boss or boss's boss is not technical.

Learning to sell your own value is very important to feel fulfilled because you add value to other people's lives and also yours. If you are not a salesperson, for your own skills you are doomed to rely only on luck, the probability of which is too low, and we feel frustrated about other people's success and also feel jealous about it.

The definition of a **salesman** is a person who is employed in the job of promoting products and services and getting people to buy them.

In our developer's world, being a good salesman is being able to show your skills and promote your ideas and your ability to get things done to the upper management, and also the developer who is working for you.

Being a salesman is being able to implement what you have learned into the project by being able to influence all stakeholders.

Being a salesman is being able to influence all your stakeholders without any friction and getting your way to move forward.

Being a salesman is making people come to you whenever there is a technical problem, where you should be the first person they think about when there is any technical problem

Identify your customer

Once you identify your own set of customers you will be able to get more things done. You will not be wasting time with people who have no influence over your growth or who just use you and are going to throw you out when not needed.

You will genuinely be focusing your loyalty on the people who are only doing good things for you and want you to grow. Customers here means people who will bring improvement to your life.

The list of people I think you can call your customers are your immediate boss, and boss's boss.

Once you identify your customer, you should start adding value to their life and it should be without expecting anything in return. If you start expecting people to praise and value your contribution, you are mostly destined to fail. You can get feedback, and then change your value-adding process, but you cannot expect anything profitable out of the transaction.

If you identify your own customer and add value to their life, you will see your life being transformed into a better living. That is how karma works. You may get some benefit from your customer, but the major benefits come from the place you didn't expect.

Positioning

Think of the last time you got an opportunity where you were not technically ready and the other person thought you were technically good and gave you the opportunity. So your opportunity has nothing to do with how talented you are, it all depends on how people perceive you in your surroundings.

> *"Position yourself well enough and circumstances will do the rest."*
>
> *– Mason Cooley*

Positioning is one thing you need to learn and do every day to shine in your field. If you don't position yourself, you are doomed to failure, despite your hard work and your knowledge.

The more you neglect positioning, the more you get frustrated, because of lack of opportunity or missing opportunities.

Positioning is a marketing **concept** that outlines what a business should do to market its product or service to its customers. In **positioning**, the marketing department creates an image for the product based on its intended audience.

You should read *'Positioning: The Battle for Your Mind'* by Al Ries & Jack Trout on how great companies positioned themselves to success and how you can leverage that knowledge to position yourself too.

In our architect world, you need to position yourself by creating an image about your knowledge and what your niche skills are. You should be on the speed dial of your stakeholder when there is a problem in your technical area.

There is a huge competition out there, there are many people who can do the same thing as you and maybe at a cheaper price or lesser salary. You need to know how you can position yourself, otherwise, you will get lost in a sea of talents.

Being first is the best way you can position yourself. Always be the first to make sure you position yourself; you are the one who knows the new technology. Position yourself that you keep updating yourself and you know the latest technology in the market, and then opportunities will keep coming to you. Even though you are not good with technology, you are proposing. Remember you can learn by doing on the job.

Always work on **imprinting** your image on your boss' mind that you are always close to the new technology and you care about the quality of the products you build. You also should make people think you are the most mature person on the team.

Make sure you never talk anything negative about anything. Even if you slip once, you will lose your ethicality. People's ideas about you will always slip into their dark side and they will think the worst of you in the worst times.

In a way, you should work on building the image that makes you look like a technically strong person and a great leader in the minds of your stakeholders, rather **than** possessing the actual skill.

You should build the skill, otherwise, when you are given the opportunity, you will not be able to make it. But getting the opportunity is the key, rather than actually executing it. Without opportunity, you don't have anything to execute, so getting a new opportunity to implement what you learned is important.

Knowledge alone is not good enough, you should position yourself in everyone's mind so that when the opportunity arises they should think of you.

Make sure your name is unique. If there are multiple people in your name, it is your duty to make your name stand out. You can add initials in your email id, or give yourself a name with an abbreviation and insist people call you by that abbreviation. Such as if your name is Jeeva Kumar S, make your name JKS, and address yourself as JKS in every situation.

The human mind tends to admire the complicated and dismiss the obvious as being too simplistic. So always keep portraying yourself as the guy who understands complicated jargon. Make sure you know the meaning too.

Enrich conflicts; conflicts of ideas are great, and respect your enemy. Keep him close to you to create conflict. When conflicts are in your workplace, respect them, and don't force out your opponents. Conflicts help you grow and make positioning easy.

> *"If people see that a principle is obvious nonsense and easy to refute, they tend to ignore it. On the other hand, if the principle is difficult to refute and it causes them to question some of their own basic assumptions with which their names may be identified, they have to go out of their way to find something wrong with it."*
>
> *– Dr. Charles Osgood*

Choose the company that positions yourself close to your technology. If you want to position yourself as an open-source technology architect working in a Microsoft solution based company, not worth it. If your company has positioned itself as a company of open source, ride on this position name, and use it for your own good.

Position with your boss who has a project which will help you position yourself. If you read successful biographies of most CEOs, they would have worked directly under any CXO and that is the reason they have got the next chance to become a CTO or CEO. This also applies to any role. Work with only bosses who will make you grow.

Friends positioning is a simple one. You might have many friends, but personal friends do not help you grow your career. Personal friends can help you in lots of ways, but never in your professional career. You might have got a job because of your friend's referral, but it will not help you move your career forward.

You should always have business friends and you should be in constant contact with them. You can get these friends in many technical events that happen around your city. Find a technical group and get yourself associated with the group and also become a volunteer in technical activities. This one activity will bring more business friends and you will be surprised by the amount of network you form and how much you get out of this single activity.

Positioning helps your career like steroids, and you will see the change if you follow even just one of the positioning techniques we discussed.

Always remember getting an opportunity is more important than the skill needed to execute the skill. Work on positioning yourself more than you work on the skill. It is very uncomfortable initially. Once your motives are authentic and you accept the idea of positioning, you will see more success.

Build a Digital Presence

93% of online experiences begin with a search engine. You will be fascinated to know how much people search about you. You will be searched when you are searching for a job, applying to speak in a speaking event, client interviews, etc. A person with a digital presence will be more probable to be selected than a person who does not show any search results on the Google page.

Digital presence helps in creating great visibility among your business friends. It establishes authority in your respective fields. Anything you put online will never go away, so your digital presence will leave an everlasting impression for years to come.

Own Website. Own a website in your name. If your domain name is already taken, then get a domain name that is closer to your name but easy to remember.

Make sure you build your niche presence online.

Own social media accounts such as Facebook, Twitter. I personally don't like Instagram because I don't think it is for techies like us. Also, make sure only to follow people who will improve your technical career; avoid requests from your relatives and friends. Because their share will only create an unnecessary distraction and waste our time. Mostly they will fight about which party is better. We all know that all of them are worse and we can't do anything about it.

Make sure you post only things that are relevant to your technical arena, don't Like, or share any other posts that are not technical. Follow the same principle with your Twitter account also. Don't follow any of your friends; only follow people who you think will add value to your technical life. If you want, keep all your personal preferences and personal posts on Facebook and not on any other social media.

Start owning a meetup group and make sure you have at least one session per month. Make sure you bring in speakers from other groups. The best way to get speakers is to go to other meetups and if you find their speaking interesting, engaging them into your group.

Start your own meetup group only if you can follow up at least one speaking engagement per month and if you don't find any speaker you should be able to speak in your meetup on a topic that is relevant to the meetup group.

In a meetup group, consistency is key. If you don't have regular meetups you will lose your members and your meetup group will not grow bigger. The bigger your meetup group, the better your digital presence, and more people will know you.

Create a Youtube channel and post videos on your channel. You can record your sessions which you speak in the meetup and post them. Don't feel shy; it is ok to have low-quality videos. Some people hate to hear their own voices. Don't worry about it. You should overcome your limitations and accept yourself.

You have to create both long and short videos. Long videos can be talking about any architecture or technology with a good demo. And short videos can be for explaining the basic concepts, tips, and tricks you follow for a technology. If you browse through Youtube, short videos that talk about what is an API have more than 11 million views. So basic videos give you more digital presence.

Whenever you have a speaking engagement, make sure you contact the attendees by some means two to three days before the speaking engagement, so they don't forget about the meetup. It also helps them mentally plan their day about their commute and other details.

You should use your Facebook, Twitter, and email wisely for your meetup. Share your speaking engagement before, during, and after the engagement. This will help you to get more speaking opportunities also.

Install Google Analytics on your website and also watch analytics on your YouTube channel and find out what works with your visitors and followers. And do more of it. Do analyze your own digital presence and improve it based on the current trends.

LinkedIn is another social media which when done right, not only creates a good digital presence but can also land your next job. Make sure you add proper details in the title of your profile. It should tell exactly what you are good at, such as .Net architect, Java architect, Java senior developer, etc. Avoid your company title. It probably will not convey much about the skill that you are good at.

Going forward, there won't be many other job search sites. Already most of the top recruiters use LinkedIn to hunt for talents for their company. So build your LinkedIn profile in a better way. Make sure you fill your key skills with diligence.

Build the Network

"You can make more friends in two months by becoming interested in other people than you can in two years by trying to get other people interested in you."

– Dale Carnegie, 'How to Win Friends and Influence People'

Your success is determined by the number of people you know. More the people who know you, more successful you are. The number of people you know directly relates to how successful financially you are. People who have seen you more often in person will trust you more and will provide you lots of opportunities for your career.

If your networking skill is good, you never need to search for your next job. All you need is to have an updated resume. People trust people whom they know personally, so your search for a job is easier by the number of people you know.

The better your relationship with people, the better you can bounce your ideas and see them materialize in the real world. You could see a lot of innovation popping up in your head when you're talking with someone with a different perspective.

The more relationships you have, the wider your perception becomes about any technology. You will learn faster when your perception is wider because your brain can relate and associate with what you learn. Good relationships bring better people to your inner circle.

If you are trustworthy, you will get lots of opportunities to make yourself better. People don't like people who are not trustworthy and they will avoid referring such persons to their friends because it will spoil their name.

People with a lesser number of relationships tend to have more stress in their lives because they only have a few people to bounce ideas off when there is a problem with both their personal and professional lives.

Learn to build relationships and add value to the relationship and the network.

People who are good in relationships tend to be emotionally intelligent and get more things done, because they know how to handle different types of people, and they accept people as they are and they don't try to change anyone.

People who are good at relationships know you cannot change anyone, but they know they can change the mood of the person. So they work only on changing the mood or analyzing the mood rather than trying to change the person.

People who are not good in relationships only talk to the people they know and they never get out of their comfort zone. They will not even go and sit in a place where they don't know anyone around.

People who are not good in relationships do not know how to start a conversation with people they meet in a technical event. Remember, technical events are full of people who are interested in the same topic as you and can help you in zillion ways.

People who are not good with people will tend to follow fight or flight response. Either they argue about something, or avoid a technical confrontation, and they will never learn anything new because they don't know how to handle differences of opinion.

Good First Impression

According to science, you make your first impression within seven seconds of meeting a person. And one will decide whether you are a trustworthy person or not in seven seconds.

People who know how to make a good first impression tend to make more friends than the ones who don't even realize there is something called a first impression.

Your physical appearance matters. You don't have to wear a tuxedo or suit to every situation, but you should make sure you wear a nice dress that is ironed and also not faded. You should never wear a flip flop unless your flip flop is good looking and is in current fashion. Wear shoes whenever possible; that gives a good first impression.

Smile: Smile is the greatest weapon you can use to make friends. When you smile at the person you meet for the first time, you bring their guard down. People will relax when they see a smiling person. You should not be smiling like a retarded person, but keep the smile as genuine as possible.

Be yourself; it all boils down to accepting yourself as who you are. If you start accepting yourself and remove all shame about yourself, it will automatically give you confidence and you will see people will start noticing you.

Good eye contact says lots about you. It says you are confident in yourself and it also says you are genuinely interested in knowing the person. Also don't stare in the eye and make people uncomfortable.

No Argument

"I have come to the conclusion that there is only one way under high heaven to get the best of an argument—and that is to avoid it. Avoid it as you would avoid rattlesnakes and earthquakes."

– Dale Carnegie, 'How to Win Friends and Influence People'

Never argue with anyone. You can never win anything out of the argument. Either you lose the argument or you will lose the relationship.

If you feel any conversation is looking like getting into an argument, end it then and there and move on. No argument is worth a relationship. Even if you win an argument, the other person will not think you are the smartest person and will not follow you.

They will only resent you because you made a fool of them in front of others. Remember arguments might help relationships grow if you are doing that over the phone, and no one is around watching who is winning and who is right. But never argue in public circumstances. Agree that his/her perspective might be right and move on.

Great people will constantly think from other people's perspectives and will switch back and forth in their shoes to figure out where they are coming from. They will support their own convention with more clarity than they are using while currently arguing, and once this happens and when the other person feels he has been understood, there is a high probability that he will accept your point too.

Ethical Leadership

Ethical leadership builds trust faster than any other characteristic of a leader. A leader who is ethical tends to implement his ideas faster than any peers. People tend to follow you even when your idea is highly impractical because they know you will support them if they fail in implementation.

Ethical leadership creates lots of synergy among peers, it not only creates creative cooperation but it also creates innovative ideas among teams because people know you have a safety net for them

Ethical leadership helps you to sleep better because you walk your talk. You don't have regret in your life because you don't give a false promise. Ethical leadership makes your life simple because you tend to not care about what people think of you; rather your work is based on an internal compass that is based on your core values.

Ethical leadership makes you the most influential person because you have more people following you because they like you for your simplicity in life.

Gandhi and Martin Luther King never had a title or an influential position, but they were followed by hundreds and thousands of people. They are being followed even now by many people because of the strength of their character.

Ethical leadership is leadership that is directed by respect for ethical beliefs and values and the dignity and rights of others.

Don't compromise your ethics for short term success

According to me, the ethical leader should have the characteristics of Trust, Honesty, Empathy, Integrity, and Humility.

Honesty

A Bird was standing in a field chatting with a bull. "I would love to be able to get to the top of the Mango tree," sighed the bird, "but I haven't got the energy."

"Well, why don't you nibble on some of my droppings?" replied the bull. "They're packed with nutrients."

The bird pecked at a lump of dung and found that it gave him enough strength to reach the first branch of the tree. The next day, after eating some more dung, he reached the second branch. And so on. Finally, after the fourth night, there he was proudly perched at the top of the tree. This was when he was spotted by a farmer who dashed into the farmhouse, emerged with a shotgun, and shot the pheasant right out of the tree.

Moral of the story: Bullshit might get you to the top, but it won't keep you there.

Once you are honest, you can influence a lot, and one more added benefit is you can sleep well. Your body, mind, and thoughts will be in equilibrium with words and actions.

Honest people tend to live longer in our current society and will be respected a lot irrespective of their position or creed. The more you cultivate honesty, the more will be your growth.

Honesty is a facet of moral character that connotes positive and virtuous attributes such as truthfulness, straightforwardness, including straightforwardness of conduct, along with the absence of lying, cheating, theft, etc.

In the book *'Radical Honesty'*, Brad Blanton talks about being abnormally honest and how truth alone will solve all your anger and frustration.

We live in a world of generalization and assumption, and the brain thinks our reality is the actual reality, and the person next to you thinks his reality is the actual reality. In that sense, we form a sense of our own perception, reality, and identity for ourselves.

When we fix ourselves with one set of identities and bias the way we see the world, then it messes up unbelievably.

For example, we fix our identity to be 'Know it all in Cloud technology', and we think the way we understand Cloud computing is the only way the Cloud works, or our understanding about the Cloud is 100% right. If someone explains a new technology or alternate way of Cloud's working, we tend to guard our understanding.

You not only lose the opportunity to learn, but also you are being dishonest, you might say one or two lies about your knowledge of the new process or technology. Once the meeting is over, you feel frustrated that you are not aware of it.

If your lack of knowledge is being pointed out, you will either get angry, or become defensive and will act in resentment toward the person who called you out as not having knowledge.

What if you are more honest in this one area, and become a person **who says you know if you know, and if you don't know that you don't know?** This one trait alone will take you to places and be the biggest catalyst in the success of your architect career.

Remember one thing; people like to flaunt about themselves and their knowledge. If you don't know about one topic and you ask them to explain, then it will make them feel good about themselves and you. It is the most important characteristic to become a charismatic leader.

Being dishonest comes from our childhood experiences and the pain we went through, when we were told about our own shortcomings. That feedback from elders or friends hurt us, and instead of taking it as feedback, we tend to go inside ourselves and don't want to hurt the same way we were hurt.

So we don't like to hurt people because we hate those who give us feedback for all different reasons, good or bad.

So don't be simply nice to people. Ask yourself whether you are nice to them because you genuinely care, or just because you want them to like you. Most likely you will lie to yourself that you care; most of the time it is you who are just an idiot who wants to be liked, and so you try to be a nice and sweet person.

When you start lying about yourself, you think people will not find out. Actually, it is the other way; people's intuitions and senses are stronger than you think. We are biologically programmed to find out deception, because if men/women who have not tuned their senses to deception will have their gene removed from the gene pool because it is bad for replication. So people who are good at understanding the other person rather than their words, tend to survive more in the changing world.

Always be candid and straightforward. Don't be a nice guy ever. Just don't over-promise. Promise only if you can follow it through and complete it.

Initially, people will be turned off or repelled by you, but it will create a huge trust and your boss will trust you more just by your words. You don't have to prove.

Remember, honesty must be shown in words, actions, and in every part of deeds from you. If you show a little bit of dishonesty anywhere, the perception about you being honest will vanish.

You should never show any signs of dishonesty in any part of your life. Even when you are talking for fun. It will limit your success if you want to move to any level more than an architect.

Let go of the security that you feel comes from your small dishonesty, that is part of you telling you want approval to feel good about yourself.

Be open to conflict; remember conflict strengthens the relationship, if you are open to a win-win outcome from the conflict.

Win-Win resolution not only betters the relationship but also creates synergy, because you will come up with solution that would not have come up if both of you would have thought about it individually.

Always be direct with anger, be honest about the conflict you have in mind with the other person, don't be nice to the face and nasty behind him.

If a person is too intimidating or gets upset, change your way of communication, but still be honest in your conversation, don't avoid conflict.

It will take more time to communicate with a person whose archetype is different from yours, or is an archetype you have not dealt with.

Remember people who are testing our honesty are the ones who make us better. You will find that when more people are testing your honesty, the more honest you become, and the more you will be tested.

Integrity

Once upon a time in China, there was a King who had no children. So he decided to find his successor from among the citizens. So he called dozens of children and gave them some seeds, and asked them to plant and water them for a year.

All the children planted their seeds and watered them. Some children had trees growing, some children had shrubs growing, but one child named Ling did not see any life out of the seed. But he still continued to water the seed for a year, and yet there was no life out of the seed.

He was worried and asked his mom about it, because it was a year after the seed was given, and he had to show his seed's growth to the King. Ling's mom told him to stick to his integrity and show the King the pot where there was no life.

The day came when everyone showed the results to the King. After seeing all the plants and trees, the King went back to the throne and told his subjects that Ling alone was truthful in his actions. The King had given boiled seeds that would not grow. The King made Ling his successor to be the next King.

Our society wants results and we want to satisfy society, so we also strive for results and give up our integrity and show some results which might or might not help our growth, as in the case of the kids other than Ling.

To be an architect with a high sense of integrity should be your highest goal. Your lifetime motto should be not to give up your integrity at any point of time, even when the time is critical. You should be cool and composed enough to say and do the right thing.

Once you don't need people's approval and liking, you automatically become a person of high integrity. Then all you need is a set of principles which we will look into in a later chapter. Following these principles will automatically take you to the places you want to go.

Those technical details we are going to see in the later chapter will give you tools that do not change with time and you can go back to the details whenever you want to make decisions.

If you do not have enough integrity, no amount of technical knowledge will help you to make yourself a great architect. All it will do is keep you as a mediocre one because you will be violating the technical principles for the appeasement of the masses to gain popularity, and eventually will lose your place in your company too, because your short term vision will hurt you in the long term.

Trustworthy

Trust reduces work, stress, and frustration. Always a major problem in our life comes with hair on top. Most of our problems, official or personal, are mostly from human issues. Trust solves lots of problems, and when not cultivated will give huge trouble or communication problems.

When trust is more, your people will accept your ideas easier. Otherwise, you will have to spend lots of time selling your idea.

When trust is high, involvement among the team will be humongous; your communication style becomes irrelevant because people understand each other without much communication.

Self-trust helps to conquer yourself, then you can conquer the world.

To become an aspiring architect, you need to build trust in every part of your life, personal, with friends and colleagues, in your company, market, and your community

In the principle-based life we spoke about, the speed of trust helps you to lead a fulfilling life.

I went through a personal phase, when I felt people don't trust me very much and I need to validate everything I tell them. I was surrounded by people who were finding fault with everything I did, and the more they didn't trust me, the more I was doing things wrong and validating their assumptions.

I wished people would trust me more and give me some more space, so I could build my competence and prove to them the worth of my work. I felt I needed a little more trust from them, so I can actually complete work. I was a little worried that life will be like this and I need either change the company or figure out a shortcut that can build trust.

Whatever I proposed as a solution or gave as an end date for my work was always scrutinized, and I wished people would trust me more and leave me alone to do my work where I didn't have to work extra to validate my solution just to prove I was going on the right path. It was very excruciating for me because I didn't have much of a mentor at that time or a boss who supported me. I was almost left alone.

When I was searching for the answer, I found the book '*The SPEED of Trust*' by Stephen M.R. Covey, son of Stephen Covey, where he came up with the process of building trust step by step. I learned a lot from it, and now I know how to build trust better. I also know it is not easy, and rather than blaming others that they don't trust you, I started changing my attitudes and behaviors which has helped me to build trust faster.

Now I can build trust in hostile environments where I have taken over the entire development and testing team which is going through huge work stress. The above diagram is taken from the book '*The speed of trust*'.

We will investigate the process of building trust, and trust me, there is no shortcut. In this, you will learn to build trust even if you have screwed up the trust by a single unfortunate event, and also how to build from there.

Self. This first step is the key to building trust in any part of your life, if you build self-trust, you can not only conquer yourself, but also the world around you. If you don't have this part of self-trust handled, no matter what you do, it will never get you anywhere.

Self-trust denotes two things, do you trust yourself, and second, are you someone others can trust? You need to spend your whole life asking this question and improving your life. Self-trust is nothing but credibility. How credible you are, is all it counts. It does not matter if people like you or not. Are you walking your talk is all that matters.

So always keep your promises, because people build hopes around your promises, however small they may be. If you have committed to something, it can be as simple as sending an email with information, make sure you would have sent it on the day you have committed.

If you cannot follow through with your commitment, make sure you apologize and honor your commitment. Don't commit anything which you cannot do. There is a small satisfaction in promising people and getting their approval about yourself, when we commit something. So people commit to many things they cannot follow through. So make sure you never make the mistake of committing and not following through with your commitment. This is the big one.

Relationship trust is all about what you do or act, rather than what you say. People don't care what you say; they unconsciously make their assumptions about you on what you do.

In order to build relationship trust in office among your peers, boss, or any stakeholders, start by talking straight, let them know you will be able to complete it or not. If you feel you are not competent, tell them you will not be able to do it in the given time.

Don't promise anything which you cannot provide for the people who report to you. Be very open about it. You might think they will leave to another project, but you will be surprised to see people will be more engaged to get the work done.

Show loyalty to your fellow mates, never steal ideas. You need to put in extra effort in letting your boss know if one of your teammates does the work or his idea worked. It is even better if he is absent in the meeting, this increases the overall morale of the team, because people know you give acknowledgment where it is due honestly, and do not do any kind of appeasement of the employee or just to look good in front of him.

Another way to improve relationship trust is to position yourself as a person who likes to grow. A person who reads reflects this automatically, because he tends to correct his perception of life, where, rather than thinking the problem is out there, he will constantly reframe the mind thinking, maybe the way we see the problem is the problem.

Third-wave organizational trust is a very important one because it deals with how you can build a culture for your organization. You can surely build a culture in your team, it is surely in your control. I have done it many times where I have joined a hostile team of architects and changed the culture to mutual trusting. It takes time but it is not hard.

If there is no organizational trust you need to pay the trust tax, there will be bureaucracy which includes cumbersome rules, regulations, policies, and procedures.

Rather than your organization focusing on continuous improvement, your organization merely adds complexity and inefficiency. There will be politics and disengagement among teams.

If there is organizational trust, then there will be accelerated growth, enhanced innovation, heightened loyalty, and better execution.

We will not look into the fourth and fifth wave Market and societal trust because it is out of the scope of our book.

You need to ask yourself four questions—Are you encouraging integrity? Do your words and actions incentivize integrity? Or can people who lie, get their way out? Are you supporting honest feedback and admitting mistakes, or you are just surrounding yourself with people who want to please you? Are you incentivizing people who admit mistakes?

Does the organization get results?. Are you helping your team deliver better, or you concentrating only on getting your name out or promoting yourself? Are you really concerned about your company making profits?

These are soul searching questions. You might say you all are good, but examine your motives for everything you do. You cannot change within a day, but wanting to change, and taking a single action to change to build organizational trust goes a long way.

Humility

Humility is not weakness, but strength under control

There were days when I thought being humble makes you weak because people can take you for granted. I used to be arrogant about replying to people and made a mess sometimes. I was just lucky to have many managers who understood me and backed me up, so I did not screw up my career.

Later I started interacting with people who really are in a very high position, and found out that humility is something you need to practice to climb the ladder, because you tend to meet people of different archetypes and humility helps to win each one of them.

Arrogance comes out of two things, one is you think you have conquered the current domain or problem, so you know what you talk about, or it is out of insecurity. Sometimes it is actively both. We try to hide the insecurity of the unknown and brush people off by our arrogance as a facade to cover our lack of knowledge.

I used to think arrogance was a good thing because I thought arrogance is a sign of confidence about your self-worth, and people see your arrogance as a sign of your competence. But I

You need great strength to be humble.

realized people are not seeing my arrogance as a sign of knowledge; they are seeing my confidence and ignoring my arrogance as a sign of immaturity.

You can be confident and still can be humble. You need to know what is being humble and what is not being humble. Being humble is not about letting people walk over you.

The list of negative humility includes the following, which is not considered as real humility, and considered only as degradation

- Talking negatively about yourself to sound humble.
- Not putting your point across in the meeting because you want to be humble.
- Accepting people's third-degree treatment so people will think how soft you are, and don't want to spoil this identity of yours formed by people.

- Not sounding your thoughts because you don't want to offend people.
- Not asking for what you want in your life.
- Changing the focus of the topic if someone gives you a real compliment.
- Passing a negative comment reduces your ability to sound humble.

List of activities that means you are really humble

- Respecting those who report to you and listening to their ideas.
- Giving credit where it is due, even if it is too small, especially when it is small.
- Taking compliments from people and thanking them graciously without any negative comments or dismissing the honest feedback given by people.
- Respecting housekeeping employees and thanking them for any work they do for you, like delivering coffee to your table, etc.
- Not snapping when the tension of the situation is high and concentrating on dissolving the tension around.
- Genuinely wanting the people reporting to you to be successful.
- Knowing communication is always brittle, you need to tell the same things more than twice for people to understand.
- Being open to people who tell you they don't know.
- Accepting to people that you cannot know everything by reading and doing once.
- Accepting that it is an architect's job to train your team members about the technology and technology choices you have decided for the project, and explaining to everyone in the team.
- Understanding everyone does not have the exposure like you and an architect's main purpose becomes making them better where they are right now.

Remember humility is not sounding humble and letting people walk over you. Humility is going beyond your own self and taking care of your team and peers who are working for you.

"True humility is not thinking less of yourself;
it is thinking of yourself less."

– Rick warren

In the next section, we will learn more about the mother of all ethics, the empathy which paves a true way to be humble. It will help to genuinely make you humble, build trust and build an army of people who can get things faster.

As an architect, humility is important because people will look up to you, and being humble helps people open up to you about the gaps in their learning. If you become a mentor and act as a mentor for your team, and convey that people work for you to learn, you automatically will sound and look like a humble person and people will respect and obey you more than you actually think.

I am writing this topic with caution. Don't act humble and avoid the things that are portrayed at the beginning of this topic that lead to degradation of yourself. You are not being humble to get the approval of people, you are being humble because you want people to open up to you and it is the result of you being in a full cup.

Don't use humility as a technique to manipulate people or get approval from peers to be a pleasing person. Self-respect is always important and you should never let anybody take it away from you.

Empathy

*"If there is any one secret of success, it lies in
the ability to get the other person's point of view
and see things from his angle as well as your own."*

– Henry Ford

Empathy is one characteristic of a leader that makes your life easy. If you practice listening with an open mind without judging, you can cross any barrier in your life. All our problems come with hair on top, if you learn to empathize with anyone, you not only solve the problem; it will automatically make you a leader.

Remember the last time you were trying to understand the problem of production issue and you were blinded on your own prejudgment and assumptions, where you ignored the inputs from the junior guy, and ended up being more frustrated. Then, after coming back to sanity, you listened to him and you were able to fix the issue within minutes.

This scenario happens many times in our lives. The other person tries to explain to us and we don't listen properly, and then we realize this is the one he was talking about all the while, and we were stupid enough to ignore him.

The above scenario is not just about improving our listening skills to live life better. The problem is not our listening skills, the problem is our inability to see things from another's perspective.

We always listen with the intent to reply, rather than to understand. All this arises because we do not want to understand people and their perspective.

If you can handle one thing, where you enter any conversation to understand where the person is coming from, you will not only become a great architect, you will also become the better leader everyone wants to work for.

The greatest good feeling you can give to any person is the feeling of being understood. Think of the last time you felt good that somebody really understood you. Who is the first person you talk to when you are feeling low in your life or feeling high in your life? You call that person because you feel they understood you better than anyone else.

Everyone knows consciously and unconsciously that when you understand people you can influence them better. But why don't they do that? It is because listening to people and understanding people takes time. And in this fast-paced world, we think understanding someone is a waste of time, we just want people to do what we say and leave us alone.

One more reason why we don't try to understand is we are afraid of being influenced by people, because once we listen and understand their problems and perceptions, we might get stuck into the realm of their life and we can be easily manipulated.

That's why we intuitively avoid understanding people's problems, but as a good leader and architect, you don't have to go in-depth into personal problems. But you should always make sure you listen to them where they come from.

In Hewlett Packard, they have an open lab stock, and a few of them were taking some parts home for their own projects. One of the managers thought it is like a license to steal, so that manager put a padlock, and it was only open on weekdays and during working hours.

HP Founder, Bill Hewlett, once working on the weekend, saw the door was padlocked, so he called the facility manager to bring a bolt cutter tool and broke the padlock. He left the note, "Don't ever lock this door again," signed Bill Hewlett.

His ideology was people use the spares to build their own side projects like a radio, or any audio system that will only come back to the company as a new idea or new hack to build a system faster.

In the same way, being influenceable looks like being a weak person where people can get what they want, but in the long run, you will gain benefits such as less turnover rate, people working late for your bad decisions, and accepting it as their responsibilities.

As Jack Welch says, 20% percent of the people will take advantage of leisure, but we tend to punish 80% of the people for the 20% of the screw-ups. So don't make rules for the 20% and force it on 80%.

I personally like the chit system of Jack Welch, where he openly says he favors people who are working good and he does give them a little extra. This system not only encourages high standards of work, but it also makes people who cannot do their job well ultimately end up disliking (or hating) their boss and their company.

When a person joins a team, you should allocate time to understand where he is coming from, what are the previous projects he has worked on, which are his favorite technologies, what is his bias against or for a technology. (Remember you also have a bias toward your favorite technology, so don't judge.)

The time that is spent in understanding looks like wasting time, but it is the one that builds the bonds faster and helps to improve the easy flow of communication later in your project. As an architect, think of the benefit of building an army of folks who will do anything you want to do just because they trust you. It all comes from making them feel they are understood. If they feel you understand them and you always walk your talk, then building an army of followers will be a cakewalk for you.

If you are not having empathy, you might be the person who cannot be easily manipulated, but you will lose the relationship building. Remember only 20% of the people will manipulate and cheat in your personal or professional life.

But we live our life based on 20% of the people in our life who misused us. So we tend to put everyone on a pedestal so we don't attain our full potential and also help others attain their full potential due to the walls we build around us because of some hurt and manipulation that happened to us.

Skills of an Architect

Drilling Down Basics

This chapter will not cover all technical details because it will be outside the scope of the book and also the volume will grow to an extreme level where it will override the purpose of writing this book. But what we will cover is why we need to know the basics, how important that is in making us better architects.

You can design better when you know certain computer science basics and will not feel left out when the computer geeks talk about the internal workings of certain technology. There are videos available that teach us what we are going to talk about. But there is not any one place that tells why you need to know the basics of computer engineering and principles.

This chapter is to address the concern I faced even though I am a computer engineer. This chapter is close to my heart and I feel very good about writing it and you will also like it. Make sure you learn this chapter and relearn it multiple times. Keep it as a cheat sheet and come back to the 'why's chapter many times until it becomes second nature.

The best way to learn all the below 'why's' and 'what', is to teach others. Don't worry about explaining it wrong, when you teach it to someone, stick to the process.

When you make a mistake while explaining or get stuck up on a concept or it is logically not getting together, it is a good thing. Don't feel bad about it. Go back and read again; this is the process I love because now you will learn better because you now formed an idea, all you need to know is whether it is right or wrong and mostly you will justify your assumption or find what the alternative to understanding is.

Trust this process; sometimes when you start reading about the one you explained wrongly or got stuck, you might find it hard when you read the concept for the first time, but after two to three times, you will get a clear view of what you want to know.

Data Structures

If you are reading this book, you should be a better problem solver; otherwise, you would not aspire to become an architect. But you might not know you are an efficient coder too. As a programmer, you know all the data structures available, and have also used each one of them. But there are lots of data structures you use, but you will not know why we use them.

Knowing the underlying data structure of every technology we use will help to make decisions better. Our whole appraisal depends on how our decisions have helped the company to scale better with better maintainable code.

A *data structure* is a particular way of organizing *data* in a computer so that it can be used effectively.

You would have known primitive data types, trivial data types, and composite data types. Primitive data types are int, bool, etc. Trivial data types are null, undefined, etc. Composite data types are objects, arrays, functions, etc. Linear data structures are stacks, heap, and Linked List.

One data structure we always overlook is the Non-linear data structure. Non-linear data structures are **trees** and **graphs.** They are used in many places in the computer science world. Explaining what is tree and graph is outside the scope of this book, but I have shared the link in the courses reference section. Make sure you complete the course to learn and understand the basics better.

Why you should know data structures in real-time scenarios.

- You will be able to choose the right data structure for a given problem, and you will never run into memory leakage problems because you understand the underlying implementation process.
- You will be able to make decisions when you have to weigh between memory and time.
- You will be able to document your decision better because you know what will be the right choice and why you made the choice.
- Binary trees are used in retrieving data for SQL databases. It is widely used for databases where you want a faster read. LSM is used in places where you want faster writing.
- Knowing about Graph data structure helps you to design your data model better, because if you are not aware of the way how the graph works, you might design a relational database rather than a graph database, so performance will be duly impacted.
- Knowing tree and graph data structure helps to understand distributed algorithms better.

Algorithms

Efficiency in the computer science world means running in a short time and using short memory as much as possible. It is called time-space complexity. Remember all the for-loops you wrote in your project and whether you wrote the for-loop that is efficient and runs faster.

If you don't understand how the basic algorithms work, and how recursion works, or how proper data structure couples with algorithms and brings down the number of lines of code, you are in great trouble. Remember, students coming out of college are extremely thorough in these algorithms, so you are going to feel ashamed if you don't know at least the gist of it.

An algorithm is a tool that provides a well-defined and efficient computational procedure to transform your input into an output. **Algorithms** help to solve computational problems.

Make sure you learn all the sort and search algorithms. I highly recommend using the Udacity course. Also make sure you create a project with your favorite programming language and then have that uploaded in your GitHub repository, so that, whenever you forget, you can refer and learn again.

You will start looking at things differently, you know when to use recursion easier and you become a slick programmer. Tip: Wherever you use a stack to perform a FIFO, then substitute with recursion.

Things you learn when you learn algorithms:

- Exit the for-loop as soon as possible by giving exit conditions, so once our work is over we don't iterate.
- Think of the amount of memory your code might take using the proper data structures and consume only the memory that is needed.
- You think in terms of writing efficient code rather than writing code to solve the problem.
- You get better at seeing the solution using recursion functions.
- You start mapping with the algorithms and your current problem and try to write a minimal code, because you know your current problem can be solved more efficiently using the right data source.
- You will also start visualizing code better if you haven't already.
- Solid **Algorithmic** knowledge and techniques separate the truly skilled programmer from the novices.
- If you start thinking in terms of algorithms, you will be able to solve the interview questions that are given in the companies that are Fortune 500 level. You will find it easy to clear those since you have already put in an effort solving those in algorithmic style.

- You will also be able to learn the questions and understand the answers that are available in all the interview questions for an architect for the first round.

There are multiple courses available online. I prefer the Udacity course UD513, where they talk about the exact amount of data structures and algorithms we need as experienced developers. The book '*Data Structures and Algorithms made easy*' by Narasimha Karumanchi, is a very good resource to get better.

Compiler Design

You should know about compiler design even if you are not a computer science graduate. Since you have taken the developer career path, you should know what you are dealing with. Knowing the compiler design will help you to understand the internal working of the computer program you are writing.

In any relationship, understanding the person is important and understanding where they are coming from is key for the longer sustenance of the relationship. In the same way, you are in a relationship with one or more computer languages, so you should understand how it works. And most of the compilers work the same way one way or another.

You don't have to be a compiler designer who has written a programming language on your own to become a great architect. But remember, if you have a resume where you wrote a compiler, then you will always get a job.

Understanding the key concepts of compiler design helps us become better architects and also makes us better at debugging our application in bad situations.

Learn the '*You don't know Js*' book, which not only teaches all nuances in Javascript but also tells how the compiler works. You will come to know facts that are bugs of the Javascript, and also known ways the Javascript works in previous versions of Javascript, before ES6.

The Js Series teaches lots of best practices and also the best way of implementing certain functionalities. It helps to see Javascript from a better perceptive, and it has helped me to code better in Javascript. Once the angular started catching up, I was able to see how things relate to each other in typescript and Javascript. It breaks lots of myths around Javascript and you will start liking Javascript more. It also gets better in JS programming. Understanding the compiler design helps to understand this book far better.

Network Concepts

You need not be an expert in network concepts, but as an architect, you should know certain basics that are very important to design your application better. In the Cloud supported world, most of the network decisions are abstract and we don't have to worry much, but knowing network concepts will help us to configure and tweak parameters that need to be addressed. Learning network concepts helps to learn Kubernetes better, and it is only when you are good at network concepts that you can get better at Kubernetes.

When you join a startup, you are expected to know all the network technology, such as setting up the Lan. When you are configuring a secure network between two applications, knowing the network concepts helps to configure in minutes rather than trying to do it in days and feeling embarrassed about not knowing much about the network even though we call ourselves IT head or in-charge, etc.

Main things you should know

- Learn all the seven layers of networks. It is very important that you understand all the protocols for each layer.
- Make sure you understand the application layer and also all the protocols available in that layer and how it works. The important ones are FTP and SMTP.
- TCP and UDP are also important protocols to know and also make sure understanding different types of handshakes is available.

- Also, learn about the virtual network and how to configure them.
- Basics such as domain and subdomain in an IP.
- Also, get in-depth knowledge of DNS because you might need to know this when setting cache rules in various parts of your system. Using cache extensively in your application in the right way will tremendously improve your application performance.
- You should also know extensively about the CDN and how it works. This will help in setting up endpoints while concentrating on proper configuration such as cache, compression, optimization, and rules engine.
- Also learn more about the setting up of Lan, what is a router, and working with firewalls in different layers.
- Make sure you know how to configure at least one firewall hardware or software; try IP filtering, packet filtering, etc.
- Learn about Ingress and Egress.
- Learn more about POE. In simple terms, A **POE switch** is a **network switch** that has Power over **Ethernet** injection built-in.
- Learn more about distributed computing and algorithms such as Leader election, and synchronization. You can understand more about your field and can do lots of wonders when learning about new technology and advanced books. https://www.univie.ac.at/ct/stefan/GIAN-Lecture-Notes-NetAlg.pdf

OOPS

You should be an expert by now in Object-Oriented Programming. But you need to know a few more nuances in OOPS. Before that, we will knock out some of the basics first and nuances next in the below list, which you should be doing as second nature.

- Think in interface, always. Always abstract the implementation. Think any piece of software will be replaced or updated or completely rewritten. So abstraction makes you better as an architect, just by not using the class directly.

- Code to an interface rather than to the implementation, make sure you use a good Dependency injection. Learn one dependency injector well and use it in all the projects. Almost all DI are good nowadays.

- Also, abstract the data and make sure encapsulation is applied at all levels of your design.

- All problems in computer science can be solved by another level of indirection, so think of indirection. Indirection means wrapping things up, so you can move the level of the problem one level up or one level down.

- Don't overuse inheritance, try composition. Inheritance derives one class from another whereas composition defines class as the sum of parts.

- Learn to refactor using OOPS concepts. You can learn lots of refactoring techniques from the book '***Refactoring***' by Martin Fowler. My favorite technique for refactoring using the OOPS concept is Replace Conditional with Polymorphism.

- Make sure you understand all three pillars of OOPS—**encapsulation**, **inheritance**, and **polymorphism.**

- Learn to model in objects; start seeing your project in models. Remember classes are about behavior and functionality.

- Create use case diagrams. Use case diagrams help a lot. They can explain things even to non-technical guys.

- Learn UML Diagrams and become an expert at them, because you might need to talk to different stakeholders. You don't have to learn all the representations, you need to just know Inheritance, Association, and Composition. With these three you can represent 99% of your project.

- Iterate your OOPS design and be ready to change it. Keep reducing the lines of code by implementing the OOPS concepts better.

- The best way to reduce lines of code every time, and not have any impact on your build is to write proper unit testing. So all you need is to run the unit testing after refactoring. It is the best way to refactor.

Functional Programming

Learning functional programming in this current software age is very important because Javascript is taking over the whole world, even in Smart TV and gaming console. Learning concepts of functional programming is very important not only for a career opportunity, but also as an architect in thinking while designing.

In some cases, certain problems need different ways of thinking while designing solutions. If you choose the right programming model for attacking different problems, you can assure the success of the project as an architect. Choosing the right programming model is also important for a successful project, which is a major duty of an architect.

Functional programming emphasizes the evaluation of function and OOPS programming emphasizes modeling as objects. In the real-time application, you can use functional programming in the space where you can see your software problem as a mathematical function. Examples are accountant software, finance systems where the state is passed around immutable states.

For example, let's take a project where you need to calculate the invoice and output the result. The invoice has various calculations that need to be done, such as product cost calculation, tax calculation, adjustment of any previous balance, etc. The amount which starts with product cost calculation will be passed to the tax calculation and the same amount will be passed to the amount adjustment calculation.

The state is the amount of the invoice which changed passing through a different system. Looking at this transaction as a real-world object is not possible like a car, vehicle, etc. Anything that **does not** exist in our real world which cannot be modeled is a good component for functional programming.

Functional programming experts claim that all software problems can be better solved in functional programming. I am always skeptical whenever people claim it cures all the diseases. But there are lots of merits to that claim, and as an architect, you should be smart enough to choose a programming model.

Functional programming supports abstraction over data and also abstraction over behavior, whereas the OOPS supports only abstraction over data. Abstraction over behavior helps in running a program in parallel.

Functional programs support parallel programming directly which is not the case with OOPS. So it is better performing in certain cases. Functional programming is used in places where you need to do some complex math, concurrency and parallelism is needed, and streaming data.

We will look into a few examples so you will understand what we are getting into. Mostly you would have done it already, and what you did not do was a functional way of solving problems.

Let us see a few features in the programming model every developer can use which are the basics of functional programming and knowledge of which helps to code better and also efficiently. Since you would have worked in Javascript, I am sure you can understand the few features we will discuss here. The only thing is, you would not have known it is named like this in the functional world. All we are doing here is updating your vocabulary, but you already know this concept.

Pure functions, is a function where the return value is only determined by its input values, without observable side effects. Think of a function that calculates Cos(X). This function will not probably have a database call or an API call. All it will do is some complex calculation to calculate the cosine value of x.

Pure functions also do not affect the global state. Any number of times you call the function with the same value, you get the same result. An impure function is when you call a function that inserts the data to the database and then returns the number of rows in the table, and you will get different results every time you call even with the same set of parameters.

As we saw in the topic on data structure and algorithms, knowing about recursion is important, and you can solve problems in recursion rather than using for-loops. Thinking about your problem in terms of recursion is a must when you are designing the functional approach to problem-solving.

Referential Transparency is a concept that means variables are **not** allowed to change their value. Think of it as the private variable you define in the class level which will change and can be used in different methods of the class. This **cannot** be done in Functional programming because it violates the global state being altered. All it means is that all variables are immutable.

Functions are First-Class and can be Higher-Order. This might sound a bit too much to understand, but think of functions as variables that can be passed around to another function. In the OOPS world remember the func keyword in c# and Function keyword in Java. They represent the passing function as a parameter. It is all the same. You would have used these concepts already.

Functional programming supports parallel programming by default. Whenever you use any map/reduce function in Javascript, you support parallelism by default because the map/reduce is the concept of the parallelism world where your small task can run in any CPU. How it can run in any CPU is because your function is a pure function and the state is not altered at any point in time. Now revisit all the important features of functional programming such as pure functions, referential transparency, and higher-order functions. These automatically support parallel programming due to no change in state, and tasks can be processed in any CPU because the state is not saved.

Take caution in choosing a different functional programming language other than Javascript (nodejs); they are not easy to learn and the curve is too high. Combining your I/O with the functional programming language becomes a daunting task, when not done with proper consideration.

Database Concepts

Database is important for any stateful application. As an architect, you are expected to build database solutions that are robust and performant. Understanding some of the basics of database concepts is very important for your architect journey. So when you decide to choose a new database or do a performance tuning in an existing database where it hinders the scaling of the project, you should know about heap and stack, which is the primary concept that comes when reading anything about databases.

A heap is a tree-based data structure in which all the nodes of the tree are in a specific order.

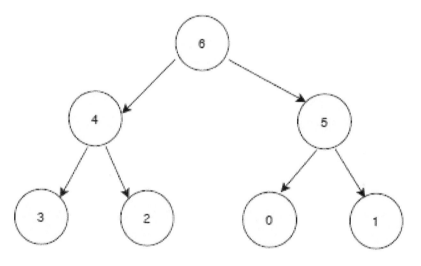

When you see the above heap, the relationship between the parent and children is that each node has greater value than any of its children. It is relevant in the database context because to understand this you need to know what is heap and how it works.

Since heap can set relationships between parent and children, it is used in indexes where the data can be traversed and accessed easily. That makes sense, but why you learn more about it is all it matters as an architect.

Binary trees are predominantly used in databases that are tuned for read performance.

Log Structured Merge (LSM) trees maintain key-value pairs. Explaining more about the LSM is outside the scope of this book. Think of it in terms of just writing a log. All logs are appended on top of each other, so the insert is always O (1). This is used in places where you need to write lots of data but the reads can be lesser.

Next time you see a database that talks about reading heavy, it is implementing the Binary Tree, and write heavy means LSM. LSM engines are the de facto standard today for handling workloads with large fast-growing data.

MongoDB comes with both Binary and LSM tree implementation. Now you can choose databases on their implementation, if you dig deeper, and based on the implementation, you can choose the databases.

You don't have to know all the databases and see how they work. Once you know what the index management algorithm is, you can choose the database. It also helps you to dig deeper into a conversation with highly skilled architects who you can talk to if you know what is Binary tree and LSM.

We saw LSM which talks about log, and remember log IS the database. Every transaction you perform in the database is written as log and log is executed. Even the replication happens by processing the log in the same order as they come in. We will not look into more about this concept; you need to understand the consensus algorithm, where knowledge about logs will help you a lot.

Talking about transactions will need a whole book altogether. I highly recommend the book, ***Designing Data-Intensive application***, to understand the nitty-gritty of transactions and other concepts of database and design.

We are not going to look into ACID and BASE properties of databases. As a developer, it is expected you know them.

CAP Theorem, Consistency, Availability, and Partition—it promises only two available in distributed systems. CA/CP/AP, but the real-time application does change the way it works. Rather than the third property cannot co-exist with the other two, Current design has changed in a way such that they take a tradeoff in all the properties a bit and make all the three properties co-exist.

Rather than abandoning the one property, you can choose something like 0.7 consistency, 0.9 availability, and 0.4 partition. It all sums up to two and it closely follows the CAP theorem. The whole concept is taking the tradeoff in consistency and availability by having eventual consistency, and working offline, we can also get the partition of network tolerance. We will look into the eventual consistency now, which is the hot topic.

Facebook or Instagram's Likes of photos or videos shows 150 and suddenly it shows 145 and after some time it shows 160 which is the final count of likes for your post or photo. Why is there so much fluctuation in the data? The first question is do you care about the accurate count? The answer is 'no'. Because all you care about is the photo, and the Likes is almost 150 of them.

What is happening here? This is called eventual consistency where you get to see the right count at the end, and in between, you might find the number going up and down. Now the eventual consistency is used in almost every application because full consistency is very costly in performance.

Can we have eventual consistency in all the applications? Hell, no. Think of your bank account running from 10 to 5000 rupees for some time, and you might end up being broke if some transaction happened at the same time. So eventual consistency may not be viable in shares, the banking sector, etc.

But the next time ask your business user, are they willing to have an eventual consistency where they can see the report faster, but the data may not be 100% accurate, but it will update after some time with an accurate count. Most times business users want to see whether users are using it and all they want to know is whether it is making progress. They want the exact details only during report generation at the end of the month. If your business users do not understand eventual consistency concepts, as an architect it is your responsibility to educate them, how the whole world including Facebook, Amazon, Instagram, etc. use this methodology and grow their business.

Learn more about streaming data, map reduce, Data systems, optimizing query, and how to choose no-SQL vs. SQL.

SOLID Principles

As an architect, you are expected to know the SOLID Principles by heart, and not only that, you should be using them during all phases of development. You should also train your peer developers to follow the SOLID principle and not violate them. No software architect can get away without knowing SOLID Principles.

At the beginning of the book, we spoke about how principles govern life, rather than learning all the tricks of the trade. If you understand the principle behind the trade, which is demand and supply, you can succeed in the trade faster. In the same way, the architect's trade trick is learning SOLID principles because it is used to design your application better for good scalability and maintenance.

If you violate the solid principle you tend to build applications that will crumble at the slightest change in requirement and bug fixes. The last time you maintained an application that is coded by someone but has very bad code, it means it has violated the SOLID principles.

If you are thinking of refactoring, use the Single responsibility which is a good place to start. We delve into each principle and come back to refactoring any project that is very tough to maintain.

If you are thorough with the SOLID principles, you can speed read this section, but the tips that are given for each section can be used as a cheat sheet while designing and developing applications.

S – Single Responsibility

This principle helps designing at all levels from class to all modules. This is the principle that should never be violated. All the bad code and spaghetti code happens when we violate this principle. If your code adheres to this principle, your code becomes easy to follow, maintain, and scale. Changes are easier, bug fixes are easier. Any developer can fix bugs in the code, and testing becomes very minimal.

The single responsibility principle (SRP) is a principle that states that every module or class should have responsibility over a single part of the functionality provided by the software, and that responsibility should be entirely encapsulated by the class, module, or function. – Wiki

There are lots of good materials out there, which do a great job of explaining this principle, but very less articles that tell us how to put things into practice.

Remember the SRP does not mean a class can do only one thing, it means it can do many things related to one. Cohesion and coupling is the underlying principle behind this principle.

If your class is creating a purchase order and also an invoice, then it violates SRP, but if the class does everything related to the Purchase order, it may not violate SRP. But remember, if there are more types of Purchase orders and you have implemented all the types of them in a single class without using inheritance or composition, then you are violating SRP.

Here are a few tricks and tips that are very useful which you can start using right away. Once you start using them, and after realizing the advantages, you will understand these principles more.

- Don't write a class of more than 80-100 lines; when you see your class going more than that, it might be a code smell. Try to refactor to a new class or move it outside your project.
- Keep your class as dumb as possible, meaning your class shouldn't do more things. If the class knows more about your business domain, then it becomes a Smarter class, a.k.a God class, which is definitely a great sign for code smell for violating a single principle. Refactor to multiple classes or separate projects.
- If you find the nesting of IF goes more than three layers, it is a code spaghetti which is a violation of the SRP principle; so try using Martin Fowler's refactoring method "Replace Conditional with Polymorphism."

- If your function is more than 20-30 lines of code, you might be violating SRP, because the rules apply to function also. Keep the function dumb, no GOD function or smart function. The best way to keep your function dumb is learning how to pass a function as a parameter in your programming language. This will keep the Business logic within the class.
- SRP should be considered while designing Microservices. Your Microservices should be designed in a single context, either it is event-driven or domain-driven context.

O – Open-Closed principle

This is my favorite principle; hope it gets to be your favorite too. Because, as an architect, if you can build solutions with this principle intact, you have succeeded in the project. All the problems occur when your project is not extensible to new requirements or you need to change many different source files for one single bug fix or change.

OCP helps to write elegant code. When written properly, it helps to minimize the number of bugs in your project. OCP when violated makes it hard to extend any functionality in this fast-paced market.

Open-Closed Principle states, an entity can allow its behavior to be extended without modifying its source code. – Wiki

Open for extension means the behavior of modules can be extended. Closed for modification means your behavior of the module and any modification do not violate the behavior on why the module or class is created.

Here are a few tricks and tips that are very useful which you can start using right away.

- Abstraction is the key here, always think in abstraction. Anytime you design any module or class, make sure you implement it using an interface.

- Whenever you need to add a new type, and you use an 'if' and add one more condition, then this is also a violation of OCP, so try to implement that 'if' with "Replace Conditional with Polymorphism". This is different from the SRP usage because there you look into the layers, and here when you see that there is even one layer of depth, but when a new type is needed, you add one more condition in a class and make a change by instantiating the other class, then you can think of abstracting the class

- Remember you cannot write any Module/Class as 100% closed, a good architect designs in such a way that modification regression issues are less. Change has to be strategic and it has to be under control. It can be one more level of abstraction that can be added once you see the changes and call them in the class. But don't over architect, with too many unused abstractions, remember YAGNI.

- There is one more abstraction that is data level abstraction, where if there is a new type added, then you might have to add a column in the table. This can be avoided if you introduce a table that can take the new type as a row rather than a column. This is also a data-driven OCP, where it is open for extension, closed for adding any new column.

- All members of a class should be private. When the member variables of a class change, every function that depends upon those variables must be changed to avoid regression. Thus, no function that depends violates the closed for modification.

Just abstracting a few classes does not make your module OCP compliant. But it is a good starting point. One level of abstraction is always necessary, not only for OCP compliance, but also for Dependency inversion which we will see later in this chapter.

The abstraction has to be thought through and it should align with business change needs. Just adding two or three layers of abstraction does not make you a good architect. You will only be killing the project if you don't know what you are doing.

Abstraction should be analyzed, and if there would be requirements in a near future, then you go for one more layer of abstraction. Don't act like an astrologer who predicts the future for 10 years. A good architect should always design for a simple but also effective module that is both quick to implement and easy to extend.

L – Liskov principle

In the SRP, you learned about writing a dumb class, and in OCP, you learned about abstraction. Liskov goes one level further. I like the saying from the internet, *"If it looks like a duck, quacks like a duck, but needs batteries – you probably have the wrong abstraction."*

A code that violates LSP, makes the code hard to debug and too confusing. Most of the time, when we have implemented the inheritance incorrectly, and developers who work for us are finding it difficult to implement our abstraction or create a new abstraction with another upper-level abstraction, then it is probably an LSP violation.

LSP means subtypes must be substitutable for their base type. Let us consider the bird is the super class and I am trying to inherit the bird with ToyBird and the bird has Quack() method and ToyBird should have battery to be passed as parameter, then the Quack (batterysource) I cannot call quack of the ToyBird with this bird instance.

So the choice of inheritance is wrong because I have a method to quack but that method is not used in my subclass and a new method quack (batterySource) is implemented. It means that the inheritance is wrong here. But is it not true, Toy bird is also a bird, and how to overcome that?

When you use inheritance, your subclass gets all the methods from the subclass. So there will be method quack () and quack (batterysource). You will not be using quack ().

You need to use composition in places where you find this kind of problem, rather than inheritance. So your electric duck will be using the duck's behaviors and also not violating the LSP. Following LSP allows us to use polymorphism more confidently. We can call our derived classes referring to their base class without concern about unexpected results.

I – Interface Segregation

This is the easiest of all the principles to understand. This principle violation tells us directly whether the interface we created is right or not. If you put the right methods to an interface and it follows cohesion and no coupling, then this principle cannot be violated.

Whenever you use an interface and any of your interface methods is not used, then it violates interface segregation. You need to make sure you divide the interface further and expose methods that are cohesive and do not violate the ISP.

Interface segregation means no client should be forced to depend on methods that it does not use.

The best way to find out in your code is to check for this code "throw new Not Implemented Exception ()"; then you need to choose a different interface. If the interface is created or comes under your control, then you need to make sure the interface is divided into smaller interfaces and exposed properly.

What is the problem, if am not using it? It means that you are unnecessarily creating dependency with behavior that you do not use. Whenever for some reason there is a problem with the interface, you are also expected to change because you have chosen the wrong interface or you have exposed the wrong interface.

As an architect, you will be writing common code or sometimes framework related code, even though this principle is easy to follow and understand, but implementing should be thought through to avoid unnecessary dependency problems that lead to changes in the interface implementations.

D – Dependency Inversion

Dependency Inversion helps in decoupling your modules. This is closely related to the Hollywood principle, Don't Call Us, We'll Call You. This principle is very much used in places where you are trying to write a plugin and it must be followed to avoid coupling.

Dependency Inversion states two rules:

- High-level modules should not depend on low-level modules. Both should depend on abstractions (e.g. interfaces).
- Abstractions should not depend on details. Details (concrete implementations) should depend on abstractions.

Here are a few tricks and tips that are very useful to both understand DI and apply it in practical applications:

- Always think of your code as a plugin where people can use it in their modules. As an architect, you will be writing more common code or core framework code at the beginning of the project.
- Expose an interface where they can implement their code, and you will be calling the interface implemented method by your developer in your common/core code.
- As an architect, the classes you exposed in your common code, must never derive from a concrete class. There can be exceptions for MVP projects.
- Any instantiation of class should either use any creational pattern or proper Dependency injection framework.
- Make sure you understand and become strong in one dependency injection framework and you never instantiate a class in your module.
- All classes when instantiated using DI framework, keep it in the constructor level. You assert the requirement for the dependency in a container-agnostic manner, meaning you're telling the class what all the dependencies are in the class

methods early. The advantage is if you are changing the DI framework for any reason, changes are very less, and because when you use setter injection inside the method, the syntax differs for every DI framework. You might think about memory; don't worry, DI will take care of it.

- One more advantage of using Constructor DI is looking at the constructor of a class, you can tell exactly what it depends upon.

Design Patterns

In this section, we will not look into the design patterns in the context of explaining things, but we will look into the concept of how to effectively use them in the everyday context of your coding to become an effective architect.

If the design patterns are effectively used and not over architected, it not only builds the maintainability of the project, but also creates a learning environment of different patterns and common vocabulary for every developer in the team to understand your code better.

Remember your developers will not praise you because you selected a super design pattern and implemented it, if it is very complex. So as an aspiring architect, you should be simplifying things and not use any design pattern when not needed. My personal experience working with great architects who have been in this industry from the punched card programming age is "Simple is better". You write code for people to understand.

Sometimes for complex problems, you need to use a decorator pattern or any enterprise pattern, but they should be handled in such a way that you write it in your core/framework code and your developer need not even have to touch that code once.

Mentoring is also part of an architect's role, and mentoring the developers on how and why you architected the way you have architected, is your first duty. Until you learn the skill of teaching your own pattern selection and architect decision to your developers, you cannot become great at your job. Most of the architects lack this quality that stops them from crossing to the next level of leading multiple architects.

You at least need to teach your developer five times before they understand your architecture and design. A smart developer might understand within one or two times of explaining. So be patient with developers and teach them about your architectural decisions and why you made those decisions.

One cannot do justice to the subject if they have to write about a Design pattern in a single book, and I am not going to try to do that. You will only learn the major design patterns that are used widely in our industry. We will not go into details on explaining the design pattern, which is the goal of this section. You will only know why you need to select a particular design pattern and how it is used in real-time applications.

Singleton pattern

This is the one pattern not only used in many cases but also the pattern that is explained first in our interview questions. There are many ways to implement the singleton pattern. The problem with the singleton pattern is if not implemented properly, it will have memory leakage or thread unsafe. I highly recommend Jon Skeet's post here that talks of four different methods to implement.

Singleton pattern is a software design pattern that restricts the instantiation of a class to one "single" instance. – Wiki

The pattern should be used in places where you can reuse the instance and creating a new instance does not make sense. Declaring the class static does the trick most of the time. Jon Skeet's article helps us to understand it better.

This pattern is mostly used in places such as getting the user data of who has logged in, which does not change often. The key idea in this pattern is to make the class itself responsible for controlling its instantiation. The hidden constructor (declared *private*) ensures that the class can never be instantiated from outside the class.

Learn more about lazy instantiation also, so you can implement it in places where your instantiation is triggered by the first reference to the static member of the nested class.

Singleton pattern is an anti-pattern because it causes the state of the object to persist, and this also violates the single responsibility principle, because the class should be taking care of the business problem it solves, instead it also solves on how to handle its own instances. These are the nuances you should know, sometimes if you design correctly, you can skip singleton classes completely. You only use it if you cannot avoid it.

For all the design pattern explanations let us take the example of creating a document that needs to be printed in both word and pdf.

Factory Pattern

This pattern is used in places where you wanted some of the class to be instantiated dynamically. Most of the time it will be an interface type that will instantiate an object at runtime, because the instance of the class might change based on some runtime parameter. They are used in places where you need to segregate the instantiation into one place because its type cannot be predetermined.

A factory method pattern is a creational pattern that uses factory methods to deal with the problem of creating objects without having to specify the exact class of the object that will be created. – Wiki

This pattern does reduce coupling between the classes by introducing the factory class which takes care of the instantiation. This pattern should be used in places where your object should be created dynamically and you might be adding more types in the future.

In case of printing the document in Word, you need a Word class and pdf class, but the method you are going to invoke is print, and class instantiation should happen dynamically, so the factory pattern does the instance creation and hands over the instance to the callee.

Facade pattern

During all our careers as architects, abstracting the complexity has been our work. We tend to hide the complexity from the implementation and expose an interface that can be consumed by the developer. Even if you take the SQL engine, the underlying architecture is very complex, but still, we run "select * from table", it brings results to us. When you check out the architecture, algorithms used will fascinate, a 500-page textbook is not enough to explain the mathematics, logic, and hardware concepts involved.

In the same way, the facade pattern helps us to hide the complexity from the exposee. It improves the readability and usability of the software library. The interface exposed provides a context-specific interface to more generic functionality.

This pattern may look like it violates the Single responsibility principle and acts as a god class, but this pattern should be thought of as a wrapper rather than an implementation class. Still, the facade pattern should not put all the complex calling of other functionalities in a single class, rather this should expose, and it is the final skin on an onion peeling method. Facade class should never have all the implementation; it should be only the wrapper.

In case of printing the word document, we will be using the interops and doing some memory management to free it from memory, etc. using multiple subsystems, and for the pdf generation you use printpdf dll, then you can expose the print method and you can give the corresponding instance.

Facade pattern and adapter pattern both do the same job of exposing an interface. We will see the difference after we understand the adapter pattern in the next section

Adapter Pattern

This pattern is used in places where you wanted interoperability between two different systems. Whenever you design a system where you need to bring different systems together, for example, a system that prints a pdf document and the one that exports word documents, and you need to expose one interface called as export, the instance changes based on the parameter whether it is a word or pdf.

Adapter pattern is a software design pattern that allows the interface of an existing class to be used as another interface. It is often used to make existing classes work with others without modifying their source code. – Wiki

Facade pattern and adapter wrap things up, but the major difference is facade pattern wraps up complex subsystems and provides an interface, but in the case of the adapter pattern, it provides only compatibility. A beautiful example, learned from the Stack Overflow, is a remote control that can be used to control TV, Set Top Box, and home theater where complex systems are put together and power, volume buttons are exposed.

Template Pattern

When considering the printing of the document either in pdf format or word format, the steps are all the same, only the printing system changes. For example when we list the steps of printing a document from a website and it is a report that shows the current month's sales projection.

Step 1:   Get the data from Database
Step 2:   Filter data and massage the data.
Step 3.   Call the print method and instance created and method called on the user choice of document format.
Step 4.   Return the file received in byte array to the website.

In the above sequence, only step 3 changes, when you want some sequence of steps that need to be followed. But if step 3 needs to be overridden then we will choose the template pattern.

Template method Pattern is one of the behavioral design patterns. The template method is a method in a superclass, usually an abstract superclass, and defines the skeleton of an operation in terms of a number of high-level steps. These steps are themselves implemented by additional helper methods in the same class as the template method.

This pattern follows the inversion of control, and also the Hollywood principle "Don't call us we'll call you". In this pattern, step 3 calls the print method of the corresponding method, rather than we usually call the print method directly by the classes.

Enterprise Pattern – CQRS Pattern

This pattern should be widely used and it should fit most of our projects. Medium scale to large scale applications use this pattern. Whenever there is a website and some jobs that run in the background, this pattern is a perfect fit. Most of the projects are architected this way, so you can even go to the extreme of saying 90% of the project can use the CQRS pattern by default.

This pattern builds scalability and decoupling automatically into the system if you implement this pattern. This should not even be thought of as a pattern, this should be thought of as a mindset in envisioning your system.

CQRS stands for Command Query Responsibility Segregation. It states that every method should either be a *command* that performs an action, or a *query* that returns data to the caller, but not both. – Wiki

Practical applications of CQRS Pattern are

- CQRS fits well with event-based programming models. It's common to see CQRS systems split into separate services communicating with Event Collaboration. This allows these services to easily take advantage of Event Sourcing.
- Since the "Add/Update/Delete" and querying database are separated, most of the applications choose to have the "Add/

Update/Delete" as a separate task that is picked up by some kind of jobs, which raises eventual consistency.

- Command and query can share models, so keeping them in the same project is a good approach, unless the project is too huge.
- Reporting has always been a bottleneck for applications, having a separate reporting database is easier with this pattern.
- The advantage is one set of developers can work on a complex domain model that is a command module that updates the DB, and another set of developers can work on the querying data for the UI. So the segregation of concern is implemented right away.
- Don't use this pattern when the domain and business rules are simple. Use the simple CRUD patterns which are sufficient enough to run the application.

Cloud patterns

Cloud Patterns is a very important section and it needs a book by itself, so I have put together a video on Youtube and you can look into that video. The Cloud design pattern is all about reliability, scalability, and availability. You can watch the video here @ https://youtu.be/h-_Ns6nmWKw

Anti-Patterns

Anti-patterns help in knowing problems that might occur when choosing a solution for a particular problem. It helps to be aware of the drawbacks that come with solutions to the problem and mitigate them when needed. This gives a vocabulary for problems of a solution.

An anti-pattern is a common response to a recurring problem that is usually ineffective and risks being highly counterproductive. – Wiki.

In this section, we will look into two types of anti-patterns. They are Development anti-patterns and Architecture anti-patterns.

Development anti-patterns

These anti-patterns are the problems that occur from the developer and development perspective. As an architect and senior developer, you should never get into this trap and also make sure, your developers are well educated about these anti-patterns.

Continuous Obsolescence or Vendor Lock-in

Technology changes every day and new releases are being available in the market by different vendors, either it is the open source or closed source like Microsoft's .Net. Multiple versions hit the market every day and it is hard to keep up. The major problem is the dependencies between different packages. Whether it is node packages or nugget packages, the version dependencies are always a nightmare. When we tried to update the version of one package, we got caught up in the dependencies of that package not being supported.

For example, if you are trying to update the version of the node package which creates pdf, it's dependent on a different math package that calculates coordinates based on browser size for responsiveness. Now when there is an update in the browser, we are now stuck with the older version of the node package and also we cannot update the browser version. This is the particular reason why some companies still use Internet Explorer, due to some vendor lock-in.

There is no straightforward solution; as an architect you should make sure, you specify the version number even in dependencies and do a proper review before adding a package to your project. One more option is to always abstract these dependencies, so you can replace the packages with a stable one at that moment.

Lava Flow

Remember the days when you saw a code in your project while fixing a bug or implementing a feature of an existing project and you know the code is obsolete and you don't want to delete or remove the code, because it might break something in production, and you don't want to be blamed for production outage. Those codes are all called Lava Flow code.

They resemble the lava of a volcano that was left by the eruption. The cause of this lava flow code is because an MVP has crept into a production ready application and the R&D project was moved to production.

Now no one wants to touch and you are also afraid. As an architect, you can do two things. Even if it is an MVP, you can do a better code review and also code better. And once the MVP has moved to the project stage, you need to put your foot down to say the code should be thrown away and we need to refactor.

You can do the refactor easily if they are in the initial stages of your application, you can fix bugs in MVP and not include any feature. Refactor the MVP in the background and define proper interfaces and system design and move the new project to production.

If you are stuck with the project which was an MVP and you get to make it better, you need to make sure, you have the stage environment perfectly ready. Then understand the code and start removing the code you feel unnecessary.

You can even put a configuration for removing the code, in production for some time if it breaks. Leave the configuration for some time and after some time delete the code and remove the configuration. But be ready to break the production and get your stakeholders signed off.

If they don't sign off, don't touch the project. Ask them to give it to someone else to take care of fixing the bugs. If you are fixing, you should do it right and avoid this anti-pattern where the a R&D code is deployed in production and is staying there forever.

Golden Hammer

"When you only have a hammer everything looks like a nail."

We should be careful, this happens in every architect's life, when we start learning new technologies. We tend to push to frame any problem we see into the solution we already know, or the one we just learned. It is a bias that hurts more than any anti-pattern. You should be very much aware of this anti-pattern.

Never suit your problem into the technology you are good with or you just learned. Always second guess and become skeptical. Even if it looks like a tailor-made solution for the given problem.

Always choose the one that is simple, even if it leaves a technology which is a great opportunity to learn. Keep it simple, become a devil's advocate of your own technology choices. This makes you more than an aspiring architect.

When you are doubtful about your own choices, you tend to think better. You get into the discipline of analyzing your own solution and this makes you a better advocate of your own solutions.

Skepticism is the key here, where your solution may be wrong. I am not talking about being insecure about proposing your solution to others thinking it is wrong. Here we are talking about being the first critic for your choice and not having confidence in proposing your solution.

Walking through a minefield

In the fast-paced world, we are expected to deliver faster than ever, because of the competitive market, and we are also implementing Agile in the wrong way. Business folks are taking advantage of the wrongly implemented Agile methodology. The latest research tells us around two to five bugs are being added for every line we add to the code.

Any change to the system that is written today in the fast-paced world is like walking through a minefield and it might break the production.

So the best way to solve this anti-pattern of changes is to test properly. Developers should become better testers, meaning they should be thinking about the edge cases. You should think of testers as a feature validator rather than actual testers.

You should take pride in releasing bugs without code. The more you release without any bugs, the more you improve your self-confidence and also trust among your peers and your boss.

You should strive to become a quality maniac and someone trying to tell there is a bug should be taken as a shame.

But how is this possible in a fast-paced world, where people want everything now? There is a solution to it. Tell them you are will be responsible for hacky code. No one will take responsibility, and slowly they give way, giving you the time you wanted to fix the code and in the way you wanted. Even I struggle with this.

Position yourself as a high-quality guy; remember the chapter in positioning. It is all about positioning, and you position yourself as a high-quality achiever in their minds, and they will automatically give you time and the quick hacky projects will not even come to you. So it is a win-win.

Mushroom Management

When you are doing mushroom management, you will leave the developer in the dark which reduces the clarity of the requirement. Mushroom management happens because of two reasons, good intention not to disturb developers, and some non-technical manager wants to hold control of the development team in his own weird ways.

Mushroom management is an assumption that the developer understood the requirements or intentionally keeps the developer in the dark about the actual requirement by not making it mandatory to communicate with end users in all way.

We will look deep in the design strategy chapters on how to bring the developers and all stakeholders into a single room with a well-defined and tested workshop, where it is not only fun but also very productive and avoids mushroom management anti-patterns.

When you are not aware of the mushroom management anti-patterns, developers will not have clarity about the overall requirement and they tend to define brittle interfaces and coupled domain concepts together. The best way is always to let developers know what are the challenges faced by the end-user using your application. The best way is to send your developer onsite and see how the end-user is using the application and let them understand their pain points.

It is not that we need to include developers in all the meetings. Any meeting of more than four to six people is not a productive meeting, it can be only an informative meeting. So in the chapter on designing, we will look into when and how to include developers in meetings in the proper way so they are not feeling it painful to attend the meeting.

Architecture anti-patterns

Architecture anti-patterns help us to identify problems in our application in the design stage. Architecture driven design and implementation will always help to build applications that scale faster. Those applications driven on thinking Architecture antipattern will be easy to change and add features because the underlying structure is concrete.

Ad Hoc Integration

This happens when there are two or more products that might make a bouquet of products and the sales team comes up with this idea, and you start integrating your multiple applications in some manner without proper abstraction for integration.

So whenever you are assigned with the project to integrate multiple applications or they want to integrate your current project with another application, think of the Ad Hoc Integration Anti-pattern.

You should be very careful in giving estimation and architecting the applications talking to each other. Think proper level of abstraction first and always think of new interfaces, don't reuse any existing interfaces.

Remember you need to complete re-engineering of the way you talk to other applications.

Cover your assets

Documents are written to show how smart you are and just to present some form of documentation to the stakeholder. These documents not only confuse the developers and stakeholders but also add extra work for updation.

Documents that are created to cover all the stakeholders' concerns will only be huge and do not add any value, they can be called Cover your assets anti-pattern (CYA).

The best way to avoid this anti-pattern is not to address all the stakeholders in the same document. Remember the document satisfies five major criteria.

- Documents are written to communicate, not to put in every thinking process.
- Document Alternatives compare between not more than two to three competing technologies.
- It should be used to record decisions in a crisp and brief manner.
- Visuals, Visuals, Visuals. Add diagrams with legends and explain them.
- The format should be easily updatable. Confluence templates are very effective, give it a try. Even Wiki pages are good, because you can check in with your source code and they are lightweight.

Architecture by Implication

This happens when an architect is overconfident about his visualization of seeing the architecture in his head and does not document his decision.

As Intel's former CEO, Andy Grove says, he does not read much of the weekly or monthly reports sent by his employees, but he is very strict on getting the reports from the leads, and says the process is more important than the output, because it is a discipline that helps the employees to put down the thought process in compiling their thoughts when creating a document.

Many architects think they can implement architecture as and when they develop, which is bad. You should put your process on paper and documents and record it. This process of planning and documenting will not only help you to communicate better, but also validate your understanding of your thought process and justify your choices.

The best way to avoid this anti-pattern is to write proper crisp documentation using viewpoints and perspectives which address stakeholders and their concerns in a well-structured way. We will look into the documentation process when looking into the chapter on documentation.

Swiss Army Knife

As the name suggests, trying to do more things in a class, does spill into every part of the code. For example, the same service bus with different topics is used for every process in your project, where you should have used a separate queue. It happens mostly due to the time crunch and also due to the Golden hammer mentality.

The best way to avoid it is to keep your own standards of fixing a size for every component in technology starting from functions, class, and the messaging system to address asynchronous challenges.

I have my own number and don't take these numbers as any kind of rule. These are based on my own experience in my life. You need to figure out your own number limit. I will not write any function that is more than 10-15 lines.

A class can go up to a maximum of 100-150 lines, and there should not be more than 4-5 jobs that work on any asynchronous messaging or streaming service such as service bus, queue, or Kafka. The project can split into two if you are working for more than two different stakeholders from different business units.

Remember this, anti-patterns address, single responsibility, interface segregation, YAGNI principle and Don't call us, we'll call you principle. You can use any one or more principles when you see yourself building or are in a mess of Swiss army knife anti-pattern.

Reinvent the wheel

This is my favorite anti-pattern. Luckily I learned this anti-pattern early in my career, which has saved me a lot of trouble. Most of the technical people who are not very successful owe it to this anti-pattern, where they try to reinvent the wheel by themselves. One main mentality you should always have is that 99.9 % of the time the problem you are trying to solve would have been solved by someone in the universe. You need to figure out the solution that is already there. That is the main job. And you need to make adjustments that suit your needs; that is where you should concentrate.

Always choose to buy, when you are given a choice between build vs. buy. Remember your aim as an architect should be to solve the stakeholder's problem. Not to get your resume weightage or learn a new technology.

You can still learn lots of new things, because once your aim is to solve the stakeholder's problems, you will be presented with problems that the latest technology will solve. Everyone wants a quick fix and a faster solution. When you try to reinvent the wheel without doing research about the solution for the problem, you become a mediocre architect.

When you don't reinvent the wheel, you will have lots of time to solve problems that are specific to your domain and project. This helps the business grow faster because you can release features faster that give an edge for your project over that of your competitor.

Reference Source: https://sourcemaking.com/antipatterns

Non-Functional Requirements

Non-Functional requirements (NFR) are as important as functional requirements, epic, stories, etc. It helps to build your system better. Identifying the NFR is one of the key roles of an architect. There are more than 50 NFR classifications available in software engineering. Good architects always choose the right NFR needed for the project.

The challenge for an architect is choosing the order of NFR that needs to be handled, choosing which NFR to opt for during the initial design of the project and which NFR can be dealt with after implementing a few user stories. Good choice of NFR defines the success of the project.

If you miss an NFR and design decisions on when to start designing the NFR, you might get into huge problems because it becomes too difficult to implement in the later stage of your project. You can learn how to choose which NFRs to implement and in which order, which is solely based on your previous experience and talking to your stakeholders and asking the right questions.

We will look into the scenario and action steps that need to be taken as an architect for the successful implementation of Non-Functional requirements.

Non-functional requirement (NFR) is a requirement that specifies criteria that can be used to judge the operation of a system, rather than specific behaviors. They are contrasted with functional requirements that define specific behavior or functions. – Wiki

A system should show a list of orders by the user is a functional requirement, how much time it should take for the page to load, and show the first 10 orders is performance NFR.

In this chapter, we will only briefly touch upon explaining the NFR, rather you will be learning about the ways you can deal with NFR in your projects with actionable takeaways.

Scalability

Scalability is one of the trickiest NFR. I have always had trouble with when to start considering them. If you consider it too early, you might build a complex system that might violate YAGNI. But if you leave it too late, you might end up burning your money in your project buying bigger hardware to handle the growth of users.

Scalability is the most important NFR, which definitely needs an architect to be present in the project. Building an MVP product is easy if the business stakeholder has a vision and has the capability to foresee a real-time problem to solve. Once the MVP is successful, the lava flow code we have written needs to scale faster based on user demands.

Scalability means the capacity to be changed in size or scale. Scalability in the software application means your system should be able to handle the increase in the amount of work by adding the hardware automatically. Autoscaling means it should handle without any human intervention. You can also say it should automatically scale down when the amount of work has reduced.

Automation is the key. You would have designed and implemented your application that can scale faster, but if it needs human intervention, then it does not solve the purpose of scaling needs.

We will look into the common ways how you can build scalable systems that can make you a better architect with some real-time examples. We will mostly consider the web application as the base.

- Always make use of CDN; it gives a huge advantage in making your application scale faster with almost zero code changes. Almost any application will have some static content such as HTML, CSS, image files, etc., so using CDN automatically copies those files to the nearest server of the user.

- Use the Static content hosting pattern available in the Cloud of your choice with the CDN connected. You not only save cost, but it is also very performant. The only problem with CDN is you need to purge the files after your release, which might take a few minutes for the files to be propagated across CDN Servers for access for the user.

- Think of API in terms of serverless technology, and serverless automatically scales. The only problem with the serverless is the cold start, there are premium plans available in the Cloud that solve this purpose too.

- Use cache extensively, every single one of them. They can give you a sense of a highly scaling solution and give you better output in a high demand situation without wasting much of the compute resources. CDN is one way of caching strategy.

  - Browser Cache
  - Client Side Cache
  - Server side Cache
  - Database cache.

- Enable autoscaling for your web application server, if serverless is not a viable choice, and make sure you also consider the time it takes for a new web application server to spin up.

- Always use a load balancer or any traffic controller for your application.

- For any type of asynchronous operation, use a messaging mechanism, so you can scale the number of jobs that listen to the job based on load.

- Keep your jobs or daemon as dumb as possible, meaning it should do only a single work and it should take minimal time as possible, this helps when the load is high.
- Don't persist your data in one single DB, choose data storage based on the data, for files choose file storage, don't dump them into SQL tables. Think of no-SQL options. No-SQL is built for horizontal scaling, it is not straight forward in most of the SQL DB available in the market.

Performance

Performance is everything in the software business. Competition is so high, if your application is not performant you are out of business. People have more choices nowadays and their span of attention is getting lesser and lesser. System design plays a key role in performance metrics. A bad design will always perform worse on load.

Performance is an indication of the responsiveness of a system to execute any action within a given time interval. People use performance and scalability synonymously, but they are different.

Performance is all about speed, throughput, Responsiveness, and scalability is all about the ability of the system to handle the load.

If the load is high, the system becomes non-performant when not designed properly and we need to scale the system to perform better.

Performance is a software metric that helps in defining your system irrespective of load. Your performance should be measured based on speed irrespective of the load. It should scale faster, so the performance metric is maintained to service the business.

You need to design your system based on the tips we discussed in the topic on scalability, and add this as a plus point to NFR with respect to speed.

- Define a metric for during the initial phases of your design and get it signed by your stakeholders.

- You should measure the metrics below. The list below is not exhaustive, these are mandatory metrics that need to be tested and validated during the testing phase.

  - Average Response Time
  - Error Rates
  - Request Rate
  - Application Availability
  - Mean time between failures
  - Mean time to recover/repair

- Choose a push mechanism rather than the polling mechanism in your application.
- Using horizontal scaling based technologies so one can utilize the power of running your process in small multiple CPUs rather than one large CPU.
- Realizing speed is relative, a good progress bar will make your app look like a quick one. That is the reason why the lift has a mirror where people get lost in checking out their appearance, and do not complain about the lift's speed.
- Use caching extensively as discussed in scaling applications.
- Setting the expectation of the throughput of your system well in advance, so people don't complain.

Testability

A good architect designs his system testable and takes the whole responsibility of turnover time in every testing type available, such as unit testing, integration testing, etc. As an architect, it is your full responsibility to keep your system testable at any point of time. This is a real NFR, where the whole responsibility falls on the architect.

A testable system should provide a concrete basement for building highly maintainable and scalable solutions. A good testable system makes refactoring easy, and you can avoid lots of regression errors in the initial stages of your development, when you have a highly testable system.

Software testability is the degree to which a software artifact supports testing in a given test context. If the testability of the software artifact is high, then finding faults in the system by means of testing is easier. – Wiki

There are ways you can improve the testability of the system. Going into every detail is outside the scope of the system, but you can learn things that will make your system more testable. If these are followed, you will automatically build projects that are testable, and your application testability will gradually increase. It needs patience and discipline to make yourself an architect who is great at building software that is testable.

You need to follow these tips to get your system testable in all stages of your project life cycle.

- Learn dependency injection (DI) and make yourself an expert in one dependency injection framework. This will automatically make your system easily unit testable. Now lots of programming languages support DI out of the box. Make use of them.

- Learn one in-memory DB framework that is available in the market, it can be SQLLite, Effort, H2, etc.

- As an architect, build fake data that are needed for unit testing, and make it very extensible for other developers to consume. You can use tools for mocking data such as Bogus, Faker, etc.

- You make it a habit to test your code changes only through unit testing. You should never use a UI for unit testing. You should only validate your fix finally using UI or postman. Once you get the discipline of writing unit tests and testing your fix, you automatically will identify the pain points your developer goes through, and you fix them and it will be easy for them to write unit tests too.

- Automate your tests and make sure your developer cannot check in the code even if one test fails.

- Never violate the testing pyramid. Write fewer tests going up the pyramid.

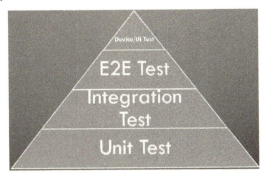

- Don't try for 100% coverage, try to get the functionality covered rather than the code. It is highly improbable and practically a waste of time to have 100% coverage.
- When you add functionality, add a test case first and then add the code. I have personally not done a full-fledged test-driven development, but have unit tested in the way that is detailed above.
- Make sure you use semantic monitoring for Integration testing. Make sure you put the proper configuration in place, so your integration testing does not harm the production environment or production data.
- Keep your E2E as minimal as possible and keep it very simple.
- Use browser stack, saucelab, visual studio app center, or any third party vendor that supports device testing.

As an architect, it is your responsibility to build, maintain, and automate the tests for your project, also you should be an example of using unit testing to build your code. Also, make a bandwagon of telling people about automated testing and its advantages almost every day.

Security

Security is one of the non-functional requirements that people won't implement until it is too late. It is the most important NFR defining an architect's capability of architecting solutions that goes through the test of time. Your system can be attacked at any time by anyone, by any means, intentionally or unintentionally. So protecting your system is one of the major challenges faced by architects.

Security is an ongoing process involving people and practices, and ensures application confidentiality, integrity, and availability. – Wiki

When you make your system too secure, you might bring down the usability of the system. Less secure you are screwed. There is no midpoint to it. Securing your application in every layer is the only way you can protect your system.

Remember, any system can be hacked and penetrated. As architects, it is our duty to make sure it is too hard to hack our system. So your hacker gets tired and walks away.

Think of two homes that has valuables in it but no door, and another home with a door that is latched and locked, and the door is latched and has a big lock in it. So door, latch, a big lock is all one layer of security. Does it mean a home with a big lock is 100% safe? No. It is safer than a home with no door. So our aim is to keep increasing the layer of security without losing the usability and performance of the system.

There are no set of rules to be followed, but there are some principles that should be followed and not violated.

- Don't trust people, hardware, software.
- Audit all users and usage.
- Implement security in every layer of software from the Physical to the Application layer.
- Always follow a least privilege approach.
- Set a time limit for every privilege provided.

There are a few best practices that are mandatory and rudimentary, that cannot be taken for granted in any part of the application and at any stage of the software life cycle.

- Always sanitize input to avoid SQL injection, Cross-site scripting, and remote file inclusion attacks.
- Always use HTTPS and enable SSL certification, even if your website does not have any payment transactions.
- Use encryption wherever applicable. Storage, API, network, etc.
- Always use request limiting, to prevent DDOS attacks. All application gateways have this feature built-in.
- Use the Encryption at REST, if your service provides them. Most of them are a few clicks away to set up.
- Make sure you keep the connection string in vaults that are only accessible by your service.
- Don't try to build a login system, use an already built-in system such as Auth0, AD B2C, etc.
- Keep your password policy as strict as possible.
- Provide Just-in access wherever possible, so you can lock down resources automatically.
- Penetration testing should be performed regularly and using external vendors, which is more cost-effective and efficient. They see our system from the outside world as our customers and hackers see them.
- Use managed services rather than the unmanaged services provided by the Cloud vendor. Managed services might look costlier, but it is worth the cost.
- Enable internet access to your services only if needed. Disable all ports if needed based on your application.
- Never share production configuration with anyone; it should be only in the application settings or in the vault.

Extensibility

Every architect's blessing in disguise is where the application that is designed and implemented is picked up in business and more customer base is added to the application exponentially.

Everyone has been there, it looks like a curse for a successful project where you will be put on the spot because the project has many issues. Remember the problem to scale a project is far better than the project without any customers. So scaling problems are actually a boon, not a curse.

Extensibility is an NFR that tests our skills as an architect. How quickly we add features to the project defines the success of the project. Extensibility is the coefficient that defines the success of the project. Extensibility defines how much your project can grow without you burning your midnight oil.

A good extensible module or project makes your developer happy because the challenges in adding or changing features become a learning curve rather than a frustration to everyday activities. When the project is extensible, you tend to push the boundaries of the speed of releases. The more extensible your project, the more your business grows in the competitive market.

Extensibility is a measure of the ability to extend a system and the level of effort required to implement the extension. Extensions can be through the addition of new functionality or through modification of existing functionality. The principle provides for enhancements without impairing existing system functions. – Wiki

Any functionality you add to the system makes the system unstable. Implementing the modern engineering practice that is discussed below will make your system less expensive to dynamic changes.

Any changes to the system will disturb the equilibrium of the system and it is for the architect to balance the equilibrium. In the book, **Building Evolutionary Architecture**, Rebecca Parson and Neal Ford talk about the role of the architect being like a unicyclist carrying boxes and trying to balance the boxes so they do not fall. It is what we do every day. Try to balance between new features and existing features.

There are multiple ways you can make your system more extensible. A well-disciplined architect does know where to draw the line on extensibility. If it is too extensible, you might fall into the YAGNI trap.

We will look into multiple ways on how to make your application extensible and the gotchas that stop your application as fast as possible.

- Beware of the anti-pattern **Vendor lock-in**, because it affects your extensibility factor much more than any other anti-pattern. Think of abstraction for every third party library or application.

- Start thinking about your system in Microservices. Understand the domain-driven design and event-driven design.

- Automate every manual work that hinders the release process. CI/CD is the best engineering process you should have to make your changes released faster. The tester should get the developer check in of code without any human intervention.

- Set up a proper rollback mechanism, so you can deploy when you find your changes break the production, you should be in a position to roll back and then fix the bug and release it again. This process of release-rollback-release should be fully automatic without human intervention.

- Choose buy strategy. When you are presented with buy vs. build choice, this goes against the first tips we spoke about. Remember the architect is like a unicyclist who tries to balance the boxes.

- Encourage developers to write unit tests and especially while fixing a bug, first unit test and then the bug fix. The advantage of having this strategy is that your system starts becoming a regression proof system.

- Always validate your assumptions. Your way of thinking may be the problem that is not allowing the system to extend and scale. Thinking about science before relativity theory, scientists were thinking in terms of Newton's law of universal gravitation, and once Einstein proposed that relativity changed everything.

In the same way, be skeptical of your own assumption of your existing knowledge.

Observability

Observability is one of the NFR that lets you sleep well and work more efficiently in your day-to-day actions. It is the NFR that should be considered from the beginning of a project, even if the project is an MVP. Observability helps in tackling bugs faster because it tells where the bugs are coming from. When implemented, you can do a time travel to figure out what happened in your application and why it happened.

When Observability is not considered in the project, you will have nightmares in finding and fixing the bugs. You will be less productive and you will always be firefighting rather than being innovative. When Observability is not properly implemented, you have to spend 12-16 hours in the office just to keep your application afloat.

In control theory, Observability is a measure of how well internal states of a system can be inferred from knowledge of its external outputs. Observability is new terminology used by DevOps teams which was called monitoring in the operations arena. I highly recommend you to read *The Practical Monitoring* by Mike Julian.

Components of Good Observability:

Data Collection. You need to collect data for Observability purposes. Different types of data are Metrics, counters, gauges, and logs. Decide on the push or pull model. You can query a service and get the data, or you can let the service push the Observability data to you. Both ways work, you can decide on a methodology based on the application which we will learn in this chapter.

Data Storage. Decide on how you are going to store the collected data, its archival process, and its lifetime. You need to think about compression and retention policies.

Visualization. Everyone loves dashboards and charts. As an architect, it is your responsibility to keep the views minimal and also highly useful. Don't write any code for this monitoring visualization, use any one of the visualization tools such as Grafana, PowerBI, etc.

Analytics and reporting. Remember analytics and reporting should be actionable, anything that does not need human intervention should not be analyzed or reported. Remember the email about your server error which everyone ignores.

These are practical minimal things you should implement to make your system observable and live a peaceful and innovative life.

- Select the right tools, don't select any monitoring tools because Amazon or Google uses them, find tools that will be used by you and not for namesake monitoring.
- Monitoring is not a job, and it cannot be manual. Build a proper alerting mechanism, so the monitoring is an automated job.
- Alert only when human intervention is needed, don't build a system that sends hundreds of emails that everyone ignores.
- Whenever we get alerts, try to find the underlying cause and fix the issue. It is ok to hack the problem and buy some time and work on the issue, but don't make it another technical debt of your project.
- Continuous improvement is the key in monitoring systems; the more you spend time on improving it day by day, the better your life becomes and fun.
- Learn Business KPIs and implement a system to track them and let business stakeholders use them to see how well the feature is used.
- Write logs as much as possible. Don't provide access even to stage resources. Let people debug issues through logs in stages. This will help lessen downtime during production releases.

- Use correlation id in your logs, to track the flow of usage and data for time travel.
- Always set up an availability test for all your applications including web app, web API, messaging services, etc.

Maintainability

As an architect, you leave a project after it's in the maintenance phase, so if you don't want some fresher or junior developer to laugh at you, or ridicule, or get frustrated with your code, you should keep your code more maintainable from day one of the project. For an MVP, the maintainability can be put off till a few successful demos.

When the maintainability is high in your project you tend to have a balanced life for yourself and the developers. Bugs are easy to fix and you can assign them to any developers, and they won't be pushing it away because they are scared of breaking production.

Maintainability is the ease with which a product can be maintained in order to correct defects or their cause, prevent unexpected working conditions, make future maintenance easier, or cope with a changed environment. – WIKI

Social psychologists and police officers tend to agree that if a window in a building is broken and is left unrepaired, all the rest of the windows will soon be broken. This is as true in nice neighborhoods as in rundown ones.

The same applies if all the code is proper, and you don't allow substandard code, then the project will be highly maintainable. But if you allow one part of the project to be broken you will end up with an extremely maintainable project.

These are the tips that need to be followed throughout the project life cycle with strict discipline. You can even sound like Hitler if anyone violates any of the below tips.

- Write code for humans. Your code should be as boring as possible. Straightforward and simple code is better than complex code.
- Choose always a simple way to implement the feature and avoid complexity. Avoid accidental complexity by all means.
- Don't compile your code without compiling it in your head once. It is a great mindset for aspiring architects. I have worked with a few developers who write the C# code in notepad, and it compiles the first time they run in the compiler.
- Code by thinking first and not by typing. Typing the code should be the end result of your analysis of the problem and edge cases.
- Try to refactor the code as many times as possible, use the Boy Scout rule for coding. Leave your **code** better than you found it.
- Write proper unit test cases. Especially if you add any complex code that is not easy to understand, so if any developer wants to fix a bug in the code in that area, they can run the unit test and see the validity of the bug fix.
- Have a well-defined CI/CD pipeline, so the release to the stage is not dependent on any person.
- Make sure you have enabled static code analyzers such as FxCop, Jtest, Linters, etc.
- Never violate the single responsibility principle we discussed in the previous chapter.
- Code review can make your code maintainable, just the thought of someone reviewing our code makes us a better developer.
- Train developers to do code review, keep them as primary reviewers, and have two code reviewers for any change. Use tools that make the code review easier and faster to give comments.
- The final tip I always suggest is to follow the 'sharpen the saw' principle, make it a habit for yourself, and also for the other developers to always learn a new way of coding.

Best Practices

"There are no best practices, it all depends."

Remember the architect's whole job is choosing the right tradeoff. When presented with the problem, he is not only presented with the need for a solution, but also the need to take a well-calculated tradeoff that comes with the selected solution.

As an architect, you have to weigh all pros and cons and you will not have all facts at the point of decision making. You need to take the judgment call based on your intuition and then you need to find the data to back it up. Intuition works best, it is not the right way if you don't have data to back it up. Discipline on gathering evidence to support our Intuition of technology choice is the challenging and interesting part of the architect's job.

Also beware of Intuition Bias, because intuition is feeling based, and if you get too attached to it, you might end up making lots of wrong decisions because of your love for technology and your knowledge rather than the needs of the business.

Always be the first person to change your decision and go back to square one. This is the one piece of advice, which if I had known earlier, would have saved lots of pain in my career. Remember the time, you made a wrong choice in technology and it was too late to turn back. If you had turned back, it would have saved countless sleepless nights. So be always critical about your own choices.

Another way to fix the Intuition bias is to brainstorm with your peers or your development team or even business stakeholders. It helps you put your thoughts in a structured way because you have to make them understand, so you tend to get more clarity toward your decisions.

Best practices are not something that can be implemented in a day and then you can forget about it. You need to figure it out every day, and with the new technology and new innovative ways of solving problems that prop up due to the open-source revolution, as an architect, you should be in a place where you learn a lot and have a hands-on on implementing the things you learned.

You have to be an implementor, mentor, and gatekeeper for best practices. There are many common best practices such as keeping the configuration outside code, following the coding standards, using dependency injection, and adding unit tests to your code.

These best practices by themselves will handle most of the problems. The above mentioned are the 20 percent practices that can fix 80% of the problems that we face every day.

A best practice is a method or technique that has been generally accepted as superior to any alternatives because it produces effective results.

All we think of here is effectiveness and not efficiency. We strive for effectiveness and efficiency will always follow. Being effective in best practices means you should be successful in producing a successful outcome of your project and not just doing things with minimum time and minimum resources.

Principles Behind Best Practices

As discussed in the previous chapter, principles govern everything, if you have the right principles, then you can take the right decisions even under very critical situations. All you have to do is find the right principle that should be applied at the right time. It helps you to validate your tradeoff and make quick and easy solutions that will have a good impact in the long term. These principles are mostly touched on by Jeffrey K Liker's Toyota way book.

Long Term Vision

Thinking long term is one of the highly effective strategies that will yield results and help you to grow your career to great heights. People who have a vision of the long term have more success than the people who have a shorter vision.

When you think in the long term, you tend to not waste your energies on petty things. Think of a guy who will work on a project for two years and a guy who wants to work for two weeks, and think of the decisions these two persons will make.

The person who will work on a project for two weeks will get things done in a hurry without caring about its consequences, because he knows he will not be held responsible because he is out in 10 working days. But the person who is going to work on a project for two years will make sure things are put in place and his decisions will be entirely different, and he will think through every decision he makes because it is going to affect his life for the next two years.

A long-term Strategy is something you want to do in the future and you live your everyday planning and implementing to have a better tomorrow. There are three strategies that can help you plan your long term vision better.

Building the A-Player team. This is the highest leverage activity. As an architect and leader, it is your responsibility to recruit and build a team with A-Players. If your team has A-Players, your life becomes simple and interesting. We will look more into the A-Player team in the latter part of this chapter. Recruiting and engaging A-Players with high quality work is the greatest challenge that improves your life and career. If you don't know how to handle A-Players, then you might end up with C-Players which will make your life busy and not productive.

Learning Culture is how every part of your team or company should work. You should treat everything you do as part of the learning curve and you are gaining experience to face changes better. As Jim Rohn says, don't wish it was easy, wish you were better. Once you set up a learning culture environment and you keep that as your long-term strategy, you build yourself and the people around you better.

Open Communication. When you have a team that talks to each other more and there is no insecurity in showing that they don't know, then it improves the overall capability of the team and also makes it a great place to work. This is one of the long-term visions you should have always in mind and you should show people and even be ready to learn from a junior developer. Be always vocal about it and ask any developer if you don't know certain things and learn from them. Encourage everyone to ask around and learn from each other.

Continuous Flow Process

Aiming for a Continuous Flow process helps us identify all the bottlenecks in our project. As an architect your aim is to set up a Continuous Flow process, so you and your team are always effective and only working on things that matter most in developing features and concentrating on mundane office chores.

Continuous flow Process is a flow production method used to manufacture, produce, or process materials without interruption.

The whole decision that you take regarding technology, architecture, or design should be based on this principle. Find the bottleneck, remove it, and move forward. You can do this to every aspect of your project, it can be creating features from a sales team or business analyst or removing bottlenecks that hinder developer productivity. It is one of the simplest principles which gives you a measure to stick to your every day's decision. If your decisions or choice hinder continuous flow, think about the decisions and revisit them.

Pull System to avoid overproduction

The Pull System to avoid overproduction concept is taken from the manufacturing division where the car manufacturer has minimum spare parts available for every part of any car, and if you need a spare part, you order them and they will start producing the spare parts. This way you don't produce what is not needed and also you don't waste space to store spare parts that are going to take lots of money and resources.

We can use the same principle here in our software industry, you can call it YAGNI, which we discussed before. You might use this principle not to code anything extra for future features. Postpone any technical decisions as much as possible, and when you take decisions for the future you tend to get into overproduction that will cause underproduction for valuable features.

Level out the workload

The leader should make the workload distributed. It can be with peers, yourself, or your running applications. Thinking in terms of leveling our workload helps you to concentrate on not burning out a single working piece of resource. The resource can be yourself, your developer in your team, or the server running your application. If you don't level out the workload, all you get is burnout.

Always think in smaller junks and how you can leverage all your resources, and get it done. Be a choreographer of your project and design your application such that the worker knows what to do and he does it very well.

You should concentrate to get the best out of every resource and no resource is idle. Let us say you are choosing two servers to run your application so that it is more fault-tolerant; there is no point in sending 80% of traffic to one server and 20% traffic to another server, so you should be at least sending 50-50 in the best case.

In the same way, there is no point in recruiting five resources in a project and giving work to two resources who work well, and almost keeping the other three not fully occupied.

It is your responsibility to split the workload and get the others trained. If they are not A-Players, release them to other projects if they are not faring well.

In my personal experience, people who are released to other projects have fared well. Not letting them go from your project out of moral considerations is a sin. You are being a bottleneck for their career growth.

Firefighting vs. Planning Well

Personally, I love this principle. When I started my career, I had not worked with a great tech lead until I traveled to Japan. People love firefighting and being busy because they feel the rush and want to feel important every day for solving the crisis that happens every day, will burns out everyone.

When I was in Cognizant with one of the Fortune 500 clients, and our project was not going smoothly, and then all hell was breaking loose, they called in a manager named Seetharaman.

He came into our project. I had just about four to five years of experience then, and I thought he was going to ask us to work more to fix bugs and get the project released. Instead, he slowed things down. He threw away most of the bugs and only took some of them to be fixed, and asked us to go home every day by 5 PM and we were able to deliver the project easier.

What he did was find the bugs that are most needed for the release. He removed all the good to have features creeped in by the testing team or the business analyst. We concentrated only on what we had promised the client to be released.

The principle of planning well should be chosen when you feel like firefighting. It feels really good to be busy and cracking things as they come up, but it will burn you out. You cannot sustain yourself in any industry if you are only firefighting. You end up with all types of medical problems.

In his book, Warren Buffett says he will not invest in companies like GM which do lots of R&D. Instead he will only invest in companies like Coke where they have already figured out what they are doing.

I am fully committed to doing projects which have lots of R&D, and my career consists of projects of those types. If I want to take the juice of Warren Buffett's advice in our industry, it means to choose projects that are slow in pace and do have lots of funding like health care, etc. You should choose domain, technology, everything where there are enough time and resources to have a peaceful life and also do lots of innovative things.

As an architect, you should be building a team of that nature. Even when there is huge pressure on your project, you should only concentrate on working not more than nine to ten hours per day. And you should have all your weekends free. Your weekends are yours, and you don't have to spill your work to the weekend.

It is a bad habit to spill your work to weekends because, as per *Parkinson's Law* the adage is that "work expands so as to fill the time available for its completion." So work for five days a week and you will find more things done. Plan well. Brainstorm well. Concentrate on getting things done at a regular pace rather than at a firefighting pace. This is also the best option to hold and recruit A-Players which we will look at later in this chapter.

Kaizen

This method is one of the methods which has made my career more successful. You should do this over and over in every part of your life. If you use it in the right way, you will make your personal and professional life better.

Your relationship with peers and family will get better. You will gain more respect and trust from everyone around you. Sometimes people even feel like you are a Godsend, and question you on how you can be so productive.

Kaizen is a Japanese business philosophy of continuous improvement of working practices, and personal efficiency. Kaizen applies to every part of your life where you want to improve. This continuous improvement principle can move mountains because you are not doing anything big bang here.

This Japanese term is made popular by Edward Deming's *14 management points*. All you have to do is take any one process and do a small improvement of it.

Let us take one part of the code which seems to have a spaghetti code of too many if's. First, write a unit test to test that method and use the refactoring technique to move it to different classes and validate the changes using the unit test's return. You have now cleaned the most trouble making part of your application.

Next time a bug occurs, you will be fixing it faster because you have cleaned that part of the code. So you always make improvements with respect to design, implementation tools, etc.

You can automate one part of the build step that is causing problems and you can move on to the next.

That is how I automated three days of the build process to 21 minutes. It was a mobile build that was taking almost three days after the code to check in and move to Testflight and android beta. I slowly started automating, and then the developer checked in the mobile code changes. Now the changes will be available in Apple Testflight and Google play store beta version for testing for testers to test without any manual intervention.

The list of best practices is very far-fetched in our industry, Best practice can become the worst practice because everything changes in this fast-paced world. People change, people's perception changes, technology changes, technology needs change. We will look into some best real-time best practices that you can follow, that will enhance your career as an architect.

Let us start with how you can get better by following the below five steps, which we have discussed extensively. This is from a different perspective to understand with respect to best practices. The best practices you need to implement to become the best in your field. Let us start on how to become the best guy in the team to implement best practices.

Becoming an A-Player

In the book '*Topgrading*', Bradford D. Smart has talked about A-Players in detail. He has coached many successful companies like GE, GM, etc. and people use the CIDS interview template that is provided by him. Recruiting and working with A-Players is the best thing you can do for yourself and for the company. You need to change your own psychology behind yourself and others to build a team of A-Players.

Let us look into more detail about recruiting and managing A-Players in the Epilogue. Now let us learn about how you can become an A-Player.

As an A-Player, your life should be balanced. Just spending 80 hours in the office and sucking up to the boss will make you look like an A-Player in your team but you are not a real A-Player. You need to find a balance between Career, Physical and Spiritual wellness, Relationships, Finance, and Recreation (pleasure and hobbies).

Don't buy more than what you can afford and pay personal or credit card loans. Keep yourself debt-free, so you can walk out of your current job any time. If a new job offers a career jump, you can take it up, even if you know it is kind of riskier than your current job. Also sometimes you might have to get a salary cut to get new technology, so spend less to save more.

Accept jobs where you can excel in your job and be an A-Player; this is where you can get the highest leverage. If you were to choose between two jobs where you have the opportunity to be an A-Player or a job with a high salary, choose an A-Player job, because once you prove to them you are an A-Player, you will automatically get a higher salary.

Find your own weakness and work on them. You should be strengthening your strengths because it helps you to get better and better and feel more confident. This weakness enhancement should happen on your weekends and spare time. Use all the time you binge-watch web series and movies, and allocate those times to get good with the basics. When we are learning about "How to learn best practices" in later chapters, you can understand this better.

Question whether a big company life is better for you, or a startup or midlevel product company works for you. In a big company, whether it is services or products, the growth is too gradual, and you cannot learn more in your job. A midsize company teaches you more in your life with respect to your job, but less on the process, so you can make a conscious choice about switching between working for a bigger company for some time and a midsize company for some time.

Get Consensus

Remember any good practice will only stay in the books or blogs if it is not accepted by your peers. At least 80% of the team should accept the good practices you proposed. Another 20% will take time to follow once they see the benefits.

Consensus is a group discussion where everyone's opinions are heard and understood, and a solution is created that respects those opinions.

There are a few steps to follow to implement your best practices in your project or company. These work best when followed in sequence. Let us take an example of implementing DevOps in your project and how you can deal with the problem in your company.

There will be many questions such as is DevOps really necessary, or if we have the tools or resources to do it. People dont like change, and we need little nudges and processes to implement best practices.

Before trying to implement any best practices, first, know your audience or stakeholders. You need to segregate your people into three:

- The group that accepts your DevOps idea without much struggle.
- The group who will ask some questions before accepting.
- The group who will never budge no matter what you do.

Do some groundwork before calling for the formal meeting by talking to some of the peers from group 1 and group 2 to understand the resistance that might occur that will help you to build a presentable use case.

Now you need to build the presentations or cases based on the first set of people who can accept and who will move forward. Especially be ready to answer the questions that will be from group 2 who will nudge some questions before accepting your best practices.

Build also cases why the best practice might not work, and talk about these to group 1 and see how they respond. You will be surprised to see how they will come up with a synergistic solution that will work. Now try the same with group 2 also. Reverse role play for your own suggestions is the key here.

Build logic into your arguments such as the amount of benefits in some sort of numbers. For example, DevOps when implemented will reduce the release process time from 4 hours to 10 minutes. Any number is good, but be sure you give the correct number, or accept that you are providing ballpark numbers. This is very important because if you give some high numbers that do not check out, your whole idea will be thrown out like a baby with the bathwater.

Once it is all done, now appeal how the best practices will bring benefits to everyone in the team, where you can go home early, don't have to log in to the slow build system that takes hours to see the log. Since you are implementing DevOps, you should be able to do it with little or no manual intervention.

Obviously, there's going to be debate throughout the process. As a leader, you tell them what is the next action step you are going to take and tell them what will be ready by next week or so. People start using the DevOps model and also start contributing to the automation of the build process. Don't leave the meeting or discussion without a next action plan. This step will make you implement things even if there is too much opposition and you know it is good for everyone.

Consistency is the King

Consistency is the best practice that you can follow from day 1, and it is also the best way to build applications that are easy to maintain. The learning curve always decreases if your code is consistent. Anyone can fix bugs in your system if your coding practices and patterns are consistent and follow proper standards.

Everything starts small. Remember you need to start somewhere, it is always best to start small and move forward, rather than thinking too big and not doing anything. Always see the whole picture but start small and then move forward.

Imitate the masters, you need to build on the shoulders of the legend, don't reinvent the wheel. Always follow the pattern that is already followed in the domain or in technology. Once you follow the standards that are widely adopted, this will very well help you to keep yourself consistent.

Have a well-focused plan, always make sure you sketch everything before you start working. Think how you can keep it consistent with what you have already built. If you are building new, then you need to imitate the masters and then follow the pattern throughout the project, starting from the project structure, coding standards, and design patterns to solving a particular problem.

Plan your documents and document your plan. You need to document the way a developer can start with the module in a project. As an architect, you take responsibility on creating style guides for CSS, coding standard for the programming language, folder structure document that defines naming conventions and folder placements. Design patterns used and the guide to implement them.

Do it even if you don't feel like it. Sometimes you feel very resistant to do something in a single pattern because it is boring. It looks like we are not being innovative. Innovation should be done after being consistent. We are not writing code to prove how smart we are; we are writing code so others can read and do some changes without resenting us when doing it. People should be happy to change our code because it is easy to read and change. That should be your motto for writing code.

Choose Thoroughly Tested Technology

Make sure you choose technology that is on the n-1 version. This means you have better support available for the version and most of the problems are ironed out already.

Some of the nuances will be addressed in the Stack Overflow and it tends to be a stable model for any project. Avoid choosing anything in the beta version for production workloads, it will sometimes bite you. Sometimes you need to choose beta version technology for production, but be extra careful.

It is always tempting to go with the beta version which has many features, but it is hardly the truth that it will work fine. I have burned my fingers lots of times. The best thing is to do a POC and keep watching the technology or package evolve. Once you know it has moved out of the beta version, you can jump in and start using the technology. That way you will be closely following your project with the latest technology.

Always make sure you choose the right version, and it should be updated in the config files on your application, which version you are using. Don't use the * or any parameter that just downloads the latest feature. It is very dangerous and will give you trouble at the wrong times.

When you have the option of choosing packages such as NuGet package or npm package, check the number of downloads, and issues list in GitHub, the last fixed issue, and also the number of downloads. Choose the one which has the latest and large number of downloads, and it tends to be more stable than the lesser downloaded packages.

Code Quality

Good quality code helps to project function better. Any good quality code makes the life of the developer easy to maintain and scale the project. Code quality is an important metric that measures the overall quality of the team. It is a direct measurement of people's skills, engagement, collaboration, and open communication. Code quality tells whether it is led by an eligible leader or by a mediocre non-techie guy.

Code quality is defined by how good your code can be based on key attributes such as Reliability, Maintainability, Testability, Portability, and Reusability. The higher the attribute, the higher the code quality.

No tool can measure code quality better than a good code review. If you are an architect you should be a good reviewer and you should set some ground rules for code review.

The basic five ground rules are:

- Developers cannot send more than 10 files for a code review. Reviewing more files in one review is humanly not possible. Keep it small and have smaller code reviews.
- There should be two reviewers for any code that should be checked in.
- Code should pass the static analyzer tester before it is assigned to the code reviewer and running the static analyzer should be automated.
- Code reviewers should be able to find the edge cases that the developer has missed in the code review. It should be thorough after understanding the requirement.
- Code review comments should be clear and concise. The aim is not to find fault, but to help each other to get better. You can even provide the link that helps the developer with any alternate approach you suggest.

There are multiple tools available in the market. FXCop, and SonarQube are widely used to measure code quality. Automate them in your build, and religiously solve the issues the tools present to you. Do not ignore them or overrule them. Remember warnings are the actual errors, and they will come and bite you at the wrong time.

Unit Testing

If the project got a good set of unit tests, it means the project has been done by very effective and efficient team members. The presence of the unit test tells about the quality of the team. As a developer, you should be writing unit testing without policing and monitoring.

Unit testing is a software testing method by which individual units of source code, sets of one or more computer program modules together with associated control data, usage procedures, and operating procedures, are tested to determine whether they are fit for use.

There are seven ground rules that need to be followed to have effective unit tests.

- You should have implemented any one Dependency framework in your project and used it in every place it is needed.
- Code coverage is not important, only feature coverage is important.
- Write unit tests first and then actual implementation, so you would have thought about all the dependency that is needed. Ironically, unit tests help us to identify the dependencies.
- If you are fixing a bug, write a unit test for that scenario and then fix the bug. This will help a lot in introducing or growing the unit test factor in the Brownfield project.
- If you are refactoring code, check whether a unit test is available, and if not available, write one with proper validation results and then refactor the code to avoid regression issues.
- Use the in-memory database, so your data is immutable and can be run multiple times without any state management problem.
- Reuse the sample data architecture you build for unit testing to integration tests also, so the code and architecture are consistent.

Performance Testing

This is one of the testing that is done after your application is gone live and it is neglected because of lots of reasons, one being the architect not asking proper questions to business stakeholders.

Performance testing is important because if your project is successful it should be able to handle the huge number of requests that come to your applications.

Your application should not become overloaded and start working. Performance is all about the speed at which your system responds. You should ask the right questions to stakeholders so you test them when the project is in a stage environment.

Performance testing is in general a testing practice performed to determine how a system performs in terms of responsiveness and stability under a particular workload. It can also serve to investigate, measure, validate, or verify other quality attributes of the system, such as scalability, reliability, and resource usage.

There are key points that should be considered for and during performance testing.

- You should talk to the customer about the performance metrics such as page load time, request response time, and document them during your design phase.
- Create a test case for performance testing when your testers are developing the test cases with the documented performance metrics.
- Test the performance testing once the build is deployed to stage. It should happen often and it is the responsibility of the architect to validate the design and also the test cases.
- Identify tools that are needed for load testing your application. For any exclusive use case create a tool or console application that can increase the load to test performance.
- Use tools like webpage test and chrome tools to test the performance metrics.
- Identify first the biggest bottleneck and fix that first, and then move to the next and fix it, and move then to the next. This is the best approach to fix performance problems.

Fitness Functions

Fitness functions protect the various architecture characteristics of the system. It helps in building evolvable architecture and system design. It helps us to compare the characteristics one over the other. Developers express fitness functions using different kinds of mechanisms such as tests or metrics.

An architectural fitness function provides an objective integrity assessment of some architectural characteristics. This concept is taken from the genetic algorithm design to define success. The fitness function defines sets of methods that validate the success of the design. For example, when you are using the RabbitMQ in your project for messaging operation, and when you want to move to Apache Kafka, then your fitness function measures the performances before and after the switchover. You run the same fitness function, which will help you to test the performance being the same, so when you evolve to different architecture you don't break the system.

It is good to identify fitness functions early in your project, so that you don't face the risks of wrong design choices that will waste lots of resources. Fitness functions can be classified into three simple categories.

- Key categories, e.g. the performance and security quality attributes for banking applications.
- Relevant categories, e.g. Code metrics around the quality of code.
- Not Relevant category. The number of bugs fixed per week, etc.

We have already discussed widely about the code quality, unit testing, and performance. All three are fitness functions that test the architecture changes so that your system can be built as evolutionary architecture rather than a reactionary architecture.

System-wide fitness functions allow architects to think about divergent concerns using the same unifying mechanism of fitness functions capturing and preserving the important architectural characteristics.

For example, the performance of a web page is supposed to respond within 2 seconds, but when the number of users is too high, the system can take a bit longer but not very long. This is where the system-wide fitness function tests the scalability fitness function and performance fitness function the overall behavior of the system.

How to Learn Best Practices

Learning best practices is easy and hard. As we discussed at the beginning of the chapter, your best practices are not always best, it depends on the situation.

As an architect, you should be able to take tradeoffs among your decisions and choose best practices that help you the most for the current situation. The best way to learn the best practices is to imitate, implement, and then innovate.

Start imitating the master; when you choose the technology, it comes with a set of best practices and implements them as said in their document.

Do not skip steps and try to finish the POC, most of the time we will waste time because we have skipped reading a few lines or missed some configurations because of overlooking.

Once you implement the POC, now you can flex change the application based on your needs. Follow the master completely and then innovate. The document you have chosen to do the POC is the master.

As a developer we do the opposite, we implement the best practices that we know from the other technology and then we are stuck as a whole. We tend to imitate the best practices for that particular technology. For example, best practices for implementing the normalization of data is one of the best practices in the SQL world.

We try to implement the same in the no-SQL world and when we are in trouble we will start following the no-SQL best practices.

Instead, you follow denormalization in the no-SQL databases first, implement it, and when you want a certain part of the application that needs normalization, you can move to normalization only for the feature of the application.

Update yourself on the key technology you are working on, subscribe to the podcast, Youtube channels and attend meetup that your key technologies are conducting, and even try to speak in any of your events.

You can learn a lot by teaching and answering the questions by the attendees which will give a different perspective of a problem.

There is no alternative to having hands-on. How much ever an architect you become, make sure you are always writing code and implementing some feature in your application. It is good to write frameworks for the project, set up a unit test library, data for unit testing, etc. It will help you to create a structure that consists of best practices and proper fitness function, so it will make the learning easier.

Look for problems that are hindering developer and business productivity and how you can make their life better. This will help your brain to automatically look for ways to do it better. This is the best way to learn any new things with respect to technology.

Talking to experts, always have a team of friends where you can talk about your practices and validate them. Have a network of people to describe, explain, and argue about a chosen practice which helps you to understand the nitty-gritty of your best practices. You will learn all its nuances by explaining it to people.

Design Tools

As an architect, you should have lots of tools to design in your own toolbox. You need to play around with different tools and find the hybrid version that is going to suit you the most. Any one tool will not be enough.

You should always sharpen your tools and be ready to change your tools if you find an effective tool to move up your design a notch. You should always take a middle ground between what works and shiny new things that promise many new advantages.

A good design tool will act as a guide when taking decisions and also helps us to validate the tradeoff. A good tool helps you design systems faster and also validate the design faster. The faster you fail in the design period and correct your assumptions better, you can save lots of time and money. A good tool will help you to measure your decisions and also gives you points to win over your stakeholders.

A Tool is an implement, used to carry out a particular function. A tool extends the ability of an individual to modify features of the surrounding environment.

A good tool is measured on three sets of attributes. They are:

- Performance
- Durability
- Value

Performance in design tools means the tools should perform better. It should address one main concern that is communicating the idea to the stakeholders. Remember different tools are needed by different stakeholders. When you talk to the business owners, you should talk in terms of how much you can save in terms of money and resources on a particular design, and in the same way, when you are talking to developers you should talk about the same problem and solution in terms of ease of implementation. Any tools should perform better based on the stakeholders.

Durability in terms of design tools means the ability to withstand change. Any tool that cannot adapt to change cannot survive the environment. Every tool cannot be a Swiss army knife. But tools that can embrace the change will help us to change the design and our scaling changes faster.

Value is the main criteria; if the tool is not doing what it is supposed to do, then there is no point in using it. Nowadays with the Agile methodology, most of the design activities are either done as just for namesake, or no design tools are used. There is a reason for the design phase and it has been widely neglected and we face anti-patterns that we discussed in the previous chapter.

There are common principles behind tools and tools must enforce some practices. A tool must always force these four principles, which are

- Brainstorming
- Showing Vs. Telling
- Listening and Inclusion
- Sustainability

Your tools should encourage and facilitate brainstorming. People should be able to voice their opinion and the tools must be conducive to record and reiterate their opinions. The tools we will see in this chapter are based on this one main principle.

Showing vs. Telling helps in communicating your ideas to a wider audience with less effort. Any visual cues to explain the problem will go longer than a long paragraph of text. Represent your solutions or challenges as any visual cues, so people can understand and remember better.

Listening and inclusion is one of the high leverage activities when designing or explaining your architecture/solution, which most architects lack a lot.

Architects think the less experienced people do not get it, so they try to force the solution on them. This is a bad strategy. All you need to do is explain first and then ask them how much they understand and explain again. Remember it takes at least three to five times of explanation for any medium to large size solution to be understood.

Sustainability is an important part of the tool that helps to scale and move faster. You need to be able to build a design that is flexible to changes and lets us even start from ground zero. Any tool that allows this approach is the right one, and one of the main criteria to handle changes faster, which is the unchanging thing in our software industry.

In the book '*Design It*' by Micheal Keeling, you will be able to learn more tools, but I have chosen nine practical Tools that can be used every day. If you need more, please refer to the book. You will learn nine Tools in this chapter and they are categorized into four categories,

- Functional Requirement
- Explore Solutions
- Design Tools
- Evaluate Design Tools

All Images are in hand drawing are on purpose to denote the creation of documentation on brainstorming

Let us consider the order example.

Consider building a pet shop online where you will be selling pets. Even though you will be learning the first two tools to gather requirements, the image below does show the architecture a little bit. We have UI, API, and database. Orders are placed asynchronously and products are displayed in the UI by directly calling the API.

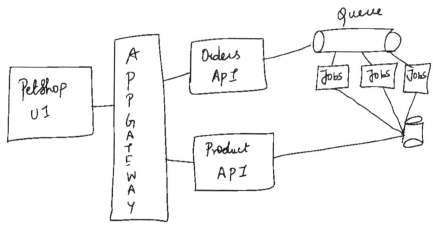

* Whiteboarding image to denote brainstorming exercise

Functional Requirements Phase Tools

This phase helps to identify functional requirements and also helps in getting the communication flow between different stakeholders, so the project can lead to success. When the different stakeholders find a smooth communication path, then the percentage of the success of the project increases tremendously.

Functional requirements tools are used in the initial phases of requirement gathering and the tools that we have chosen make this exercise great fun and effective. These tools will help not only to build requirements, but they will also help the developers and architects to better understand the business needs.

A good functional tool should be able to well define the problem, identify concerns such as constraints, quality attributes, Functional requirements, and other influencers such as time, cost, availability of knowledge, etc.

Goal Questions Metrics Workshop

This is the workshop which when handled properly will not only define the requirement, but also help the stakeholders understand the requirement. It is a straightforward workshop, define a goal, let stakeholders ask questions about the goal, and define metrics to measure the completion of the goal.

Benefits
- Measure Goals
- Flexible approach

Stakeholders
- All stakeholder(s) can participate
- Two to five max., one from each level

Preparation and Materials
- Whiteboard
- Goals that need to be discussed.

Steps
- Write the goal far left of the whiteboard
- Prompt participants to provide questions
- Identify the metrics needed to answer the question and answer them

GGN Work Shop

Goals	Questions	Answers
Build a System for selling Pets	Can Customer have a Profile?	Yes, User should have a Profile
	Can user buy also Pet products?	No, Initial Mvp only for Pets
	How will user pay?	Use Payment gateway, COD also should be available
	What reports should be Created?	Sales/Forecast reports needed
	Is order asynchronous/Synchronous?	Orders can be asynchronous Process, user Can be notified about progress
	Where Can I get Product data	Data warehouse team will expose an API

*Whiteboarding image to denote brainstorming exercise

Goal: Build a System for selling pets.

This goal provokes questions among the team. We can start with normal questions that are available in all web applications and slowly move to domain-specific questions. In the above image, there is a transition between common questions to domain-specific questions

Exercise: Create a GQM for the application that should replicate all functionality like the Instagram photo app.

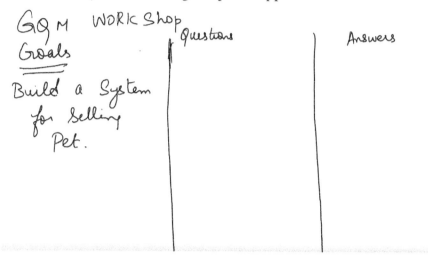

Quality Attribute Web

This exercise helps to create quality attributes, i.e. non-functional requirements. The last exercise helps to build the functional requirement and this will help you to build the non-functional requirement almost out of thin air. It is one of the interesting and fun exercises where people showcase their technical expertise, and coming out of this exercise people will feel more accomplished and feel good about themselves.

Quality attributes are all non-functional requirements. They include attributes such as Security, Maintainability, Testability, Reusability, Availability, Performance, Reliability, Scalability, Cost, etc.

Benefits
- Guide all stakeholders to think of quality attributes instead of features
- Flexible approach

Stakeholders

- All stakeholder(s) can participate
- Two to five max, one from each level

Preparation and Materials

- Whiteboard and sticky notes
- Quality attributes that should be discussed.

Steps

- Write all the quality attributes as a spider web on the board with sticky notes
- Brainstorm concerns
- Classify and write the concerns in the appropriate place

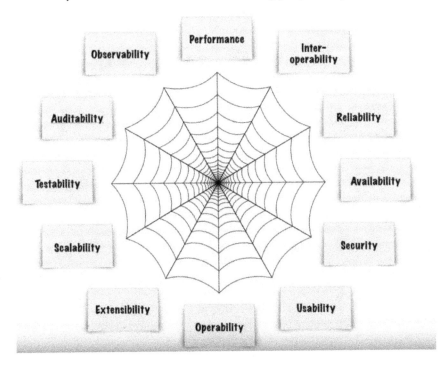

Choose not more than four to six attributes and you can do this quality attribute exercise, and as an architect, you should choose the quality attribute based on the stages of the project. It is always best to choose the observability, reliability, scalability, and security questions in the initial stages of the project.

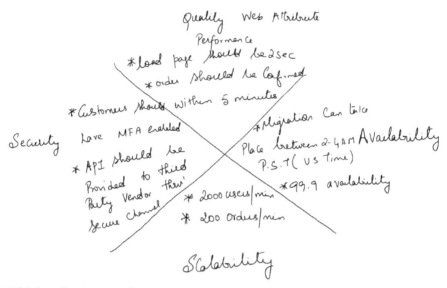

* Whiteboarding image to denote brainstorming exercise

Exercise: Create a Quality web attribute for the application that should replicate all functionality like the Instagram photo app. Just add only details for security, performance, availability, and scalability.

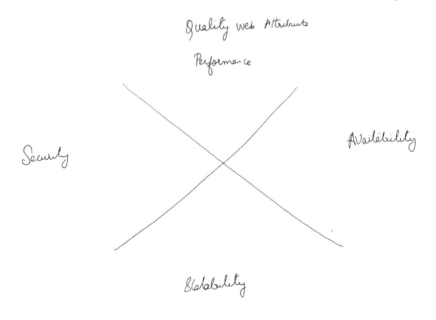

Explore Solutions Phase Tools

This phase helps to explore the underlying solutions for the problem defined and understood in the above phase. This phase helps to deep dive into the problem with the solutions in hand and remove the bias and fallacy that might occur due to the limitation of the knowledge of the architect.

As an architect, we are only limited to the solution with our existing knowledge. We can only discover solutions, we cannot invent any solution. This exercise helps you to get the solution and problem cycle, so you can understand more about the problem with the existing solution in your mind. In the case of a pet shop, you will only think in terms of SQL, if you don't have knowledge of no-SQL, and if you have just learned the no-SQL and are burning inside, you might try to solve the problem with no-SQL options.

As we were discussing in all the previous chapters, make sure you play devil's advocate and don't fall into any anti-pattern. Anything that is fancy and cool might be overkill. So you need to weigh the balance and choose the solution that is simple and fits almost exactly in solving the problem. Rarely any solutions or technology will fit the problem exactly.

There might be some tapes and bandages and not too much. Those bandages should be removable in a change of technology or newer versions of technology.

There are four ways you can understand the problem and reiterate the solutions that fit your design and implementation decisions.

- Identify multiple design concepts and engineering approaches.
- Understand the domain concepts.
- Identify solutions.
- Redefine the problem and reiterate.

These tools will help you to identify the solutions from your knowledge of solutions, and understand the problem better and also stretch your knowledge a little bit more than when you started.

Remember you cannot learn anything completely new, you can only learn by comparing and stretch from what you last learned.

Class Responsibility Collaborator (CRC) Cards

This tool helps you to reiterate through your design alternatives. It also helps you discuss the gaps in your solution and also to sell your design ideas to the group. This exercise is the extension of the Class Responsibility Collaborator by Kent Beck and Ward Cunningham.

I highly recommend you to check out the '*Design it*' book by Micheal Keeling to learn more about this tool.

Benefits
- Quickly iterate through design alternatives
- Create group buy-in and Identify potential Gaps in architecture

Stakeholders
- Development team
- Two to five people max

Preparation and Materials
- Index cards and markers
- Components that need to be discussed

Steps
- Introduce the goals
- Read the functional requirement

    Identify the component name, its responsibilities, and collaborators

CRC Card

* Whiteboarding image to denote brainstorming exercise

In the above example, we have a product, order, Cart service class taken as an example. Now we have added the responsibilities for each and every service and its corresponding collaborator. The order needs to work with the product class to reduce the available product count, so the product class is a collaborator for Order. And in the same way Cart service has the order and product and order as collaborators. Responsibilities are self-explanatory.

Exercise: Create a CRC Card for the Instagram photo app. Identify three classes, their responsibilities, and their collaborators.

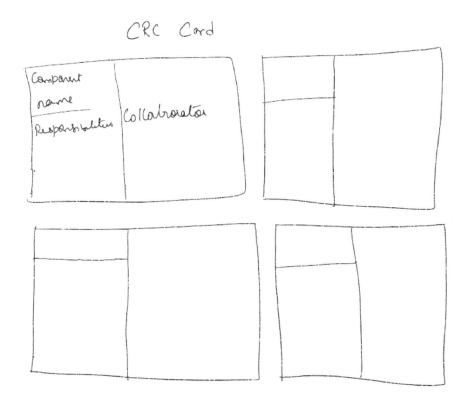

Event Storming

This exercise helps in visualizing the events that occur in your current project. This is a new way of approaching design. There used to be a time when we used to design based on use cases, then came the domain-driven design, and finally, it is now event-driven design. No design model is good or bad because any design is better than no design, evolving your design is key.

This approach helps you to visualize the given problem at hand and dig deeper. The main advantage of this workshop exercise is that it helps you find edge cases. Since it involves the domain experts, you will even get the NFR edge cases into the limelight.

Benefits
- Visualize learning opportunities
- Identify assumptions and edge cases

Stakeholders

- The development team and Domain expert
- Two to five People max

Preparation and Materials

- Index cards and markers
- Events and processes that need to be discussed

Steps

- Create an event map and assign a color for each event
- Place the events in order
- Review events and iterate

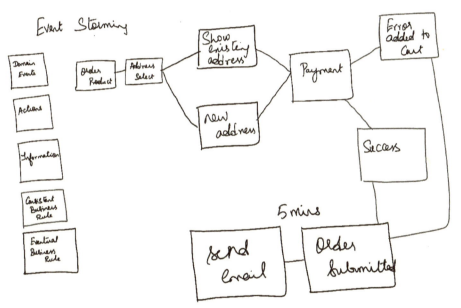

*Whiteboarding image to denote brainstorming exercise

Event storming consists of identifying five major components.

- Domain Events
- Actions
- Information

- Consistent business Rules
- Eventual Business Rules.

In the event storming exercise we have given different colors for different events, red for Domain-based events, e.g. order a product, actions are in orange, which means the selecting the address by the user, and information is given in green, the information displayed to the user, like suggesting address. Business rules are given in red to denote the validation rules for the actions, and Pink for eventual business Rules such as sending an email on unavailability or order availability, etc.

Exercise: Create a CRC Card for the Instagram photo app. Identify all the storming events, take the event of a user liking a photo, and how internally the event gets triggered in the Instagram app and the API.

Event Storming– instagram Photo app

Design or Make

The next phase is the design or make phase where we dive deep into the actual work. This phase helps us to get our act together and start working on artifacts generation or any work that starts the work of artification generation. Software artifacts include use cases, class diagrams, UML models, and design documents.

This phase helps to record decisions and communicate the same to other stakeholders. This phase will mostly be an architect's contribution where architects should create artifacts using tools.

Architecture haiku

This tool helps in recording the overall solutions. This tool will help in prioritizing the non-functional requirements, and the rationale behind design decisions. Record also the technical constraints that might hinder the project progress and how we can overcome them. Keep it as brief as possible. It has to be completed in one single page, so keep it crisp, simple, and clear.

Benefits
- Think through the essential parts of the architecture
- The frame of reference for other documentation

Stakeholders
- Architects mostly

Preparation and Materials
- Use a single piece of paper

Steps
- Identify business goals and important quality attributes
- Identify architecture pattern used
- Record key decisions and their rationale

We will consider the same pet shop system where the business goals are written on one side of the page and key decisions and rationale on the other side. In the sample exercise, you can give the rationale behind the decisions and record the decision.

We have also recorded the constraint behind our key decisions. Also, we have identified the top quality attributes and architectural patterns as well as the rationale behind the decisions.

Architecture HAIKU

Business Goals	Key decisions and Rationale
* Build system to sell Pets Online * Cut the sales Cost upto 30 - 40 %	* Cloud Provider - Azure * Serverless architecture to save Cost * Use Open Source Technologies such as .net Core, angular etc * Azure cheaper than Aws/GCP
Top Quality attributes Security → Availability → Performance Architectural Patterns REST & SOA	* AD B2C for Security * Kubernetes facilitates Canary deployment for better availability * Use REST, Graph-QL, GRPC for better protocol Consumption

* Whiteboarding image to denote brainstorming exercise

Exercise: Create an Architecture Haiku for the Instagram photo app. Identify all Business goals and key decisions and constraints.

Modular decomposition Diagram

This tool helps in getting your work into implementation. This tool is one step closer to the implementation phase and it is one of the interesting and challenging exercises to perform. It needs concentration and focus. If you can finish this exercise, this tool will build less coupling and high coherence in the project.

You can save lots of night outs if you do this exercise. Remember to always be ready to ditch this decomposition diagram and move to a different diagram, if you feel your understanding has changed.

Benefits
- Maps refinement in architecture
- Reduces complexity and prompt system thinking in architecture

Stakeholders
- Mostly Architects

Preparation and Materials
- Use a single piece of paper

- Add paper if you want to add details to the larger diagrams, breaking them into more modular.

Steps
- Draw a tree, parent nodes is your project
- Identify leaf nodes
- Make sure leaf nodes are not connected directly with other leaf nodes

This tool helps to identify and break down the pet shop app into multiple modular components of UI, API, Jobs, and more components in each component. Add modules to the leaf of the tree and keep moving forward.

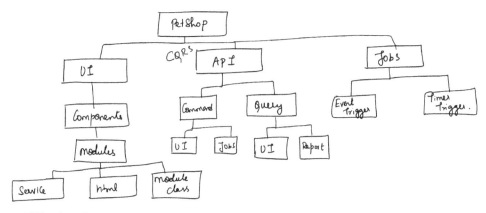

*Whiteboarding image to denote brainstorming exercise

Exercise: Create a Modular decomposition diagram for the Instagram photo app. Add a child to the Instagram app as UI, API, and jobs and add more details to the tree, till you can further modularize.

Instagram App

Validate Design

The last phase of the design is evaluating the created design. This phase tool helps us to check whether our design is implemented correctly or if there are any violations. If there are violations, how can we prevent them, and also how to mitigate them, so it does not spoil the overall architecture. This phase is a recurring phase.

Our design will not be 100 % right and developers will be changing design due to requirements or a better understanding of requirements. This flexibility is a must and it will help the developer to own the design and make sure he is part of the problem-solving.

There are multiple ways to validate your design. We will look into only three of the major tools.

Code Review

This is one of the high leverage activities in which you should train your whole team. Code review helps you to get quality into your project and team without any problem. Code review is one of the important activities that has been neglected sometimes because of high pressure. If you really want to make your project very successful, then code review helps you get there.

If you want to sum up two things that you can follow right away, don't check in any code without any review, even if the code is written by you. Just knowing that someone will review your code will let you do things right and not take shortcuts when solving the problem. You will research and write the right code for the bug fix or a module.

Second, the fastest way to train your team is to have two code reviewers for any code review. You can be the default code reviewer, and make sure you check how the other code reviewer has reviewed. This will bring a sense of authority in looking over code changes which will automatically make the code better and better on every code review.

Benefits
- Understand the developer's understanding of architecture

- Creates a teachable moment
- Allow developers to choose their way still not losing the connection with architecture
- Identify style issues
- Good code review can catch bugs and edge cases

Stakeholders

- Developer peers, architects, always more than one person
  Preparation and Materials
- Use proper code review tools available in most of the Git repos such as GitHub, Bamboo, and Azure DevOps. Use them wisely.

Steps

Your code review should check for these four parts in every code review.

- Correctness
  - Are there any violation of patterns
- Consistency
  - Check using Static analyzers such as FxCop, SonarQube, CodeRush
- Testability
  - Unit test available, especially for edge cases. Proper bootstrapping of testing data.
- Modifiability/Maintainability

Decision Matrix

Recording design alternatives is one of the activities that we miss when we design or implement our application. A new joinee, or new senior architect, or even CTO comes to our project and asks a few questions about the justification behind technology choices. We will not be able to answer, because we cannot hold everything in memory.

Recording this decision making is very important because you never know how things will change and your ass will be handed to you in a meeting if you don't record these. As absent-minded as we are, we tend to forget things, and the decision matrix is one of the simplest ways to record decisions that can be used at any point of time and makes us look like great architects.

Benefits
- Used to compare a variety of decisions
- Visualize relative strengths
- Facilitate open discussions about tradeoffs with stakeholders

Stakeholders
- The architect prepares and other stakeholders review
- Preparation and Materials
- Proper documentation format in the architecture document

Steps
- Identify evaluation factors
- Explain the scoring method (rubric).
- Fill the matrix
- Share and discuss with stakeholders

This tool is to create a simple matrix that represents the decision recording process. It is just adding the ranking of the particular decisions. You can have a legend, it can be simple +, – and zero denoting neutral.

Decision Matrix

	Queue	Service Bus	Event Grid	Legend
Availability	O	O	+	0 - neutral
Performance	–	–	+	⊕ - Positive
Security	–	+	+	⊖ - negative
Scalability	+	+	++	
Maintainab-lity	+	–	++	
Buildability	+++	–	– (new technology)	

* Whiteboarding image to denote brainstorming exercise

The example explains the three asynchronous technologies that we can use in the pet store and how we thought about each quality attribute and we ranked them accordingly. You can add details about the technology you choose and why you rejected the other technologies in a couple of lines to document your thought process.

Exercise: Create a Decision matrix diagram for the Instagram photo app. Choose any three technologies that you want to compare and decide on. Don't worry about even the validity of the decision; this process is just giving you the discipline of documenting your decision in the easiest way, so you don't have to go through the pain of explaining or forget the explanation of the decision making process. This exercise will remove the complaints of no documentation available about your architecture or your module.

Decision Matrix

Availability			
Performance			
Security			
Scalability			
Maintainab- -ity			
Buildability			

Legend
0 - neutral
⊕ - Positive
⊖ - negative

Risk Storming

This tool is used to identify the risks in your architecture. It helps you to find the problems in your design in the early part of your development cycle, which not only reduces cost but also reduces the overall stress for every developer, because with the bad design, you might end up burning the midnight oil.

Bring all the decisions to the table and have an open mind while discussing the risks involved. Use the brainstorming rules which we discussed in the previous sections, to be non-judgmental and non-justifying your decisions in design when people raise their concern over a certain design or certain technology usage. Be open and let them write on the board or sticky notes and bring their own views and ideas of risks into the limelight.

Your job should be to just choose the next topic when the current topic has exhausted the risks involved.

Benefits
- Quickly identify the risks in the proposed architecture

- Constraint risk identification
- The platform for all team members to elevate the concern and decide the right path

Stakeholders
- Three to five Developers
- Preparation and Materials
- Whiteboard, Sticky notes, and markers

Steps
- Sketch relevant views that are part of the discussion
- Brainstorm risks
- Assign risks to each view
- Prioritize and discuss the identified risks
- Develop mitigation strategies

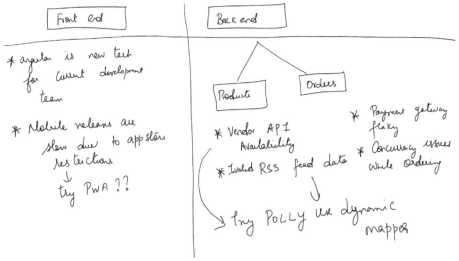

*Whiteboarding image to denote brainstorming exercise

In the above example, we discuss the front and backend technologies that have risks involved such as the new technology, not much knowledge from the developer, and how to mitigate the risk by alternate decisions.

Exercise: Create a Risk Storm diagram for the Instagram photo app. Discuss the risk involved in the app design choice. For the front end, the app has to work in a mobile, desktop browser, and also as a PWA. Choose any technology that you can use to build your app on all types of devices. Write the technology and write the risk of choosing the technology.

For the backend, choose technology like C#, Node js, or Java, and discuss the multiple packages you might have to use inside the Instagram app like messaging, performance, monitoring, and what are all the risks with respect to the packages or the design choices.

Risk   Storming

```
┌──────────────────┐        ┌──────────────────┐
│   Front end      │        │   Backend        │
└──────────────────┘        └──────────────────┘
```

All the tools discussed are the tip of the iceberg; explore more tools from 'Design it'. But make the tools discussed as second nature and try them small first and build a mental map of how you can use these tools and who all can be a better partner for brainstorming.

Discuss with the team. Start very small, and once you get hold of the tool, you can use it extensively. Remember, brainstorming is the underlying principle and how you use the tool or what tools you use does not matter much, every tool must make you and the team members communicate more among yourselves.

The next main underlying reason to use multiple tools is to make the understanding of the domain and technical problem better by all stakeholders. Developers and businesses should be in the thought process and you should act as a bridge in building the communication platform between them, so the project will be successful.

Your tool should find the issues sooner rather than later. Collaborate often and use the same tool many times. Remember all we need is to let the communication flow between team members and the success of the project will be inevitable. So start using the tools one by one.

Documentation

When I started to search for techniques and tips for becoming an architect, I stumbled on documentation. I learned from multiple sources that an architect creates the architecture document, and when I read some of the documents it never made sense.

All I inferred is how dumb I was, not to understand the diagrams and concepts explained. But I was not alone, except the architect, no one really understood well or completely. Then I thought I am in a group of dumb people, maybe there is a set of people who are really smart, and I can never get there.

Then I started to read about all the ways about documentation and building software architecture. Most of the books are only academic, which meant nothing but a bunch of definitions and vague examples that have no implication in the real world.

This chapter is to address the problem of documentation. None of the methods are invented by me, but I have done multiple workshops on documentation and everyone felt better and good at writing architecture documents at the end of the workshops.

Documentation is one of the activities every architect avoids or is not very happy about it. The real reason behind documentation being hard is only one thing. We are trying to satisfy all the stakeholders at the same time. Documenting for all the stakeholders in a single document such as Business analyst, developer, CXO, and operation/support team will go nowhere. It will only sit in the sharepoint or file repository and nobody wants to update or modify it.

I have gone through the same journey, where I am either stuck or procrastinating the document writing, because trying to address all stakeholders in one diagram and one paragraph is really hard and not at all useful.

After lots of research, I figured out that you cannot build any one section that can cover all stakeholders. This was like a revelation for me. It is also justified in real time because any document maintained by the corresponding team or stakeholders seems to be more useful than the huge architecture document which is referenced in every meeting.

When I got hold of the book '*Software Systems Architecture: Working with Stakeholders Using Viewpoints and Perspectives*' by Nick Rozanski and Eoin Woods, I understood I had got all the documentation wrong.

The things I mainly learned from this book are that documentation is all about recording important decisions. It should be the only place where people can go and refer and use, it need not be one document. It should be updatable at any point of time and by anyone. The tool you use for documentation should be easy and extensible.

The domain concepts and boundaries for any section should be clear and should be defined properly. Every section should address only one concept and it should be clear.

Mindsets of Documentation

In a document everything will change, even the whole document structure, so be ready to change it. If you are adding images into the document, those images should be easily changed and added back again easily. Add revision number to the document and also enable revision properties that are available in the document repo like Google docs, etc.

The document is not to show how smart you are. We think if we write very simple documents and everybody understands them, they will figure out we are imposters. Please keep that insecurity aside when writing documents.

Keeping it simple takes more brain than keeping it hard. So leave yourself out of the equation and remember you are validated in the long term, and short term validation is immaterial. They might not think you are smart when you show a document that is easy to read and understand.

But on the next project, they will ask you to share your template so their team can write a better document like yours. That's where you shine. Documentation is delayed gratification, where you might not get a name or fame for writing an understandable document.

Over Architecting is one of the major problems of architecture documents. We think if it doesn't include everything that is even a little relevant to the requirement, it might not look like a good architecture document. Get that out of your mindset.

The document should have only details which you are going to implement and maybe a little more. For example, if you are not going to use the queue mechanism for your transaction and will currently use only API based transaction, skip documentation of the queue mechanism. You can draw diagrams and record your decisions on API whether it is REST or GraphQL. But leave a note, that if scaling becomes a concern, we need to move to a QUEUE mechanism.

Leaving a note is a very important record because it will convey to the stakeholders that you have actually thought through and you have taken the decision with the right data in hand. You can also use the decision matrix here, so you can convey, the decision was conscious and not an ignorant one.

Principles of Architecture Document

Seven principles govern the principles of architecture. These seven principles are the ones I have used and helped me in getting my life better. As we discussed in almost all the chapters, principles will help you to make decisions in challenging and ambiguous times.

Addressing Stakeholder Concerns:

This is one of the main principles we always violate. We write architecture or design architecture to look smart or brainy in the eyes of others or look shiny in our resume. They call it resume driven design. You don't write documents for yourself, it is for others. So addressing stakeholders' concerns and understanding them takes the first priority.

Effective Communication (KISS)

Keep it simple and simpler. Your document should be very plain English and the respective stakeholders should understand their section without any hassle. Talk in diagrams, add a legend to the diagram, add numbers to the flow of sequence, and explain each number. Stakeholders should be able to get what you are trying to convey.

One diagram or one paragraph or one section should convey a message to one type of stakeholders like developers, or architects, or Business analysts. Don't combine any section or diagram or paragraph to address different types of stakeholders at once.

Structured and Fluid

Always use structured documentation, which is also fluid. Structure to maintain the way the communication is flowing, and fluid to make changes easily. You can use the template we used in this chapter or find your own. First, start with some good structure and start finding the friction that is available in the template which is voiding the structure and fluidity.

Change the template according to your needs or preference later. Keep in mind your architecture documentation should be used by other architects one day.

Pragmatic Concerns

Practical approaches and real-time scenarios make the documentation fun and easy to understand. You should always come from the places where you can explain the new technology that is analogous to the existing one and how they are the same and yet different from one another. This helps in making the document more pragmatic and easy to understand. Real-time usage in other projects such as Netflix and Amazon or Google will help people to investigate more about the decisions. Always great architects use already tested strategy and technology. Leave the innovation of new strategy to companies like Thoughtworks, Google, and Amazon. Copy and improve the documentation and don't shy away from pointing out the source your architecture is influenced from.

Viewpoints and Perspectives

Viewpoints and perspectives give you a method to identify all the missed requirements and also to have a corresponding artifact which is a diagram or a document that represents both functional and non-functional requirements. It helps you to identify the main functional elements, how they interact with each other, software, hardware, needed operation, and environment for the successful running of our application.

ViewPoints

Definition: A *view* is a representation of one or more structural aspects of an architecture that illustrates how the architecture addresses one or more concerns held by one or more of its stakeholders.

Perspectives

Definition. An architectural perspective is a collection of activities, tactics, and guidelines that are used to ensure that a system exhibits a particular set of related quality properties that require consideration across a number of the system's architectural views.

In this chapter, we see how you can leverage viewpoints and perspectives to create documents that can convey information to different stakeholders and also keep records of our technical and non-technical decisions. This document can also be used to communicate and educate new joiners into our team and act as a reference point when we are explaining the architecture of the project.

Viewpoints help us to address the concerns of every stakeholder through different models. Concerns are nothing but a requirement, an objective, or an intention for the architecture. Models are abstraction aspects of architecture. For example, from a functional viewpoint, external interfaces are a concern, and box diagrams are models. We will look into details with every viewpoint in detail.

There are seven types of viewpoints.

- Context
- Functional
- Information
- Concurrency
- Development
- Deployment
- Operational

We will consider the same pet shop example we used in the design tools chapter. We are trying to document the pet shop online application using the viewpoints. We will skip the context viewpoint for the sake of brevity.

Functional Viewpoints

This is the first viewpoint that captures the function requirements at a very high level and you can use this viewpoint to understand the system. It is one of the viewpoints very tough to design but once a model is created it is simple to explain the functionality.

Definition: Describes the system's runtime functional elements and their responsibilities, interfaces, and primary interactions.

Addressed Concerns: The main concerns that are handled in the viewpoint are

- Functional capabilities
- External interfaces
- Internal structure

Addressed Model: functional structure model contains the following elements

- Functional Elements
- Interfaces
- Connectors
- External Entities

Functional Elements are the ones that address the responsibility that is taken care of by the part of the system. In the diagram, product catalog, Order and order processor and order fulfillment are functional elements that address the system.

Interfaces. An interface is a well-defined mechanism by which the functions of an element can be accessed by other elements. E.g. The database can be accessed by the system through API.

External Entities represent other systems, software programs, and hardware devices that your system communicates with. In the pet shop example, for orders, the payment gateway will be an external vendor.

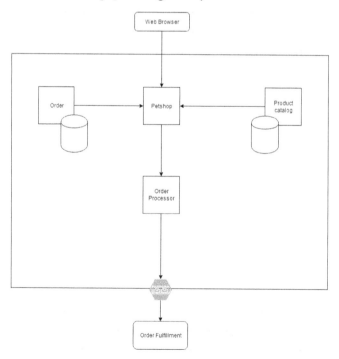

Exercise: Create a Box and lines diagram for the Instagram photo app. Find the functional elements, interfaces, and external entities. For starters, the Photo process that resizes and applies filters is one functional element and you can name it Image Processor.

In the viewpoint, we will handle three different models to represent the viewpoint. As the first step, the table identifies the elements and their responsibilities.

Elements	Responsibilities
Login System	Login should be validated and the admin should be able to view the add-products page. Customer should be able to access the order page
Pets Catalog	The system should allow pets and also search for pets based on roles
Orders System	Orders system should allow users to order a product and also track the progress of the delivery
Mail System	The system should be able to send emails to customers whenever there is a status change in their orders. The system should email the admin if there is a product count that goes down a threshold inventory quantity

Exercise: Fill the below table, with the identified elements and their responsibilities for the Instagram photo app.

Elements	Responsibilities

Identify Interfaces

Develop interfaces using the design by contract approach. This table is self-explanatory and you can just skim to understand better. The identified interfaces add pre/post conditions to the elements, their side effects, and protocol that is exposed as an interface by the elements.

Elements	Precondition	Postcondition	Side effect	Protocol interface
Login System	The user will be unauthenticated, he needs to provide login credentials	Authenticated users will be able to access the orders and products based on their roles	NA	Web API
Pets Catalog	User should be authenticated	Customers can view the product. Admin can add pets	NA	Web API
Order	Users should be authenticated	Orders should be added to the system	The product should be reduced to the number of products ordered	Messaging queue
Mail	The order should be placed or status is changed	Mail sent status updated	NA	Messaging queue

Exercise: Fill the below table, with the identified Interfaces for the Instagram photo app.

Elements	Precondition	Postcondition	Side effect	Protocol interface

Identify External Entities

This table lists out all the external systems such as hardware and software programs that the current system will interact with.

Elements	External Entity
Login System	Azure AD B2C or Auth0
Pets catalog	NA
Order	Paypal, Payment Gateway
Mail	Sendgrid

Exercise: Fill the below table, with the identified Interfaces for the Instagram photo app.

Elements	External Entity

Information Viewpoint

It drives the shape of other system structures such as the information structure, concurrency structure, and deployment structure. Basically, everything you do with a database or any storage. This viewpoint helps to identify data-related activity that pertains to the requirement. This is almost like designing the database design and recording it. If you are good with database design, this viewpoint will be very easy to understand.

Definition: Information viewpoint describes the way that the system stores, manipulates, manages, and distributes information.

Stakeholders: Primarily users, acquirers, developers, testers, and maintainers, but most stakeholders have some level of interest.

Static data structure models

It defines the static structure of the data. It uses the entity-relationship modeling technique to represent its models. To identify the relationships, cardinality, and attributes in this exercise, we have designed the user, product, orders, and shipment.

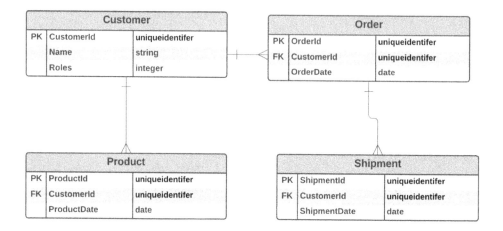

Exercise: Identify the tables that will be needed for the Instagram photo app and also their respective columns.

Information life cycle models

These models analyze the way the data values change over time, this example shows how the product is searched and checked out and also the searching functionality.

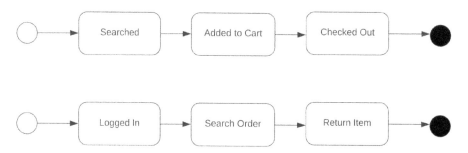

Exercise: Identify the two lifecycles in Instagram photo apps and draw how the flow of data happens, for example, what happens when the user wants to upload a photo and also what happens when someone likes a photo/video.

Concurrency Viewpoint (Exercise Skipped)

Describes the concurrency structure of the system, mapping functional elements to concurrency units to clearly identify the parts of the system that can execute concurrently, and shows how this is coordinated and controlled. Due to the Cloud and other technology innovations, this can be skipped.

Stakeholders: Communicators, developers, testers, and some administrators.

Processes

Process group

Threads

Inter-process communication

Development Viewpoint (Exercise Skipped)

This is where you identify your technologies, modules, and how they talk to each other. You can denote multiple ways to represent this model. This will be mostly used by the developer and you would have had a pretty decent idea on how to design this section, so I am skipping this on purpose.

Identify and classify the modules

Identify the module dependencies

Identify the layering Rules – Can modules call other modules or they can call modules in their own layer

Deployment Viewpoint (Exercise Skipped)

Design the Network

Estimate the capacity

Operational Viewpoint

Do not skip this viewpoint. As an architect, this will help you distinguish yourself from a mediocre architect to a great architect. This article is consciously and intentionally kept long for you to identify every parameter and design accordingly. Otherwise, you will build a product that will not give a good name, because during the release time you will face lots of issues which you will be blamed for.

Definition: Describes how the system will be operated, administered, and supported when it is running in its production environment.

Stakeholders: System administrators, production engineers, developers, testers, communicators, and assessors.

This example explains the operational viewpoint that needs to be identified for the pet shop application.

Identify the installation groups

Identify users who will be affected by this system or module or project.

Web User:

Phase I will have only search functionality available for products and the user will be ordering the product by calling the customer support team.

Phase II will have both search and checkout facilities, but we should still be able to order products through support calls for three months after Phase II is rolled out.

Customer Support:

Phase I will be able to search for pets. So we need to make sure the customer support team is trained in helping the customer to buy pets that they have searched for online.

Phase II will have both search and checkout of products; customer support should have been trained on the system.

Cloud Administrator:

Cloud administrators should be available round the clock, so administrators should be working in shifts.

IT Administrator:

The current IT administrator should be phased out after Phase II because all our applications will be moved to the Cloud. Proper training should be given to IT administrators so they learn Cloud-native administration with the newly recruited Cloud administrators.

Backup Strategy

We need to enable backup in the SQL and Cosmos DB. We should take a physical copy and store it in our on-premise server. Database encryption should be enabled to safeguard our on-premise backup.

Configuration Management

Configuration Groups

DBMS Parameters will only be saved in the Key vault and the connection string will not be saved in any source control.

Web Parameters can be saved in application settings in azure. There should be no deployment changes for the parameter. We should use Build once deploy everywhere strategy.

Migration Plan

Pets database will be first migrated in Phase I and orders database will be migrated in Phase II. Only the past 12 months of orders data will be migrated to the new system as confirmed with business owners.

Support strategy

The customer support team will be taking calls during office hours from 8:00 AM to 6:00 PM. For non-business hours we will have our Chatbot enabled and it will answer the FAQ questions, and other questions will be created as a ticket where the customer support person can come with the reply the next day.

All SLA of support tickets will be as per the company standards.

Exercise: Fill in all the areas that are left blank for Instagram photo apps. This will give you a good exercise on thinking through the complete process of building a highly scalable application.

Identify the installation groups

Web User:

_____

_____

_____

_____

Customer Support:

_____

_____

_____

_____

Cloud Administrator:

_____

_____

_____

_____

IT Administrator:

_____

_____

_____

Backup Strategy

_____

_____

_____

_____

Configuration Management

_____

_____

_____

_____

Configuration Groups

_____

_____

_____

_____

Migration Plan

_____

_____

_____

_____

Support strategy

_____

_____

_____

_____

Perspective or ities or NFR's

_____

_____

_____

This is a highly fun-filled activity and once you get the hang of it, this activity will help you to go to the office with a *josh* of facing challenges with your full swing. I really love solving non-functional requirements because it is a place that will help you to implement all that you learned, starting from implementing a new language feature that improves the performance to changing the whole architecture to improve performance.

Handling perspectives helps me to keep myself on my toes and also learn a lot of technology which will help my technology to actually grow. This is the place you need to talk to your stakeholder and have a thorough understanding of the system and the amount of money they are willing to spend.

An architectural perspective is a collection of activities, tactics, and guidelines that are used to ensure that a system exhibits a particular set of related quality properties that require consideration across a number of the system's architectural views. E.g. Performance, scalability, usability, reliability, availability, etc.

Performance and scalability

The ability of the system to predictably execute within its mandated performance profile and to handle increased processing volumes. We have used only two perspectives to keep it simple and focused, but you can use the same tabular column for other perspectives also.

Concerns	Orders	Products
Throughput	10 Concurrent orders should be processed in 5 seconds. 500 Concurrent orders should be processed in 20 seconds	10000 Concurrent users should be able to search for products in 2 seconds. 100000 Concurrent users should be able to search for products in 20 seconds
Response time	350 transaction per minute and 98% of the transaction should return to the user within 5 seconds	Retrieve of any search should not take more than 2 seconds
Turnaround time	Mail about the status change should reach the customer within 5 minutes	Any change in a product that is available in the cart of the user should be notified within 2 minutes

Exercise: Identify all the concerns of performance and scalability for Instagram photo apps. For the sake of exercise, you can fill the throughput, response time, and turnaround time.

Performance and scalability

The ability of the system to predictably execute within its mandated performance profile and to handle increased processing volumes.

Concerns		
Throughput		
Response time		
Turnaround time		

Future of an Architect

"The best way to predict the future is to create it."

– Peter F. Drucker

Becoming a great aspiring architect is a journey, and it is one of the milestones which should be celebrated, but you should not stop there. Achieving the milestone opens up a huge door of opportunities and challenges. Sometimes you will wish you were a senior developer who is respected and challenges are affordable and more refreshing. Once you become a seasoned architect, your company and peers will trust and expect more out of your day.

People around you expect you to know everything. They expect you to give a foolproof solution and you are expected to explain any two different technologies at any point of time.

Your contacts will grow because of your knowledge and you will feel more incompetent, because the average IQ of the people you meet will be way higher than yours. You should handle the imposter syndrome and also the feeling of insecurity every day. Equipping yourself is part of your journey.

Remember, success in moving from architect to technical director or VP or even CTO is all about handling yourself, in case of huge challenges. You will have a wild ride, but that is worth it. Every day you will feel you should have stayed as a developer.

I have put together seven quality traits that have helped me to move from architect to Technical director to VP of engineering. I am still an amateur; I still have the imposter syndrome. I still feel I should have handled the situation better.

I still wake up in the middle of the night on some challenges. But these traits have made me better. They have reduced my stress and helped me to handle the people who work for me and the people I work for.

The seven traits are

- Long Term vision
- Expressing your idea to non-tech stakeholders
- Building Networks
- Recruiting A-Player
- Productivity Tools/Time management
- Technology Vision
- Domain Expert

Long Term vision

This is one of the high leverage activities which we have discussed a lot in our book. You should define your own long term vision. This will help you to oversee and ignore and neglect some ego that is bruised by some of your colleagues. You will stop reacting because you have a 5-year or 10-year vision and you don't want to ruin it because of your own ego bruising.

Given below are the traits of a long term thinker. You are not carried away by the smaller losses, these traits will make you a long term person. These are shortcuts and tips to get there. It is the path, not the destination, but will surely help you get to your happy place.

1. You cannot achieve anything more long term by hurting someone's ego, you might have short term success, but you will always fail long term. **Catching more** flies with **honey** than with vinegar is a concept that should be part of your thinking habit.

2. Always go for Win-Win negotiation, your strength is only derived from your team, so you should always look out for

building your network and recruiting people. We will discuss more about this in the recruiting A-Player. Always any person who you work with should learn or get a better end of the bargain than you get. You need to work with more people and so you can get a smaller benefit from the bargain, but since you work with many people you will end up having a greater benefit than anyone else.

3. Have a chit system for your employees who work better. I learned this from Jack Welch, former CEO of GE. He says "prime the chit system", which means you need to give as much as possible to the person who has potential and who performs well in your team. Should everyone be treated the same? Yes, they should be treated the same by treating them the way they respond to the most. Don't fall into the trap of fitting everyone in a single rule and then losing an A-Player. If you are going to give the same treatment to the A-Player as you treat your C-Player, you will lose a lot in the long term because the A-Player will leave your company.

4. Accept people as they are and don't try to change them. Remember you can only change the mood of the person, not the type of the person, so always think of making the emotions around you better, so you can build and get what you want in life. Don't get carried away by thinking you can talk and get things done. That is a very ineffective method, people do what you say but with a grudge. Always walk your talk and be a more trustable person, so it will help you build empires in the long term. Integrity is the key.

5. Use the H.A.L.T system while making decisions, don't take any decision when you are Hungry, Angry, Lonely (makes you vulnerable), and Tired. Long term thinkers always take decisions slowly but will stick to them for longer. Short-term thinkers snap into a decision but they don't stick with it longer.

6. Keep current trends with the market, how it turns. If you are working in open-source technologies, then have friends in a

closed community like Microsoft and Apple. If you work in closed technology, have a network in open source, learn how the innovation works on that end.

7. You are all your team strength and if you don't learn to build and keep a great team, you cannot grow great in your career. Always make sure you have a network of at least five to seven people who will come with you or join a new project. The best way to do it is by mentoring at least 25-30 people, so you can have people who will join your project because they will be mentored more.

These lists are not extensive. These will help you to have the mindset to have a better long term vision while taking decisions and living your life forward.

Expressing Your Ideas to Non-Technical Stakeholders

If you learn to communicate your ideas to your non-technical stakeholders, then you will tend to grow faster in your career, because that is where the funds come from. You need to solve real-time problems that are valuable and bring monetary benefits to the company. If you are the person who understands how to talk to people on their terms, you tend to have more influence in the company.

You will be the person who will be called in a meeting to know your take on things before taking a decision. You will become more powerful because people want to know what you think about the major decision that is going to be taken.

Given below are the traits to learn and practice, so you can increase your circle of influence. Expressing your ideas to non-tech stakeholders means influencing your boss or any other members in a team by explaining to them your ideas in a way they can understand, so they support to carry forward or implement your ideas such as adapting new technology throughout the organization or paying for some software that will give returns in the long term.

- Learn psychology, understand Maslow's principle more. A good way to understand anyone is to see the world of others from the way they see, rather than compelling them to see how you are seeing it. Always understand how they perceive the world.

- Be a good listener. Understand their background and what industry they come from. My previous board of directors had a civil engineering background. So when I explain any software process, I need to find the analogy of how it fits in their world. If you are talking to a stakeholder who is good at sports, then you need to learn sports metaphors so you can explain in their terms.

- Dumb your idea down. Dumb idea down so they don't have to think too much. All they have to say is yes or no. Always take the positives and negatives of your idea to them. Let them see both sides of the coin and give them the control to decide based on your facts.

- Always be ready. The key stakeholders will let you know what their plans are for two to three years forward. Listen carefully whenever they say anything about the future of the company. This will give a glimpse of where they want to take the company. Now let your idea talk in terms that support their long-term goal.

- Long and short term benefits. Always explain to them about the long term and short term benefits. The idea here is to see the results in the imaginary eye, so it is easy for them to be synergistic. Be open to their ideas and be ready to change your strategy.

- All ideas will not be accepted. Only 20% of your ideas will be accepted and the remaining might go down the drain. Pitching ideas is not about getting them accepted and you being celebrated as a genius. Pitching an idea is all about understanding the stakeholder's needs and trying to fit your role and adding value to the company. It takes time to increase your 20% acceptance rate to 40-50%.

- Results alone matter. If you can show results, only then will all the above tips work. Without results, everything you say is just a theory. So always make sure you have done what they have asked you specifically. You should finish what they have told you when they last met you. That's how you build trust to invest in your ideas.

Don't ever look down on them or show any signs of showing disrespect if they are not technically savvy. You have to be extremely careful to adjust your behavior so you will never come in as a show-off and they don't get it. It's all about you complimenting your strength to their vision and you should always keep in mind they are experts in other fields and you respect them for what they have achieved in their respective fields.

Building Networks

As per a study by Harvard Business School, Building Network helps give you three unique advantages:

- private information,
- access to diverse skill sets, and
- power.

It will propel your career, you will be able to get things done faster. You will have lots of people on your phone contacts, where you can contact them when you need to know any drawbacks about the technology or where to go when you are in need. Networks help you not only to boost your skill, but help you to increase credibility.

Humans tend to always trust referrals from people whom they already trust. This way, if someone tells good things about you, and you are being introduced by them, then you are most likely to get things done from them.

Building networks means knowing people in diverse fields, so you can help others and also yourself in case of any need. The tips that are discussed might seem to be manipulating people, but they are not.

It is the way the world and the human psyche work; if you intend to help people a lot, these tips are just a way to move your objective faster.

- Helping others. You should always strive for helping people on getting what they want and that should be your motive and motto. Yes, you will need from others but that should be secondary. Remember you should be used by your network more than you use them. You should have a bigger network, so you get only 5% of the benefit from a person you benefit from, but he gets a 95% benefit from you. Still, it is ok. You have to know 100 different people so you get five times more benefits and you have helped 500 times more.

- Diagnose your network. Always make sure you have diverse set of people. Different gender, different technology and also some non-technical people in your network. This will not only improve perspective but also add lots of business value to your own profile

- Go to places. Make sure you always go to lots of places where you can find people you aspire or want to become. Just going to a local party does not help your professional network. Attend conferences, meetups, and workshops in multiple fields, and feel free to talk to the speakers and event organizers and offer to help. If you go to certain meetups or events consistently then you will make friends and you can grow your network faster. Consistency is the key.

- Shared activities. After you have set your motive right, diagnosed your network, and found the place you can meet the people you want to become, be ready to do shared activities with those you want to network with. It can be dinner after the workshop, meetup, or event. It can be hanging out somewhere over the weekend or any other shared activities that they do with their friends.

- Identify brokers. It is difficult to get acquaintances with people who already have lots to offer, because everyone wants their attention. So always identify people who can get you introduced to them.

- Be a broker. Your altruistic brain should always look out for improving the lives of the people you network with. If you can find someone who can be a great help to one of your friends' networks, feel free to introduce them. Especially if friends in your network are stuck in a problem, and you know other people in the network can help, go out on a limb to connect them together.

- Being Specific. Networking is for mutual benefits. You should also not be wasting your networked friends' time. Don't ask them any vague questions or vague help, where they have to do lots of work to help you. You do the homework, and then call them or meet them to validate your solution or get advice. They are not your psychologist, don't talk about your vices and virtues, and waste their time. Your communication should be clear and to the point and they should know you respect their time.

Building networks have lots of tips but the key is always mutual benefits. You should always approach the relationship about what you can give to them to make their lives better. Doing homework about the person is also one of the high leverage activities to get their attention. But don't praise them like an idiot, to show you wanted something from them.

Recruiting A-Players

Recruiting A-Players will help you to grow in your career faster. The more you know how to handle and recruit A-Players, the better you will be able to get things faster. You can go home in peace, if you know the fire is burning, because those A-Players you trust will have a solution in the morning. Mostly as a good architect, we tend to offer help, but these players might not need them. Leaving them alone is what they want. Your habits and people skills will help you hold A-Players.

The more A-Players there are in your team, the more A-Players you can recruit, and the more business and revenue for your company you will make. If you don't have enough A-Players in your team, you will also lose the current A-Players and even end up losing the team and project. So success with recruiting and holding A-Players is always the Key.

These are the practices I follow to recruit and hold A-Players in my team.

- Always look out for smart people everywhere you go. Make sure you let them know you think they are smart. Don't do the praise like a loser who wants something from them. Be genuine and be specific, why you are praising what they did. Be impressed and don't try to impress.
- Network outside your current technology. If you are working in angular, network in react world. If you are in the Java world, network in the .Net world, and vice versa. This way you will improve your own skill and you can validate people in your current technology. Because you have to do your best to judge a good A-Player.
- Leave your ego and try to learn from people you think are smart. Ask them how they learned how to do certain things. Be open in public about their smartness and accomplishment.
- See them not for what they are now, but see them for what they will be after 10 years and interact with them and push them to be the guy you have envisioned. A-Players like being pushed to the edge of their talents.

- Use the CIDS interviewing process to know them better. It is a good tool to know your future employee better. It takes more than two to three hours, but it is worth the time spent to understand your team. And what type of work they have already done and how you can give them both challenging and also better work with the history of work they have done.
- Don't accept C-Players. The main reason A-Players leave is you are ok with C-Players' activity. The more you accept their behavior and ask an A-Player to fix the problem created by the C-Player, A-Players will get frustrated and leave the company once it reaches the acceptable level.
- More freedom. You should be able to support A-Players and let them take responsibility and try new things. You should build a safety net but you should never poke into their work, because they will get frustrated.

Productivity Tools/Time Management

As an architect, getting more things done in less time is key to success. That is the reason you are getting paid more than a senior developer. You should have lots of productivity tools and time management tricks that help to look savvy in front of the non-technical and technically savvy people. Knowing tools and their proper use is one of the key attributes of the architect. But once you reach more than the architect's level, you should be able to tweak the tool and time management skills to fare better in your next level.

Productivity tools that are discussed in the chapter "A Leader in an architect" will help you get to any level, all you need is to tweak and follow the process explained in the chapter.

In this section, we will only look into small tips and tricks that will be able to give very high leverage. Use these tips as stepping stones, but you need to follow the details provided in Chapter 4, so you can deal with any situation on your own.

Remember productivity is all about focusing on one work and not moving from it until it is done.

The seven major tips that will help you get more productive and get you high leverage are:

- Learn meditation. It helps you to learn to reign in your wavering mind and once you do that kind of exercise every day, you will realize, you are wavering from the work that you wanted to concentrate on. This will help you get back to the work. Remember you want to get a task done, but you went to search about it in Google and you wavered to some other useless task and you find you wasted 15-20 minutes. Becoming conscious of your wavering mind is an exercise that becomes easier when you meditate.

- You tend to get disturbed by everyone in the office and you are needed by everyone to take a decision, or everyone wants your input. Find a place you want to hide in your office. Even if you don't have a place to hide, make sure you have a spot where when you work, nobody will disturb you. The best way is to tell people not to make any disturbance if you move to that spot. This is a way of training people not to disturb you which will help you get more things done.

- Always go to a meeting with a book and a pen. This might sound like a cliche, but we think we are smart people who can hold everything in mind. Actually, you cannot, until you are superhuman. Just scribbling the main points will help you to recap the meeting and get things done without missing them.

- Always ask your people to come prepared when they talk to you. No unstructured conversation should be allowed. You can have a casual conversation with your team who directly reports to you. If they are not directly reporting to you, they should set up a meeting. Remember you should be freely accessible but not always available to others' whims and fancies.

- I learned this technique from Scott Hanselman. If you find yourself sending the same information to more than two people through email, you should create a blog or create a Wiki page because that way you can ask them to refer to the page. This will save lots of time and those Wiki pages become your knowledge Pandora's box.

- Associating with only like-minded people is one of the highly productive activities. In the office, never talk about politics or any other topics. Those are time wasters. You can say those help me to build a relationship. Yes, it will help you build relationships. But don't do it during office hours, do it when you are out with them for dinner or lunch or taking them for a drink. On the office campus, no chit chat with anyone who is not directly reporting to you.

- It takes time to figure out to be productive. You are not going to be productive within a day. You need to find out which are all the activities that make you unproductive. You need to improve every day and find what the clutter that makes you unproductive is. Find everything that makes you feel productive and do that over and over.

Technology Vision

Technology vision helps you to stay focused in your career and helps you achieve both low hanging fruit and also goals that will take a decade to just see results. You will forgo your ego, if you have technology vision, because you know everything will even out sometimes. A good technology vision will help you schedule each day of yours so you know you are moving on the right path.

Technology vision is a strategy you formulate for yourself that will help your business to sustain all the changes in technology trends without being left out, and also measures KPI that is accepted by all the stakeholders.

In this section, we will not be writing a technology vision statement, but you can write one of your own; there are lots of resources available on the internet to write one. Here we will look into how you can handle improving yourself to become a person who has a technology vision, and improve yourself every day.

- Learning at least five to six books on the latest technology trends every year is a must. I learned about quantum computing. Did I understand everything? No, but it has helped me to increase my perception of computing power. I might not see a viable quantum computing in my lifetime, but have understood how things work in our computer industry. Algorithms are written first and then computers were invented later. The technology I am interested right now is chaos engineering, cyborgs, drones, Augmented reality, etc.

- Meeting new people and testing the waters in your surroundings, you should be constantly talking and attending lots of meetups and conferences, and meet young and mature people and see how technology is moving forward.

- Networking and recruiting A-Players, your work is always about recruiting people. Think of recruiting as an everyday activity. Refer *Bradford* D. Smart, Topgrading for more details.

- No ego fights; don't fight with anyone because you have been left out of the mail or important meeting. It might be even intentional to strip off power from you. Handle the conflicts gracefully, don't take decisions based on your ego. Always ask whether it is ego talking or genuinely there is a problem you need to concentrate on leaving out. Remember everything will even out after some time, concentrate on improving yourself. I am not saying to be naive and someone takes your ship which you have built; am telling you to let go of ego and have a better futuristic vision.

- Find your business Key performance index (KPI). Without making money you cannot survive in the business. You need to constantly measure company KPI and monitor so you can move. Read '*Blitzscaling*' by Reid Hoffman on how to build your product faster.

- Learn to balance between the R & D team and also the Engineering team. You need to understand how both teams work and also have a thorough understanding of how you drive them.

- Code for one hour a day, keep your hands dirty, even if you have become CTO of your company. This activity not only helps you understand the pain of the developers, but also helps you to understand how the development is evolving every day with new tools, technology, and mindsets.

Domain Expert

Expertise in domain gains respect from non-technical peers; it helps them feel that you understand them. It communicates indirect empathy for your non-technical stakeholders.

It helps you to bring revenue to the company by building products that sell because you understand the product and customer. You will be included in all decision making because you bring value to the company both technically and in sales.

These tips will speed you up, whenever you move into a new domain.

- When you are new to the domain, search for "dummies – learning made easy" books. You will learn a lot and you will understand the common words that will be used in the meeting. So your mind will not waver, when they initially talk to you.

- Remember when you are new to the domain, it takes time, and be patient with yourself. Don't shy away from the initial meetings because it is boring. Take your time, do your homework about the domain and try to find the similarity between domains that you already know. Comparing and learning is very easy.

- Try a module or fix a bug initially in your new project, so you can understand the current structure of the code. Every domain needs a different way of architecture and some of the technology is created for a particular domain. For example, Actor model architecture is used in customer support call transfer software. You cannot use the same architecture in the retail industry.

- Refer to Chapter 3 for positioning. Your goal is to position yourself as a domain expert. If you want to grow beyond an architect, you should be able to come across as a domain expert and people should feel you are one.

- Talk to customers often and make sure you can do a site visit. Ask your boss that you want to visit customers for a short visit. Most of the good bosses will love it when they hear you want to visit customers because you can mold your product to suit customer needs.

- Always look out for technology that solves your specific domain problems and invest your time in knowing them. You should have hands-on on those technologies.

Conclusion

This book has been a journey and it has taken two and a half years to complete this book. It was a huge learning experience, because when I started writing about a topic, my knowledge of which I was very confident about, I was only humbled by my ignorance. So I had to research a lot, so that it could be very structured and useful for the readers.

This book is one of a kind, because I wish I had this book during those 10 years when I wanted my career to progress in the architecture path. You can use this book in many ways; this book is specifically designed to be modular, with lots of how to's.

Every topic is modular, because you can read one chapter and start working on it in your life. It was written after talking to lots of researchers and experts and taking instances out of my personal experience.

Every topic that is written in this book has a real-time application that can be applied easily. There is not a single place where anything is abstract. Even in the first chapter, I have made sure you can take away something that has practical implications.

Always remember to take responsibility for yourself and for others who are working with you. Once you drive the responsibility paradigm into your heart, you can always figure out how to execute in any time frame. All it needs is patience and persistence.

This book is written after having been naive in office politics and how it negatively impacted me. I have suffered a lot from being naive, so this book helps you to get through the phase of ignorance. I still don't consider myself anywhere close to understanding all the politics, all I know is that hard work will eventually average out any amount of politics.

This book is written for people like you and me who want to be successful ethically. No part of this book talks about anything unethical. We all know karma is a bitch. What goes around comes around. But also forgive yourself, if you have done anything unkind to anyone in your life, and move on. Do more kind actions than you did unkind actions.

Learning is the key in the journey of an architect. Keep learning and do things that you have learned. It helps you keep yourself afloat. It is mandatory just to get through your current role. You need to spend your weekends also to move ahead in your career.

As an architect, your strength is what your team strength is. So while building your team, learn a few people management techniques. Always have your team members' wellness in your mind. As Richard Branson says, train them well, so they can leave you anytime, and treat them well so they never leave.

Learn the basics over and over. It takes time. It took me at least five books to understand the algorithms and time complexity. Understanding solid principles took me five years. So be patient in your learning.

Writing a document is tough, writing so everyone can understand is an even tougher thing to do. You can become good only by writing more documents. The exercises that are given in the chapters seem very simple, but it has taken me years to bring a template that is easy to complete.

Remember technical capability is not enough, you need to first change yourself, understand yourself and the emotions that are triggered.

Once you understand yourself, you can easily understand others. Keep improving yourself every day.

All the best on your journey from an expert senior developer to an architect.

Books – References

Chapter 1
The 7 Habits of Highly Effective People by Stephen R. Covey
Man's Search for Meaning by Viktor Frankl
The Power of Habit by Charles Duhigg
Think Fast and Slow by Daniel Kahneman
Focus: The Hidden Driver of Excellence by Daniel Goleman
The Psychology of Achievement by Brian Tracy
What to Say When You Talk to Your Self by Shad Helmstetter, PhD
Think and Grow Rich by Napoleon Hill

Chapter 2
The 48 Laws of Power by American author Robert Greene
The SPEED of Trust: The One Thing that Changes Everything by Stephen M.R. Covey
How to Win Friends & Influence People by Dale Carnegie
Meeting the Shadow: The Hidden Power of the Dark Side of Human Nature by Connie Zweig & Jeremiah Abrams
Silent Power by Stuart Wilde
Who moved my cheese by Dr. Spencer
Zen Mind, Beginner's Mind: Informal Talks on Zen Meditation by Shunryu Suzuki

Hit Refresh by Satya Nadella
Body Language by Julius Fast
The Presentation Secrets of Steve Jobs: How to Be Insanely Great in Front of Any Audience by Carmine Gallo

Chapter 3

Mastery (The Modern Machiavellian) by Robert Greene
Good to Great: Why Some Companies Make the Leap and Others Don't by Jim Collins
Steve Jobs: The Exclusive Biography by Walter Isaacson
The Cartoon Introduction to Statistics by Grady Klein, Alan Dabney
Positioning: The Battle for Your Mind by Al Ries & Jack Trout
Influence: The Psychology of Persuasion by Robert B. Cialdini
Framework Design Guidelines: Conventions, Idioms, and Patterns by Krzysztof Cwalina & Brad Abrams
Phoenix Project: A Novel about It, DevOps, and Helping Your Business Win by Gene Kim and Kevin Behr
The 80/20 Principle: The Secret to Achieving More with Less by Richard Koch
Radical Honesty: How to Transform Your Life by Telling the Truth by Brad Blanton

Chapter 4

Data Structures and Algorithms Made Easy: Data Structures and Algorithmic Puzzles by Narasimha Karumanchi
Udacity Course: *https://classroom.udacity.com/courses/ud513*
You Don't Know JS: 6 Volume Set by Kyle Simpson
Designing Data-Intensive Applications: The Big Ideas Behind Reliable, Scalable, and Maintainable by Martin Kleppmann
Head First Design Patterns by Eric Freeman, Elisabeth Robson, Bert Bates, Kathy Sierra
Building Evolutionary Architectures: Support Constant Change by Rebecca Parson & Neal Ford

The Toyota Way: 14 Management Principles from the World's Greatest Manufacturer by Jeffrey K. Liker

Topgrading, 3rd Edition: The Proven Hiring and Promoting Method That Turbocharges Company Performance by Bradford D. Smart

Design It!: From Programmer to Software Architect by Michael Keeling

Software Systems Architecture: Working With Stakeholders Using Viewpoints and Perspectives by Nick Rozanski & Eóin Woods

Chapter 5

The Effective Executive: The Definitive Guide to Getting the Right Things Done by Peter F. Drucker

Winning: The Ultimate Business How-To Book by Jack Welch & Suzy Welch

Emotional Intelligence, Why It Can Matter More Than IQ by Daniel Goleman

The Start-up of You: Adapt to the Future, Invest in Yourself, and Transform Your Career by Reid Hoffman & Ben Casnocha

Topgrading, 3rd Edition: The Proven Hiring and Promoting Method That Turbocharges Company Performance by Bradford D. Smart

Blitzscaling: The Lightning-Fast Path to Building Massively Valuable Companies by Reid Hoffman and Chris Yeh

www.ingramcontent.com/pod-product-compliance
Lightning Source LLC
Chambersburg PA
CBHW031235050326
40690CB00007B/814